AMERICAN POETRY
OF THE
TWENTIETH CENTURY

AMERICAN POETRY OF THE TWENTIETH CENTURY

Edited by
RICHARD GRAY

*Lecturer in the Department of Literature,
University of Essex*

CAMBRIDGE UNIVERSITY PRESS

CAMBRIDGE

LONDON NEW YORK NEW ROCHELLE

MELBOURNE SYDNEY

Published by the Press Syndicate of the University of Cambridge
The Pitt Building, Trumpington Street, Cambridge CB2 1RP
32 East 57th Street, New York, NY 10022, USA
296 Beaconsfield Parade, Middle Park, Melbourne 3206, Australia

Library of Congress catalogue card number: 75-21033

ISBN 0 521 20516 6 hard covers
ISBN 0 521 09874 2 paperback

First published 1976
Reprinted 1980

Printed in Great Britain at the
University Press, Cambridge

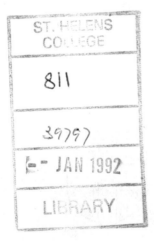
(this copyright page continues opposite)

ACKNOWLEDGEMENTS

The editor and publisher would like to make acknowledgements as follows with regard to the quotation of copyright material:

EDWIN ARLINGTON ROBINSON 'Eros Turannos' and lines from 'The Man Against the Sky' reprinted with permission of Macmillan Publishing Co., Inc. from *Collected Poems* by Edwin Arlington Robinson, Copyright 1916 by Edwin Arlington Robinson, renewed 1944 by Ruth Nivison; 'Mr Flood's Party' reprinted with permission of Macmillan Publishing Co., Inc. from *Collected Poems* by Edwin Arlington Robinson, Copyright 1921 by Edwin Arlington Robinson, renewed 1949 by Ruth Nivison; 'The Sheaves' and 'New England' reprinted with permission of Macmillan Publishing Co., Inc. from *Collected Poems* by Edwin Arlington Robinson, Copyright 1925 by Edwin Arlington Robinson, renewed 1953 by Ruth Nivison and Barbara R. Holt. 'Richard Cory' and 'George Crabbe' by Edwin Arlington Robinson are reprinted by permission of Charles Scribner's Sons from *The Children of the Night*; 'How Annandale Went Out' (copyright 1910 Charles Scribner's Sons) and 'Miniver Cheevy' (copyright 1907 Charles Scribner's Sons) are reprinted by permission of Charles Scribner's Sons from *The Town Down the River*.

HART CRANE 'Black Tambourine', 'Chaplinesque', lines from 'For the Marriage of Faustus and Helen', 'At Melville's Tomb', 'Voyages' I, II, III and VI, 'Royal Palm' and lines from 'The Bridge' from *The Collected Poems and Selected Letters and Prose of Hart Crane* are reprinted by permission of the author, Oxford University Press and Liveright, Publishing, New York, Copyright © 1933, 1958, 1966 by Liveright Publishing Corporation.

JOHN CROWE RANSOM the poems from *Selected Poems of John Crowe Ransom* are reprinted by permission of Eyre and Spottiswoode Ltd. 'Winter Remembered', 'Bells for John Whiteside's Daughter', 'Parting at Dawn' and 'Captain Carpenter', Copyright 1924 by Alfred A. Knopf, Inc. and renewed 1952 by John Crowe Ransom, reprinted from *Selected Poems*, third edition, by John Crowe Ransom, by permission of Alfred A. Knopf, Inc.; 'Dead Boy', and 'Blue Girls', Copyright 1927 by Alfred A. Knopf, Inc. and renewed 1955 by John Crowe Ransom, reprinted from *Selected Poems*, third edition, by John Crowe Ransom, by permission of Alfred A. Knopf, Inc.; 'Vision by Sweetwater' and 'Antique Harvesters', Copyright 1927 by Alfred A. Knopf, Inc. and renewed 1955 by John Crowe Ransom, reprinted from *Selected Poems*, third edition, by John Crowe Ransom, by permission of Alfred A. Knopf, Inc.; 'Painted Head', Copyright 1934 by Alfred A. Knopf, Inc. and renewed 1962 by John Crowe Ransom, reprinted from *Selected Poems*, third edition, by John Crowe Ransom, by permission of Alfred A. Knopf, Inc.

E. E. CUMMINGS   the ten poems from *Complete Poems of E. E. Cummings* are reprinted by permission of MacGibbon & Kee. 'in Just' and 'Buffalo Bill's defunct', Copyright, 1923, 1951, by E. E. Cummings, reprinted from his volume, *Complete Poems 1913–1962*, by permission of Harcourt Brace Jovanovich, Inc.; 'Dick Mid's large bluish face', Copyright, 1925, by E. E. Cummings, reprinted from his volume *Complete Poems 1913–1962*, by permission of Harcourt Brace Jovanovich, Inc.; 'next to of course god america i', Copyright, 1926, by Horace Liveright, Copyright, 1954, by E. E. Cummings, reprinted from *Complete Poems 1913–1962* by E. E. Cummings by permission of Harcourt Brace Jovanovich, Inc.; 'somewhere i have never travelled', Copyright, 1931, 1959, by E. E. Cummings, reprinted from his volume, *Complete Poems 1913–1962*, by permission of Harcourt Brace Jovanovich, Inc.; 'In) all those who got', Copyright, 1935, by E. E. Cummings, Copyright 1963, by Marion Morehouse Cummings, reprinted from *Complete Poems 1913–1962* by E. E. Cummings by permission of Harcourt Brace Jovanovich, Inc.; 'My father moved through dooms of love', Copyright, 1940, by E. E. Cummings, Copyright, 1968, by Marion Morehouse Cummings, reprinted from *Complete Poems 1913–1962* by E. E. Cummings by permission of Harcourt Brace Jovanovich, Inc.; 'enter no (silence is the blood whose flesh)', © 1963 by Marion Morehouse Cummings, reprinted from *Complete Poems 1913–1962* by E. E. Cummings by permission of Harcourt Brace Jovanovich, Inc.; 'afloat on some', Copyright, 1944, by E. E. Cummings, Copyright, 1972 by Nancy Andrews, reprinted from *Complete Poems 1913–1962* by E. E. Cummings by permission of Harcourt Brace Jovanovich, Inc.; 'since feeling is first', Copyright, 1926, by Horace Liveright, Copyright 1954, by E. E. Cummings, reprinted from *Complete Poems 1913–1962* by E. E. Cummings by permission of Harcourt Brace Jovanovich, Inc.

ROBINSON JEFFERS   'Divinely Superfluous Beauty', 'To the Stonecutters', 'Continent's End' and lines from 'Roan Stallion', Copyright 1925 and renewed 1953 by Robinson Jeffers, reprinted from *The Selected Poetry of Robinson Jeffers*, by permission of Random House, Inc.; 'Hurt Hawks', Copyright 1928 and renewed 1956 by Robinson Jeffers, reprinted from *The Selected Poetry of Robinson Jeffers*, by permission of Random House, Inc.; 'The Eye', Copyright 1941, 1944 and renewed 1969, 1972 by Donnan Jeffers and Garth Jeffers, reprinted from *Selected Poems* by Robinson Jeffers, by permission of Random House, Inc.; 'My Burial Place', Copyright © 1963 by Garth Jeffers and Donnan Jeffers, reprinted from *The Beginning and the End and Other Poems* by Robinson Jeffers, by permission of Random House, Inc.

ROBERT LOWELL   'Children of Light', 'The Holy Innocents' and 'Colloquy in Black Rock', from *Poems 1938–1949* reprinted by permission of Faber and Faber Ltd; the same poems from *Lord Weary's Castle*, Copyright, 1946, by Robert Lowell, are reprinted by permission of Harcourt Brace Jovanovich, Inc. 'Beyond the Alps', 'For Sale', 'To Speak of the Woe that is in Marriage' and 'Skunk Hour', from *Life Studies* reprinted by permission of Faber and Faber Ltd; the same poems reprinted with the permission of Farrar, Straus & Giroux, Inc. from Robert Lowell's *Life Studies*, Copyright © 1956, 1959 by Robert Lowell. 'For the Union Dead' from the volume, *For the Union Dead*, reprinted by permission of Faber and Faber Ltd; the same poem reprinted with the permission of Farrar, Straus & Giroux, Inc. from Robert Lowell's *For the Union Dead*, Copyright © 1960 by Robert Lowell. 'Reading Myself' from *Notebooks*, reprinted by permission of Faber and Faber Ltd; the same poem reprinted with the permission of Farrar, Straus & Giroux, Inc. from Robert Lowell's *Notebooks*, Copyright © 1967, 1968, 1969, 1970 by Robert Lowell.

MARIANNE MOORE   the poems from *The Complete Poems of Marianne Moore* are reprinted by permission of Faber and Faber Ltd. 'No Swan So Fine', 'The Frigate Pelican', 'Poetry', 'When I Buy Pictures', 'A Grave', 'An Egyptian Pulled Glass Bottle in the Shape of a Fish' and 'To a Snail' are reprinted with permission of Macmillan Publishing Co., Inc. from *Collected Poems* by Marianne Moore, Copyright 1935 by Marianne Moore, renewed 1963 by Marianne Moore and T. S. Eliot; 'What are Years?' is reprinted with permission of Macmillan Publishing Co., Inc. from *Collected Poems* by Marianne Moore, Copyright 1941 by Marianne Moore, renewed 1969 by Marianne Moore; 'The Steeple Jack', reprinted with permission of Macmillan Publishing Co., Inc. from *Collected Poems* by Marianne Moore, Copyright 1951 by Marianne Moore. 'Melchior Vulpius' from *The Complete Poems of Marianne Moore*, Copyright © 1959 by Marianne Moore, reprinted by permission of The Viking Press, Inc.

THEODORE ROETHKE   the poems from *Collected Poems of Theodore Roethke* are reprinted by permission of Faber and Faber Ltd. 'Open House', Copyright 1941 by Theodore Roethke; 'Cuttings' and 'Cuttings (later)', Copyright 1948 by Theodore Roethke; 'Night Crow', Copyright 1944 by Saturday Review Association Inc.; 'Unfold! Unfold!', Copyright 1949 by Theodore Roethke; 'Memory', Copyright © 1956 by The Atlantic Monthly Company; 'First Meditation', Copyright © 1955 by Theodore Roethke; 'The Moment', Copyright © 1963 by Beatrice Roethke as Administratrix of the Estate of Theodore Roethke; 'Once More, the Round', Copyright © 1962 by Beatrice Roethke as Administratrix of the Estate of Theodore Roethke all from the book *Collected Poems of Theodore Roethke* are reprinted by permission of Doubleday & Company Inc.

CARL SANDBURG   'Chicago', 'A Fence', 'Ice Handler', 'Fog' and 'Gone' from *Chicago Poems* by Carl Sandburg, Copyright 1916, by Holt, Rinehart and Winston, Inc., Copyright 1944, by Carl Sandburg, reprinted by permission of Harcourt Brace Jovanovich, Inc.; 'Sunset from Omaha Hotel Window', 'Still Life', 'Band Concert' and 'New Feet' from *Cornhuskers* by Carl Sandburg, Copyright, 1918, by Holt, Rinehart and Winston, Inc., Copyright, 1946, by Carl Sandburg, reprinted by permission of Harcourt Brace Jovanovich, Inc.; 'More Country People' from *Good Morning, America*, Copyright, 1928, 1956, by Carl Sandburg, reprinted by permission of Harcourt Brace Jovanovich, Inc.; lines from 'The People, Yes' from *The People, Yes* by Carl Sandburg, Copyright, 1936, by Harcourt Brace Jovanovich, Inc., Copyright, 1964, by Carl Sandburg, reprinted by permission of the publishers; 'Waiting for the Chariot', Copyright, 1950, by Carl Sandburg, reprinted from his volume, *Complete Poems*, by permission of Harcourt Brace Jovanovich, Inc.

WALLACE STEVENS   the poems from *Collected Poems of Wallace Stevens* are reprinted by permission of Faber and Faber Ltd. 'The Snow Man', 'A High-Toned Old Christian Woman', 'Sunday Morning', 'Bantams in Pinewoods', 'Anecdote of the Jar', 'Life is Motion', and 'Thirteen Ways of Looking at a Blackbird', Copyright 1923 and renewed 1951 by Wallace Stevens, are reprinted from *The Collected Poems of Wallace Stevens* by permission of Alfred A. Knopf, Inc.; 'The Idea of Order at Key West', and lines from 'The Man with the Blue Guitar', Copyright 1936 by Wallace Stevens and renewed 1964 by Holly Stevens, are reprinted from *The Collected Poems of Wallace Stevens* by permission of Alfred Knopf, Inc.; lines from 'Notes Toward a Supreme Fiction', Copyright 1942 by Wallace Stevens, are reprinted from *The Collected Poems of Wallace Stevens* by permission of Alfred Knopf, Inc.; 'Final Soliloquy of the Interior Paramour', Copyright 1957 by Wallace Stevens reprinted from *The Collected Poems of Wallace Stevens* by permission of Alfred Knopf, Inc.

WILLIAM CARLOS WILLIAMS   'The Revelation', 'Sea-Trout and Butterfish', 'Proletarian Portrait', 'Tract', 'The Widow's Lament in Springtime', lines from 'Spring and All', and 'Young Sycamore' from William Carlos Williams' *Collected Earlier Poems*, Copyright 1938 by New Directions Publishing Corporation, reprinted by permission of New Directions Publishing Corporation; 'Raleigh was Right' and 'The Night Rider' from William Carlos Williams' *Collected Later Poems*, Copyright 1944, 1948 by William Carlos Williams, are reprinted by permission of New Directions Publishing Corporation; 'Preface to *Paterson*, Book 1' from William Carlos Williams' *Paterson*, Copyright 1946 by William Carlos Williams, is reprinted by permission of New Directions Corporation; 'The Descent', 'The Orchestra', 'A Negro Woman', lines from 'Asphodel, that Greeny Flower' and 'Pictures from Brueghel: Poems I and II' from William Carlos Williams' *Pictures from Brueghel and Other Poems*, Copyright 1948, 1954, © 1962 by William Carlos Williams, are reprinted by permission of New Directions Publishing Corporation.

CONTENTS

[ix]

A NOTE ON THE SELECTIONS

In preparing this anthology I have adopted roughly the same procedure as Allen Freer and John Andrew, the editors of *The Cambridge Book of English Verse, 1900–1939*, and Alan Bold, the editor of *The Cambridge Book of English Verse, 1939–1975*. That is to say, I have included only those who seem to me to be the most important American poets in the period covered; and I have made the kind of selection from their work that will, I hope, give the reader a reasonable idea both of the interests and techniques of the individual poets and of the major developments in modern American verse. As to the period: I have confined myself to writers whose first volumes were published before the end of the Second World War. Consequently, one or two writers from the 'second generation' are included (i.e. Theodore Roethke and Robert Lowell), but not people like Charles Olson (who, although of the same generation as Roethke and Lowell, did not publish his first collection of verse until the 1950s) or more recent poets such as Robert Duncan. In some ways I regret this: but to have adopted a different procedure would, I believe, have been to involve myself in making a series of rather premature (and necessarily very personal) historical and literary judgements. It would, in fact, have been to turn this book into something quite different.

One word more: there are three major American poets of the period whose work is not represented here, T. S. Eliot, Ezra Pound, and Robert Frost. The reasons for this are simple. Selections from the work of Eliot and Pound are to be found in the Freer and Andrew volume mentioned above; and I can only recommend that the reader interested in obtaining a really thorough idea of the subject refer to this. As for Frost's work, the permission fees for this popular poet proved too high to be afforded.

June 1975   R.G.

INTRODUCTION

About three hundred and fifty years ago, a few English merchants set out to colonise, and then to exploit, the New World across the Atlantic Ocean. They knew what they wanted: a profitable source of income and, in some instances, a chance of spreading the Word among the unregenerate of the wilderness as well. What they did not know, however, was that the 'Virgin Country' to which they were committing themselves would change them as much as they would change it. The same holds true for the settlers who followed afterwards, among them the many whose purpose it was actually to continue the way of life and religious worship forbidden them in the old country. Whatever their reasons for going, and whether they liked it or not, the men who migrated to America in those early years soon found themselves subjected to a process of psychic transformation, which made of them new beings with what one of them, de Crèvecoeur, called 'new principles...new ideas...new opinions'. They became, in fact, Americans.

It is one thing to possess a new identity, but quite another to know what that identity is. The acquisition of self-knowledge is a difficult task at any time and for the man in the New World it was especially so, because his was a developing environment. Even while he was considering what America was, and what he as an American was, both were changing rapidly. True, a few things were clear. It was possible, for instance, to assert with some measure of confidence that the American was a man who had opted out of society in anything but its simplest form. He had left Europe behind, and its comparatively sophisticated social framework, to light out for a territory in which he could act as the arbiter of his own fate: his own judge and jury as well as his own witness. He had, in a sense, repudiated the past or, as later more Freudian analysts would have it, the image of the father, and with it those institutions, the products of history, which at once constrained the European and gave him a reassuring sense of his purposes. The classic hero who was beginning to emerge in the literature of the new country was himself an illustration of this. He was Natty Bumppo alone in

[xv]

the wilderness, or Ahab alone in his struggle with Moby Dick. He was Huckleberry Finn howling against his aunt's intention to 'adopt and sivilize' him, or Walt Whitman insisting '*I* was the man, *I* suffered, *I* was there.' In his literature as elsewhere, the American did not envisage himself working out a relationship with society, in the manner of a Tom Jones or a Becky Sharp: but rather as singled out from the ranks of men, a unique being. The object of his song and study became his isolated self, as if his own psyche contained all of life that was relevant to him.

Once he had placed himself in isolation, though, the American was still faced with the same problem: who and what was he? In effect, he had only made the problem more difficult to solve because he had denied the traditional means of defining the self – the means supplied by relationships with others – as a prelude to self-definition. The problem seemed even worse for the American *writer*. He had his hero, to whom the special quality of isolation pertained and in whom the conflicts of the drama were to be focussed. But what was the nature of this isolation, and what shape were these conflicts to assume? How could a character or persona be created if the creator did not know to begin with who or what that character should be? Was it possible to define the Self without reference to the Other? And could anyone even begin to write as an American if an American language had not been evolved? For language, as the semanticists never tire of telling us, exists in a state of mutual dependence with personality, shaped by it and helping to shape it in turn; and so to have a language of one's own is to have something which is at once a proof of and, to some extent, a means to self-definition. It would perhaps not be exaggerating too much to say that the discovery of a language, a unique and characteristic 'voice', is one of the most important steps which can be taken towards the discovery of identity.

This, of course, is the crucial point. The ultimate problem with which the American writer is confronted is the evolution of a language. He has to invent a form which will answer to his general needs, emotional and imaginative, and a style which will be as true to his own sense of life as he can make it. With some reservations, that perhaps could be described as the task of the European writer as well: but it is exactly those reservations which are important here. Whatever the degree of his originality, the European does, even now, seem to start from

something. There is the sense of a staple idiom to which he is
giving his own inflections and which endows his work with a
substance, or sense of belonging, which it would not otherwise
have. The American, on the other hand, appears to start almost
from scratch. Despite specific debts which one writer may owe
to another, the debt that William Carlos Williams owes to Walt
Whitman for instance, or the one that Hart Crane has
acknowledged to both Whitman and Poe, each of them appears
to be evolving his own means of expression as he goes along. And
despite the fact that the degree of overt experimentalism may
vary – Wallace Stevens, for example, is obviously a much more
experimental poet than Robert Frost – a belief in originality, and
the unique demands of the individual, remains something of
a constant. Williams and Crane, Stevens and Frost, Marianne
Moore and Robinson Jeffers: all, in their way, seem to be
committed to what Ezra Pound once called the breaking of new
wood – searching out a style that will help them to define the
truth about themselves. To every one of them consequently,
and their kind, can be applied a remark that was once made
about the New England poet Emily Dickinson: that he, or she,
writes as if nobody else had ever written before.

The point I am making about American literature depends –
it is perhaps obvious by now – upon a paradox. There is a tradition of a kind here, but it is a tradition of the new. American
writing, and American verse writing in particular, has existed
from the very beginning at the extreme edge of Romanticism
(an edge, it might be added, which European literature has only
recently even begun to approach); where the only recognition
shared is a recognition of difference, where one of the few prece-
dents accepted is the rejection of precedent, and where Truth
and Beauty are identified with a procedure of constant metamorphosis. As a result, the one genuine way in which the
American *can* acknowledge his participation in a common cultural effort is by behaving as a supreme individualist. He pays
his greatest respects to his past in rebelling from it, and the
best compliment he could to his nation by denying its authority
over him. It is a strange situation, even an ironic one, stemming
ultimately from the contradictions implicit in the idea of freedom; and neither its strangeness nor its ironies have been lost
on the writers of the previous generation.

They *were* lost once upon a time, however, and this brings us to the story of modern American verse: that surge of activity and revolutionary experiment which, after rescuing the national literature from virtual stagnation, went on to produce some of the finest creative work this century has seen. The beginnings of the story can be located fairly precisely, in the period just before and during the First World War when, as D. H. Lawrence once put it, 'The old world ended' – or as Virginia Woolf remarked, no less apocalyptically, human nature began to change. As the references to Lawrence and Woolf suggest, some of the larger occasions for the American poetic 'renaissance' were not exclusively national: they crossed boundaries and belonged to the 'modernist' movement in Western art and literature as a whole. But since it is the immediate facts of that 'renaissance' we are concerned with here, its *home* roots, emergence, and consequences, we shall have regretfully to leave those occasions untraced. To chart the trajectory of 'modernism' – except, that is, to say that it served eventually to bring the European artist rather closer to the American, in his sense of loneliness and limitless possibility: this, considering that our subject is the 'American-ness' of American poetry, its qualities as a distinctive body of writing, would be at best an irrelevance and at worst an enormous distraction.

Anyway, to return to the story of modern American verse: it starts, as many good American stories do, with a situation approaching crisis. The closing decade of the nineteenth century and the opening decade of the twentieth were what is now generally known as a 'twilight interval', when the poets of the nation – such as they were – appeared to lack any real sense of direction. Emily Dickinson had died in 1886, Walt Whitman in 1892, and with them had gone that willingness to experiment, an immense belief in the future and a sense of the open road, which had been largely responsible for the great poetry written in the eighty or ninety years following the founding of the new republic. Admittedly, this 'twilight interval' was also the period in which Edwin Arlington Robinson published his first volumes, and Ezra Pound began a life of poetic discovery. But Robinson, Pound, and the few people like them who were beginning to write in a new vein hardly occupied the public attention. They were kept waiting in the wings while the stage was given over to mediocrities: poets mouthing nothing except a genteel delight in the gypsy life, or a reverence for some polite version of the Ideal. Reversing the paradox mentioned earlier, we could perhaps say that these 'little sonnet-men' (as Robinson called them) really betrayed their ignorance of their American inheritance by embracing a gospel of conformity. They sang songs that were pale copies of their predecessors', they used received ideas and conventional forms of expression; and in doing all this they only succeeded in demonstrating how little they belonged in the company of those they supposedly imitated – great innovators like Poe and Dickinson, Whitman and Thoreau.

The change came, as I have suggested, about 1910–15. Let us say 1912, for that was the year which saw the first edition of *Poetry: A Magazine of Verse*. Published by Harriet Monroe in Chicago, it became a kind of focus for the new movement in poetry both because of the immense body of significant work it included within its own pages and because its success encouraged imitators. In an indirect way it was and is the progenitor of all those 'little magazines' which have, perhaps, had more to do with the promotion of modern American poetry than any other medium: among them, *Others* and *The Dial* in New York, *The Double Dealer* and *The Fugitive* in the South, *The Midland* and *The Prairie Schooner* in the West, and such expatriate journals as *Broom, Secession, transition*, and (for a time) *The Little Review. Poetry*, while it still flourishes, has descendants even today, ranging from established and quite respectable publications like the *Transatlantic Review* to those mimeograph sheets which are a feature of nearly every large community in which an interest in literature is to be found. For all its subsequent reputation, however, its early issues were greeted with suspicion: it was regarded as a strange phenomenon, especially so because its founder made no further demand on her contributors than that they should write good, distinctive verse. And the suspicions seemed confirmed when, in the course of its first few years, it published such radical and diverse experimenters as William Carlos Williams and T. S. Eliot, Wallace Stevens, Carl Sandburg, and Hart Crane. Here at last were the new voices of which American poetry had been starved for nearly a generation; and the instinctive reaction of the literary establishment – an unsurprising reaction, really, when one considers that it was fighting for its own survival – was astonishment followed by attack.

Battle was being joined, meanwhile, on other fronts than

Chicago. In London, for example, a small group of expatriate writers had gathered around the figure of Ezra Pound. Individually, apart from Pound and the poetess H.D., they were not to achieve anything of major significance. But collectively they were responsible for what seems in retrospect to have been one of the most important movements in modern literature: Imagism. The term 'Imagism' was apparently invented by Pound and used for the first time in print, appropriately enough, in the pages of *Poetry* – for which Pound was acting as foreign editor. Soon after this first appearance a full length article on the subject was published, again in *Poetry*. Written by F. S. Flint, another member of the London group, it announced the Imagist programme: three 'rules' which all Imagists, and by implication all good poets, were supposed to follow. These were:

(1) Direct treatment of the 'thing' whether subjective or objective.

(2) To use absolutely no word that did [*sic*] not contribute to the presentation.

(3) As regarding the rhythm: to compose in sequence of the musical phrase not in sequence of a metronome.

Later, in 1915, an anthology of Imagist poetry was published in England; and, after the American writer and heiress Amy Lowell assumed control of the movement, two further anthologies appeared in 1916 and 1917. But the further history of Imagism need not detain us here. What matters for our purposes is not the movement as such, and the work it may immediately have encouraged, but its *ideas*. Like *Poetry*, Imagism provided a focus, only this time an ideological focus rather than a practical one. It served to crystallise certain tendencies, certain notions about the nature and purposes of poetic experiment, which had been developing in a rather scattered fashion over the previous decade – to organise, to define, and so to promote them. As one, highly articulate product of the forces that were shaping the new poetry, it gave due notice of where American writers were bound and the kinds of distinction they were likely to achieve.

Take the first of the Imagist 'rules', for example, the rule demanding that the poet pay attention, have a proper respect for the concrete fact: this was clearly issued as a challenge to a previous generation which had cherished the vague. Poetry, the argument went, had for too long thrived upon rhetorical gestures, the ethereal and the abstract. It now had to be brought back to earth; and the best way of doing this, so the Imagists thought, was to stick closely to the object or experience being described – and hardly ever, if at all, to move from this to *explicit* generalisation. If the poet did wish (as the philosopher of the Imagist movement, T. E. Hulme, put it) to 'glide into an abstract process' he had to make it seem inevitable, a natural result of his meditation on chosen particulars. Immediately, several modern American poets spring to mind, as people whose work illustrates quite directly the power of this belief in the concrete: Robert Frost, for instance, whose own brand of subtle pragmatism is reflected in lines like,

> The fact is the sweetest dream that nature knows,

or William Carlos Williams, who demanded from quite early on in his writing career that there should be

> No ideas but in things.

But – and this is the crucial point – we need not necessarily confine ourselves to such immediate and obvious examples in order to show how pervasive this belief has been. Even Hart Crane, who is surely the most unworldly and mystical of modern American writers, wanted to anchor his mysticism *in* mundane experience. His favourite metaphor for the speculative flight, indeed, was the bridge: something which crosses the other element, water, reaches towards heaven, yet keeps both feet firmly planted on earth. He would never have dreamed of simply rejecting the ordinary, as earlier followers of the Ideal had done; and the fact that he would not have done so suggests the strength, the almost incalculable influence, of an idea to which Pound, Flint, and their companions were among the first (in this century at least) to give memorable expression.

It would be possible to go on and show how the other two Imagist 'rules' reflected contemporary preoccupations; so much so that they, equally with the first 'rule', were to be implemented (in various, idiosyncratic ways) by most major American poets of the 'renaissance'. How the concern for a functional speech, for example (that is to say, a speech which achieves a maximum effect with the minimum possible resources), was to produce both the robust colloquialism of Carl Sandburg and the precious, precise diction of Wallace Stevens. Or how the belief in a flexible verse-form (which is in turn the symptom of a broader commitment to an open, unpremeditated structure) was to find expression alike in the language experiments of Cummings, Roethke, and Moore and in the less extreme but no less original voice which sounds through the work of John Crowe Ransom or Robinson Jeffers. But this, perhaps, is unnecessary. The exemplary status of Imagism is I hope clear by now, as is the general thrust of its ideas; and time compels us to move on to the later story of American verse – so as to glance, however briefly, at some of the fresh episodes added to it by other decades and other forces. Here, the career of Ezra Pound after he had left the Imagist group is interesting again because it can serve us, in a sense, as a paradigm. From Imagism Pound moved on to Vorticism, in which the object was seen as a kind of dynamo 'from which, and through which, and into which ideas are constantly rushing'; and then from Vorticism he moved on to ever more extreme and personal forms of experiment. At the same time as this was going on, his home was on the move too: from London he travelled to Paris, from Paris to Italy, from Italy to the United States (and forced confinement), and then from the United States back to Italy. His whole life was, as he recognised, that of the voyager and the exile: which was why, surely, the figure of Odysseus exerted such a powerful attraction for him.

Odysseus could have been adopted as an alter ego by many other American writers between the Wars, and especially the writers of the twenties. For this, as nearly everybody knows, was the age of the expatriate when novelists like Ernest Hemingway and poets like E. E. Cummings took advantage of a favourable rate of exchange to return to Europe. There they hoped, just as Pound did, that they could work out their 'American-ness' in a new context. Away from their native land, they could perhaps bring fresh terms of reference to bear upon it: they could compare the New World now with the Old, from which it had sprung. Settled in Paris, in Rome or possibly London, they might discover what Hart Crane was later to call 'new thresholds, new anatomies': there would be new experiences available to them, and new ways of organising experience too, any or all of which they might develop according to their particular intentions. Whether they participated in some of the experimental movements which flourished during this period, such as Vorticism and Futurism, Dadaism and Surrealism; or whether they were more interested in the established cultural patterns of their new surrounds, the net effect of their journey was an expansion of sensibility and a refinement of style. In their different ways they added, and added significantly, to their own personal vocabularies.

But what precisely were these vocabularies to be used for? How were the American poet's interests and allegiances affected by his self-imposed exile? Gertrude Stein was, I think, quite close to an answer when, in talking about expatriatism, she declared:

> ...writers have two countries, the one where they belong and the one in which they live really. The second one is romantic, it is separate from themselves, it is not real but it is really there.

Developing this suggestion a little further we could perhaps say that, for the American poet living in the 1920s, the first country Stein refers to was the place where he had been born: a world of big business and economic boom in which, as one contemporary observer put it, 'each citizen functions with pride in the... conspiracy against the individual'. The second country, on the other hand, was the place where he *might* have been born. It was another America entirely, that land of perfect freedom which was and is as much a product of the mind as a geographical location. And it was in order to realise this *second* America, in his imagination and then in his verse, that the poet felt obliged to detach himself from his given, his native land. He had to leave the America he had known because, more than ever before, it appeared to have betrayed the American Dream. He had to travel abroad, not because he wished to abandon his inheritance, but because he wanted above all to keep a firm hold upon it, and cope dispassionately with the problems it had created. Like so many others before him the American poet-exile was in effect living out a paradox, never closer to home than when he was asserting his distance from it.

Few poets stayed abroad as long as Pound did, however. For people like E. E. Cummings and Hart Crane expatriation was no more than one stage in a continually fructifying process of departure and return, and as a *general* phenomenon it had faded by the end of the twenties, another victim of the Depression. Steadily accompanying it from the first, and eventually superseding it in the thirties, was another impulse which we can associate with such different writers as Robinson Jeffers and Robert Frost, John Crowe Ransom and William Carlos Williams – and which Williams himself described so eloquently in one of his later essays. 'Place', he said (by which he meant the home-place),

is the only reality, the true core of the universal...We live only in one place ...but far from being bound by it, only through it do we realize our freedom...we do not have to abandon the familiar and known to achieve distinction...rather in [our] place, if we only make ourselves sufficiently aware of it, do we join with others in other places.

The poet, Williams was arguing, had to discover the imperatives of conscience in and through his own locality: he had to articulate the dream of freedom within a regional, or at the very most an American, context. This was nativism of a quite uncompromising kind, and it seemed to define the situation in terms very different from the ones favoured by the expatriates.

Were the terms all that different, though? Was (and is) nativism, perhaps, really no more than another reading of an age-old American situation; different from expatriatism, certainly – but different only in its *approach*, rather than in the problems it dealt with and the solutions it reached? For the 'place' Williams celebrated did not, he admitted, actually exist anywhere. Like the Old South that John Crowe Ransom occasionally eulogised, it was a product of myth; or, to be more accurate, *a product of the poet's language*. Williams, Ransom, and their kind simply used their environment as raw material, out of which they could evolve a more perfect idea of locality. They abstracted a few possibilities from the world around them and then transformed these into a vision of the Great Good place, a modern and geographically more circumscribed equivalent of the American Dream. That is why Williams begins his great epic of place, *Paterson*, in the way that he does – with these lines:

> Paterson lies in the valley under the Passaic Falls
> its spent waters forming the outline of his back. He
> lies on his right side, head near the thunder
> of the waters filling his dreams! Eternally asleep,
> his dreams walk about the city where he persists
> incognito.

Paterson the town here becomes Paterson the man, or rather Paterson the active mind, a type of the myth-making process.

The city is internalised, in other words, and in the event metamorphosed into Williams' very own and golden city; a place where, to go back to that quotation from Gertrude Stein, the poet and his reader can 'live really' – and where they can, hopefully, fulfil themselves. This is not pure escapism. Williams is well aware of the gap between ideal and actual and, as these lines suggest, is trying to use his epic to grapple with some of the problems it produces. But neither is it a conventional form of regionalism, in which the writer simply celebrates the *established* identity of a particular locale. It is, rather, regionalism or nativism of an extraordinarily American kind. Just like the expatriates, and indeed like so many of his predecessors, the American nativist tries to create a better country, and a better identity for himself, there on the page – in the forms and arguments of his verse. He takes the geography of his surroundings and, by concentrating on certain hints and guesses he discovers there, draws us an utterly new map.

The first three decades of the poetic 'renaissance' in America are fairly easy to trace, at least in the broad terms I have been using here. The first decade was marked, as we have seen, by innovation and experiment, the exploration of new forms; the second, by a further expansion of frontiers, verbal and geographical; and the third, by a rediscovery of the American place. The subsequent three decades 1940–70, however, offer many more problems. They are difficult to locate, except as concerns details and personalities, because no definitive pattern seems as yet to have emerged. One reason for this is, of course, our own proximity to the later period. We are too close even to the immediately post-war years, really, to be able to tell what their major tendencies were. And another reason, no less important, is that by the 1940s the great generation of American poets – the generation that includes all but two of the poets in this anthology – had gone their own way: into death (Hart Crane), into eccentricity and self-parody (Robinson Jeffers, Robert Frost), or into some very special form of achievement which was, in turn, the product of years of personal experiment (Wallace Stevens, William Carlos Williams). Even to the minimal extent of opposition to an entrenched literary establishment, they no longer functioned in common; and such interests as they *had* once shared seemed, many of them, no longer relevant to a 'second generation' of writers born in the early part of this century.

Difficult as it is, though, to establish the exact contours of these past three decades, one thing remains eminently clear: that good work continues to be written – and work which belongs quite firmly, I think, to the American tradition of the new. The revolution in the national verse may (as William Carlos Williams has suggested) be well accomplished by now: but far from lapsing into post-revolutionary inertia, overshadowed by their elders' accomplishments, most poets still seem to be committed to experiment. They have managed, somehow, to sustain a posture of vigorous and highly articulate rebellion. Take, for example, these opening lines from poems by the two (very different) writers of the 'second generation' included in this anthology, Theodore Roethke and Robert Lowell:

> Many arrivals make us live: the tree becoming
> Green, a bird tipping the topmost bough,
> A seed pushing itself beyond itself,
> The mole making its way through darkest ground,
> The worm, intrepid scholar of the soil –
> Do these analogies perplex? A sky with clouds,
> The motion of the moon, and waves at play,
> A sea-wind pausing in a summer tree.
>   (Roethke, 'The Manifestation')

> O to break loose, like the chinook
> salmon jumping and falling back,
> nosing up to the impossible
> stone and bone-crushing waterfall –
> raw-jawed, weak-fleshed there, stopped by ten
> steps of the roaring ladder, and then
> to clear the top on the last try,
> alive enough to spawn and die.

> Stop, back off. The salmon breaks
> water, and now my body wakes
> to feel the unpolluted joy
> and criminal leisure of a boy...
>   (Lowell, 'Waking Early Sunday Morning')

These two passages (and, indeed, the poems from which they are taken) have little enough in common, but what they do have is quite fundamental. For both show values being fashioned in and by the process of writing. The fluid arrangements which Roethke has favoured here, and the disciplined freedom of the verse-structure chosen by Lowell, are each of them being used essentially in an act of discovery – discovery of the self, that is, and of the priorities to which that self is committed. Extraordinarily undulant, the lines work their way between a number of alternatives, never confining themselves to any one for very long and creating a sense of order out of the sheer dynamics of their movement. No fixed conclusion is reached, nor even hinted at. Instead, the poet tries to weave an identity out of the entire fabric of his language, its meanings, its rhythms, and its associations; to achieve the type of self-definition which hardly exists apart from the words he uses and which, consequently, remains unavailable to explanation or paraphrase.

This kind of process (it is perhaps worth repeating it just one more time) is exactly what American poets have always had in mind when talking about the need to devise their own style: what Walt Whitman, for example, meant when he called his entire life's work 'a language experiment'; what William Carlos Williams meant when he claimed that he wanted to 'unravel' the common speech; and what today a writer like Robert Creeley means when he says, 'The process of definition is the intent of the poem.' Behind all of these statements, and ones like them, lies the belief that words alone can offer the poet the means to an identity, and that in working out the right way to arrange those words – the right way for him, that is – he is working out the geometry of himself as well. The process is a continuous one, of course. The individual alters from moment to moment and so, by inference, the speech which serves to define him and his experiences must alter in some way too. If it does not, a failure of self-knowledge can result, with the personal style degenerating into idiosyncrasy, an exercise in literary pastiche. The hollow rhetoric that resounds through the later work of Carl Sandburg, the willed eccentricity of some of Marianne Moore's more recent verse, and the mask of the wry country philosopher that Robert Frost rarely lets slip in his final volumes, are, all of them, quite depressing illustrations of this. In such cases, it seems clear, words are not being used in a quest for identity, but only to attach to the writer an identity which is no longer his. And that, after all, must be the cardinal sin in a literature which draws most of its energies from a studied evasion of such fixity; in which, to borrow a line from a contemporary American poem, the one thing that does not change is the will to change.

EDWIN ARLINGTON ROBINSON

Edwin Arlington Robinson was born in 1869 in Head Tide, Maine, but shortly after his birth the family moved to the neighbouring town of Gardiner, which was to become the setting for many of his poems. From 1884 until 1888 he attended Gardiner High School and it was there that he became enamoured of ancient Greek and Latin literature, as well as of what he called 'the music of English verse'. These loves were to remain with him for the rest of his life and provided a major formative influence. As he later explained to a friend, they helped to make him 'a classicist in poetic composition', one who believed that 'the accepted media for the masters of the past' should 'continue to be used for the future'.

In 1891 Robinson enrolled at Harvard University but two years later, before he could complete his courses, he was summoned home suddenly by the death of his father. Then began what were, perhaps, the worst years Robinson was ever to know, in which a series of disasters followed one upon another with such rapidity that he was sometimes tempted to refer to his existence as 'a living hell'. His brother Dean, it was discovered, was addicted to morphine. His brother Herman lost most of the family inheritance in the financial panic of 1893. Robinson himself was the victim of an unhappy love affair; and began seriously to suffer from an ear infection which, he feared, might make him lose his mind. Worst of all, his mother died in circumstances so ghastly that they were to mark the poet for the rest of his life. The cause of her death was black diphtheria and, fearing contamination, the doctor, the undertaker, and the priest refused to come anywhere near her. It was therefore left to her relatives, and to Edwin in particular, to perform most of the necessary offices.

Even then Robinson did not surrender entirely to his habitual pessimism. Release of a practical kind was offered him by his writing, which bore fruit with the appearance of his first volume of verse, *The Torrent and the Night Before*, published privately in 1896. And quite apart from this, Robinson had found some

[1]

philosophical support in the thought of Carlyle, Emerson and Swedenborg, whose idealism helped to confirm him in his own belief that 'there is a good deal to live for' – although, he was careful to add, 'man has to go through hell really to find it'. Acting on a rediscovered sense of purpose he decided to make a new start, and in 1897 left Gardiner for New York.

In New York Robinson prepared a second edition of his poems, entitled *The Children of the Night*, but it was no more successful than the first. This was followed in 1902 by *Captain Craig*, a novel in verse, the publication of which was paid for, without his knowledge, by friends of the family. Once before Robinson had been forced to seek paid employment, in 1899 when he worked briefly in an office at Harvard, and after the appearance of *Captain Craig* he took another job, this time as clock-checker on the construction of the New York subway. Almost destitute by now and discouraged by the apparent lack of interest in his verse, he began to seek relief in heavy drinking.

The turning-point in Robinson's career came in 1905 when President Theodore Roosevelt, impressed by *The Children of the Night*, obtained a sinecure for him at the New York Customs House. At last comfortably provided for, Robinson could return to his writing, producing first a series of plays and then, in 1910, *The Town Down the River*, a new volume of verse. In 1911 things were made still easier for him when he was invited to spend his summers at the MacDowell Colony, in New Hampshire. It thereafter became a habit with him to write his poems there and then return to New York for the rest of the year, where he revised his work, met other writers and friends, and occasionally visited the theatre. Financial success still eluded him but in 1916 *The Man Against the Sky* brought him his first real critical acclaim; and in 1917 *Merlin*, the first in a trilogy of poems based on the legend of King Arthur, more or less confirmed his reputation.

By the third decade of this century Robinson was established as a major poet. A *Collected Poems* appeared in 1921 and received the Pulitzer Prize. In the following year he received an honorary degree from Yale University, and what was perhaps most surprising of all, *Tristram*, published in 1927 as the last volume in the Arthurian trilogy, became a national bestseller; so popularity on a large scale finally came Robinson's way. He had never courted it, but he had earned it; and it remained his as he continued, indefatigably, to produce a volume a year until his death in 1935.

FURTHER READING

Anderson, Wallace L. *Edwin Arlington Robinson: a Critical Introduction.* Cambridge, Mass., 1968.

Barnard, Ellsworth (ed.). *Edwin Arlington Robinson: Centenary Essays.* Athens, Georgia, 1970.

Coxe, Louise O. *Edwin Arlington Robinson: the Life of Poetry.* New York, 1969.

Fussell, E. S. *Edwin Arlington Robinson: the Literary Background of a Traditional Poet.* Berkeley, Calif., 1954.

Smith, Chard P. *Where the Light Falls: a Portrait of Edwin Arlington Robinson.* New York, 1965.

Winters, Yvor. *Edwin Arlington Robinson.* Norfolk, Conn., 1946.

Richard Cory

Whenever Richard Cory went down town,
We people on the pavement looked at him:
He was a gentleman from sole to crown,
Clean favored, and imperially slim.

And he was always quietly arrayed,   5
And he was always human when he talked;
But still he fluttered pulses when he said,
'Good-morning,' and he glittered when he walked.

And he was rich—yes, richer than a king—
And admirably schooled in every grace: 10
In fine, we thought that he was everything
To make us wish that we were in his place.

So on we worked, and waited for the light,
And went without the meat, and cursed the bread;
And Richard Cory, one calm summer night,   15
Went home and put a bullet through his head.

George Crabbe

Give him the darkest inch your shelf allows,
Hide him in lonely garrets, if you will,—
But his hard, human pulse is throbbing still
With the sure strength that fearless truth endows.

In spite of all fine science disavows,   5
Of his plain excellence and stubborn skill
There yet remains what fashion cannot kill,
Though years have thinned the laurel from his brows.

Whether or not we read him, we can feel
From time to time the vigor of his name   10
Against us like a finger for the shame
And emptiness of what our souls reveal
In books that are as altars where we kneel
To consecrate the flicker, not the flame.

How Annandale Went Out

'They called it Annandale—and I was there
To flourish, to find words, and to attend:
Liar, physician, hypocrite, and friend,
I watched him; and the sight was not so fair
As one or two that I have seen elsewhere: 5
An apparatus not for me to mend—
A wreck, with hell between him and the end,
Remained of Annandale; and I was there.

'I knew the ruin as I knew the man;
So put the two together, if you can,   10
Remembering the worst you know of me.
Now view yourself as I was, on the spot—
With a slight kind of engine. Do you see?
Like this...You wouldn't hang me? I thought not.'

Miniver Cheevy

Miniver Cheevy, child of scorn,
    Grew lean while he assailed the seasons;
He wept that he was ever born,
    And he had reasons.

Miniver loved the days of old   5
    When swords were bright and steeds were prancing;
The vision of a warrior bold
    Would set him dancing.

Miniver sighed for what was not,
  And dreamed, and rested from his labors;   10
He dreamed of Thebes and Camelot,
  And Priam's neighbors.

Miniver mourned the ripe renown
  That made so many a name so fragrant;
He mourned Romance, now on the town,   15
  And Art, a vagrant.

Miniver loved the Medici,
  Albeit he had never seen one;
He would have sinned incessantly
  Could he have been one.   20

Miniver cursed the commonplace
  And eyed a khaki suit with loathing;
He missed the mediaeval grace
  Of iron clothing.

Miniver scorned the gold he sought,   25
  But sore annoyed was he without it;
Miniver thought, and thought, and thought,
  And thought about it.

Miniver Cheevy, born too late,
  Scratched his head and kept on thinking;   30
Miniver coughed, and called it fate,
  And kept on drinking.

Eros Turannos

She fears him, and will always ask
  What fated her to choose him;
She meets in his engaging mask
  All reasons to refuse him;
But what she meets and what she fears   5
Are less than are the downward years,
Drawn slowly to the foamless weirs
  Of age, were she to lose him.

Between a blurred sagacity
  That once had power to sound him,   10

And Love, that will not let him be
   The Judas that she found him,
Her pride assuages her almost,
   As if it were alone the cost.—
He sees that he will not be lost,   15
   And waits and looks around him.

A sense of ocean and old trees
   Envelops and allures him;
Tradition, touching all he sees,
   Beguiles and reassures him;   20
And all her doubts of what he says
Are dimmed with what she knows of days—
Till even prejudice delays
   And fades, and she secures him.

The falling leaf inaugurates   25
   The reign of her confusion;
The pounding wave reverberates
   The dirge of her illusion;
And home, where passion lived and died,
Becomes a place where she can hide,   30
While all the town and harbor side
   Vibrate with her seclusion.

We tell you, tapping on our brows,
   The story as it should be,—
As if the story of a house   35
   Were told, or ever could be;
We'll have no kindly veil between
Her visions and those we have seen,—
As if we guessed what hers have been,
   Or what they are or would be.   40

Meanwhile we do no harm; for they
   That with a god have striven,
Not hearing much of what we say,
   Take what the god has given;
Though like waves breaking it may be,   45
Or like a changed familiar tree,
Or like a stairway to the sea
   Where down the blind are driven.

from 'The Man Against the Sky'

Between me and the sunset, like a dome
Against the glory of a world on fire,
Now burned a sudden hill,
Bleak, round, and high, by flame-lit height made higher,
With nothing on it for the flame to kill   5
Save one who moved and was alone up there
To loom before the chaos and the glare
As if he were the last god going home
Unto his last desire.

Dark, marvelous, and inscrutable he moved on   10
Till down the fiery distance he was gone,
Like one of those eternal, remote things
That range across a man's imaginings
When a sure music fills him and he knows
What he may say thereafter to few men,—   15
The touch of ages having wrought
An echo and a glimpse of what he thought
A phantom or a legend until then;
For whether lighted over ways that save,
Or lured from all repose,   20
If he go on too far to find a grave,
Mostly alone he goes.

Even he, who stood where I had found him,
On high with fire all round him,
Who move along the molten west,   25
And over the round hill's crest
That seemed half ready with him to go down,
Flame-bitten and flame-cleft,
As if there were to be no last thing left
Of a nameless unimaginable town,—   30
Even he who climbed and vanished may have taken
Down to the perils of a depth not known,
From death defended though by men forsaken,
The bread that every man must eat alone;
He may have walked while others hardly dared   35
Look on to see him stand where many fell;
And upward out of that, as out of hell,

He may have sung and striven
To mount where more of him shall yet be given,
Bereft of all retreat,   40
To sevenfold heat,—
As on a day when three in Dura shared
The furnace, and were spared
For glory by that king of Babylon
Who made himself so great that God, who heard,   45
Covered him with long feathers, like a bird.

Again, he may have gone down easily,
By comfortable altitudes, and found,
As always, underneath him solid ground
Whereon to be sufficient and to stand   50
Possessed already of the promised land,
Far stretched and fair to see:
A good sight, verily,
And one to make the eyes of her who bore him
Shine glad with hidden tears.   55

   . . . . . .

Or with an even likelihood,
He may have met with atrabilious eyes
The fires of time on equal terms and passed
Indifferently down, until at last
His only kind of grandeur would have been,   60
Apparently, in being seen.
He may have had for evil or for good
No argument; he may have had no care
For what without himself went anywhere
To failure or to glory, and least of all   65
For such a stale, flamboyant miracle;
He may have been the prophet of an art
Immovable to old idolatries;
He may have been a player without a part,
Annoyed that even the sun should have the skies   70
For such a flaming way to advertise ...

   . . . . . .

Or, mounting with infirm unsearching tread,
His hopes to chaos led,

He may have stumbled up there from the past,
And with an aching strangeness viewed the last　75
　Abysmal conflagration of his dreams ...

　　　.　.　.　.　.　.

And at his heart there may have gnawed
Sick memories of a dead faith foiled and flawed
And long dishonored by the living death
Assigned alike by chance　80
To brutes and hierophants ...

　　　.　.　.　.　.　.

Or maybe there, like many another one
Who might have stood aloft and looked ahead,
Black-dawn against wild red,
He may have built, unawed by fiery gules　85
That in him no commotion stirred,
A living reason out of molecules
Why molecules occurred,
And one for smiling when he might have sighed
Had he seen far enough,　90
And in the same inevitable stuff
Discovered an odd reason too for pride
In being what he must have been by laws
Infrangible and for no kind of cause.

　　　.　.　.　.　.　.

Whatever the dark road he may have taken,　95
This man who stood on high
And faced alone the sky,
Whatever drove or lured or guided him,—
A vision answering a faith unshaken,
An easy trust assumed of easy trials,　100
A sick negation born of weak denials,
A crazed abhorrence of an old condition,
A blind attendance on a brief ambition,—
Whatever stayed him or derided him,
His way was even as ours;　105
And we, with all our wounds and all our powers,
Must each await alone at his own height
Another darkness or another light;
And there, of our poor self dominion reft,

If inference and reason shun   110
Hell, Heaven, and Oblivion,
May thwarted will (perforce precarious,
But for our conservation better thus)
Have no misgiving left
Of doing yet what here we leave undone?   115
Or if unto the last of these we cleave,
Believing or protesting we believe
In such an idle and ephemeral
Florescence of the diabolical,—
If, robbed of two fond old enormities,   120
Our being had no onward auguries,
What then were this great love of ours to say
For launching other lives to voyage again
A little farther into time and pain,
A little faster in a futile chase   125
For a kingdom and a power and a Race
That would have still in sight
A manifest end of ashes and eternal night?
Is this the music of the toys we shake
So loud,—as if there might be no mistake   130
Somewhere in our indomitable will?
Are we no greater than the noise we make
Along one blind atomic pilgrimage
Whereon by crass chance billeted we go
Because our brains and bones and cartilage   135
Will have it so?
If this we say, then let us all be still
About our share in it, and live and die
More quietly thereby.

Where was he going, this man against the sky?   140
You know not, nor do I.
But this we know, if we know anything:
That we may laugh and fight and sing
And of our transience here make offering
To an orient Word that will not be erased,   145
Or, save in incommunicable gleams
Too permanent for dreams,
Be found or known.

              .   .   .   .   .   .

Shall we, because Eternity records
Too vast an answer for the time-born words   150
We spell, whereof so many are dead that once
In our capricious lexicons
Were so alive and final, hear no more
The Word itself, the living word
That none alive has ever heard   155
Or ever spelt,
And few have ever felt
Without the fears and old surrenderings
And terrors that began
When Death let fall a feather from his wings   160
And humbled the first man?
Because the weight of our humility,
Wherefrom we gain
A little wisdom and much pain,
Falls here too sore and there too tedious,   165
Are we in anguish or complacency,
Not looking far enough ahead
To see by what mad couriers we are led
Along the roads of the ridiculous,
To pity ourselves and laugh at faith   170
And while we curse life bear it?
And if we see the soul's dead end in death,
Are we to fear it?
What folly is here that has not yet a name
Unless we say outright that we are liars?   175
What have we seen beyond our sunset fires
That lights again the way by which we came?
Why pay we such a price, and one we give
So clamoringly, for each racked empty day
That leads one more last human hope away,   180
As quiet fiends would lead past our crazed eyes
Our children to an unseen sacrifice?
If after all that we have lived and thought,
All comes to Nought,—
If there be nothing after Now,   185
And we be nothing anyhow,
And we know that,—why live?
'Twere sure but weaklings' vain distress
To suffer dungeons where so many doors

Will open on the cold eternal shores   190
That look sheer down
To the dark tideless floods of Nothingness
Where all who know may drown.

Mr. Flood's Party

Old Eben Flood, climbing alone one night
Over the hill between the town below
And the forsaken upland hermitage
That held as much as he should ever know
On earth again of home, paused warily.   5
The road was his with not a native near;
And Eben, having leisure, said aloud,
For no man else in Tilbury Town to hear:

'Well, Mr. Flood, we have the harvest moon
Again, and we may not have many more;   10
The bird is on the wing, the poet says,
And you and I have said it here before.
Drink to the bird.' He raised up to the light
The jug that he had gone so far to fill,
And answered huskily: 'Well, Mr. Flood,   15
Since you propose it, I believe I will.'

Alone, as if enduring to the end
A valiant armor of scarred hopes outworn,
He stood there in the middle of the road
Like Roland's ghost winding a silent horn.   20
Below him, in the town among the trees,
Where friends of other days had honored him,
A phantom salutation of the dead
Rang thinly till old Eben's eyes were dim.

Then, as a mother lays her sleeping child   25
Down tenderly, fearing it may awake,
He set the jug down slowly at his feet
With trembling care, knowing that most things break
And only when assured that on firm earth
It stood, as the uncertain lives of men   30
Assuredly did not, he paced away,
And with his hand extended paused again:

'Well, Mr. Flood, we have not met like this
In a long time; and many a change has come
To both of us, I fear, since last it was   35
We had a drop together. Welcome home!'
Convivially returning with himself,
Again he raised the jug up to the light;
And with an acquiescent quaver said:
'Well, Mr. Flood, if you insist, I might.   40

'Only a very little, Mr. Flood—
For auld lang syne. No more, sir; that will do.'
So, for the time, apparently it did,
And Eben evidently thought so too;
For soon amid the silver loneliness   45
Of night he lifted up his voice and sang,
Secure, with only two moons listening,
Until the whole harmonious landscape rang—

'For auld lang syne.' The weary throat gave out,
The last word wavered, and the song was done.   50
He raised again the jug regretfully
And shook his head, and was again alone.
There was not much that was ahead of him,
And there was nothing in the town below—
Where strangers would have shut the many doors   55
That many friends had opened long ago.

The Sheaves

Where long the shadows of the wind had rolled,
Green wheat was yielding to the change assigned;
And as by some vast magic undivined
The world was turning slowly into gold.
Like nothing that was ever bought or sold   5
It waited there, the body and the mind;
And with a mighty meaning of a kind
That tells the more the more it is not told.

So in a land where all days are not fair,
Fair days went on till on another day   10
A thousand golden sheaves were lying there,

Shining and still, but not for long to stay—
As if a thousand girls with golden hair
Might rise from where they slept and go away.

New England

Here where the wind is always north-north-east
And children learn to walk on frozen toes,
Wonder begets an envy of all those
Who boil elsewhere with such a lyric yeast
Of love that you will hear them at a feast   5
Where demons would appeal for some repose,
Still clamoring where the chalice overflows
And crying wildest who have drunk the least.

Passion is here a soilure of the wits,
We're told, and Love a cross for them to bear;   10
Joy shivers in the corner where she knits
And Conscience always has the rocking-chair,
Cheerful as when she tortured into fits
The first cat that was ever killed by Care.

CARL SANDBURG

At the time of Carl Sandburg's birth, in 1878, both of his parents were still registered as immigrants from Sweden. Like most immigrants they were very poor, remaining so throughout Sandburg's childhood, and because of this the boy was forced to leave school when he was still only thirteen and find employment. He worked in his home town of Galesburg, Illinois, for a while, then travelled across the West, working at all kinds of trades including those of milkman, salesman, stage hand, sign painter, and brickmaker. In 1898 he returned to Galesburg but stayed there only a few months before enlisting in the army. The Spanish-American War had just broken out, and Sandburg was immediately sent on active duty to Puerto Rico where, incidentally, he found time to act as a foreign correspondent for the Galesburg newspaper and so gain his first experience as a journalist.

Upon returning to the United States, Sandburg left the army and enrolled at Lombard College. He worked hard and began to write poetry in his spare moments, some of which was published under the auspices of his professor in 1904: but before he had completed his studies he suddenly withdrew from the university, without any apparent reason for doing so, and took up a job as a travelling salesman. Soon afterwards he returned to journalism, as a roving reporter, and proved so diligent in all he was required to do that he was appointed to an editorial position on a Chicago newspaper. Chicago now became his adopted home. He plunged enthusiastically into the life of the city, and in particular into its political life, forming close connections with branches of the reform party; and within a year of moving there he had become quite prominent in local affairs. For a while, after his marriage in 1908, he lived in Milwaukee, working first as secretary to the mayor and then as editor of the local newspaper, but by 1913 he was back in Chicago again – and this time more committed to the life of the poet than to any of his nominal duties.

Chicago, when Sandburg returned to it, was in the midst of what later came to be termed a 'renaissance'; an increase of cultural activity, and of interest in the arts generally, which was in part a consequence of its being established as the unofficial capital of the Mid-West. It had a new university, founded in 1892, and a new symphony orchestra. It had its own little theatre, and a bohemian quarter to which came writers like Vachel Lindsay, Edgar Lee Masters, and Sherwood Anderson. Above all, in 1912 it had become the home of *Poetry*, a magazine founded by Harriet Monroe with the avowed aim of publishing the best in modern verse (see Introduction). It was to *Poetry* that Sandburg sent some of his recent work, which was eagerly accepted and published, with much acclaim, early in 1914. Two years later his *Chicago Poems* appeared as a volume and this, quickly followed by *Cornhuskers* in 1918, established him as a revolutionary – not to say controversial – new voice. The year of 1918 also saw Sandburg appointed as an assistant editor on the Chicago *Daily News*, a job which gave him financial security and which he kept until the pressure of his creative work forced him to retire from it in 1932.

Several more volumes of poetry appeared over the next few years, among them *Smoke and Steel* in 1920 and *Slabs of the Sunburnt West* in 1922. These confirmed Sandburg's reputation as the poet of the common people. Meanwhile, Sandburg was developing that reputation in other ways by finding new means of expressing populist values. There was, for example, his monumental biography of Abraham Lincoln, begun in 1919 and not finished until 1939, which presents Lincoln as an embodiment of the American Dream, and there was also his work in the folk tradition: specifically, his collection of traditional ballads, *American Songbag* (1927) and his re-working of folk song and idiom in *The People, Yes*, a long poem published in 1936.

By the time *The People, Yes* appeared in print Sandburg was not only a recognised poet, he was (like Robert Frost) something of a national monument as well – a man whose work, and whose personality as it was presented in that work, was deemed to express the best possibilities of the American people. One palpable indication of this is the way he was showered, in his old age, with innumerable awards and honorary degrees, including a Pulitzer Prize for his *Collected Poems* (1950). Less palpable, perhaps, but no less telling was the immense popularity he came to enjoy: long before he died in 1967 his writing – much of it – had become part of a common

stock of knowledge available to every American, and his name
had grown familiar to a public otherwise unacquainted with the
creators of modern verse.

FURTHER READING

Allen, Gay Wilson. *Carl Sandburg.* Minneapolis, Minn., 1972.
Detzer, Karl. *Carl Sandburg: a Study in Personality and Background.* New
    York, 1941.
Golden, Harry. *Carl Sandburg.* Cleveland, Ohio, 1961.
Sandburg, Crowder. *Carl Sandburg.* New York, 1963.
Van Doren, Mark. *Carl Sandburg.* Washington, 1969.

Chicago

Hog Butcher for the World,
Tool Maker, Stacker of Wheat,
Player with Railroads and the Nation's Freight Handler;
Stormy, husky, brawling,
City of the Big Shoulders: 5

They tell me you are wicked and I believe them, for I have seen
    your painted women under the gas lamps luring the farm boys.
And they tell me you are crooked and I answer: Yes, it is true
    I have seen the gunman kill and go free to kill again.
And they tell me you are brutal and my reply is: On the faces
    of women and children I have seen the marks of wanton
    hunger.
And having answered so I turn once more to those who sneer
    at this my city, and I give them back the sneer and say to
    them:
Come and show me another city with lifted head singing so
    proud to be alive and coarse and strong and cunning.   10
Flinging magnetic curses amid the toil of piling job on job, here
    is a tall bold slugger set vivid against the little soft cities;
Fierce as a dog with tongue lapping for action, cunning as a
    savage pitted against the wilderness,
        Bareheaded,
        Shoveling,
        Wrecking,   15
        Planning,
        Building, breaking, rebuilding,

Under the smoke, dust all over his mouth, laughing with white
teeth,
Under the terrible burden of destiny laughing as a young man
laughs,
Laughing even as an ignorant fighter laughs who has never lost
a battle,   20
Bragging and laughing that under his wrist is the pulse, and
under his ribs the heart of the people,
Laughing!
Laughing the stormy, husky, brawling laughter of Youth, half-
naked, sweating, proud to be Hog Butcher, Tool Maker,
Stacker of Wheat, Player with Railroads and Freight Handler
to the Nation.

A Fence

Now the stone house on the lake front is finished and the work-
men are beginning the fence.
The palings are made of iron bars with steel points that can
stab the life out of any man who falls on them.
As a fence, it is a masterpiece, and will shut off the rabble and
all vagabonds and hungry men and all wandering children
looking for a place to play.
Passing through the bars and over the steel points will go nothing except Death and the Rain and Tomorrow.

Ice Handler

I know an ice handler who wears a flannel shirt with pearl
buttons the size of a dollar,
And he lugs a hundred-pound hunk into a saloon icebox, helps
himself to cold ham and rye bread,
Tells the bartender it's hotter than yesterday and will be hotter
yet tomorrow, by Jesus,
And is on his way with his head in the air and a hard pair of fists.
He spends a dollar or so every Saturday night on a two hundred
pound woman who washes dishes in the Hotel Morrison.   5

He remembers when the union was organized he broke the noses
of two scabs and loosened the nuts so the wheels came off six
different wagons one morning, and he came around and
watched the ice melt in the street.

All he was sorry for was one of the scabs bit him on the knuckles
of the right hand so they bled when he came around to the
saloon to tell the boys about it.

Fog

The fog comes
on little cat feet.

It sits looking
over harbor and city
on silent haunches   5
and then moves on.

Gone

Everybody loved Chick Lorimer in our town.
    Far off
    Everybody loved her.
So we all love a wild girl keeping a hold
    On a dream she wants.   5
Nobody knows now where Chick Lorimer went.
Nobody knows why she packed her trunk...a few old things
And is gone,
    Gone with her little chin
    Thrust ahead of her   10
    And her soft hair blowing careless
    From under a wide hat,
Dancer, singer, a laughing passionate lover.

Were there ten men or a hundred hunting Chick?
Were there five men or fifty with aching hearts?   15
    Everybody loved Chick Lorimer.
    Nobody knows where she's gone.

Sunset from Omaha Hotel Window

Into the blue river hills
The red sun runners go
And the long sand changes
And today is a goner
And today is not worth haggling over.   5

    Here in Omaha
    The gloaming is bitter
    As in Chicago
    Or Kenosha.

The long sand changes.   10
Today is a goner.
Time knocks in another brass nail.
Another yellow plunger shoots the dark.
    Constellations
    Wheeling over Omaha   15
    As in Chicago
    Or Kenosha.

The long sand is gone
    and all the talk is stars.
They circle in a dome over Nebraska.   20

Still Life

Cool your heels on the rail of an observation car.
Let the engineer open her up for ninety miles an hour.
Take in the prairie right and left, rolling land and new hay crops,
    swaths of new hay laid in the sun.
A gray village flecks by and the horses hitched in front of the
    post office never blink an eye.
A barnyard and fifteen Holstein cows, dabs of white on a black
    wall map, never blink an eye.   5
A signalman in a tower, the outpost of Kansas City, keeps his
    place at a window with the serenity of a bronze statue on a
    dark night when lovers pass whispering.

Band Concert

Band concert public square Nebraska city. Flowing and circling
dresses, summer-white dresses. Faces, flesh tints flung like
sprays of cherry blossoms. And gigglers, God knows, gigglers,
rivaling the pony whinnies of the Livery Stable Blues.

Cowboy rags and nigger rags. And boys driving sorrel horses
hurl a cornfield laughter at the girls in dresses, summer-white
dresses. Amid the cornet staccato and the tuba oompa,
gigglers, God knows, gigglers daffy with life's razzle dazzle.

Slow good-night melodies and Home Sweet Home. And the
snare drummer bookkeeper in a hardware store nods hello to
the daughter of a railroad conductor—a giggler, God knows,
a giggler—and the summer-white dresses filter fanwise out
of the public square.

The crushed strawberries of ice cream soda places, the night
wind in cottonwoods and willows, the lattice shadows of
doorsteps and porches, these know more of the story.

New Feet

Empty battlefields keep their phantoms.
Grass crawls over old gun wheels
And a nodding Canada thistle flings a purple
Into the summer's southwest wind,
Wrapping a root in the rust of a bayonet,   5
Reaching a blossom in rust of shrapnel.

More Country People

The six pigs at the breast of their mother
Equal six spots of young brown against a big spot of old brown.
The bleating of the sheep was an arithmetic
Of the long wool coat thick after winter.

The collar of white hair hung on the neck of the black hog,   5
The roosters of the Buff Cochin people strutted.

Cherry branches stuck their blossoms against the sky.
Elbows joined elbows of white blossoms.
Zigzags blent into a mass.
'Look once at us—today is the day we call today.'   10

from 'The People, Yes'

The people will live on.
The learning and blundering people will live on.
They will be tricked and sold and again sold
And go back to the nourishing earth for rootholds,
The people so peculiar in renewal and comeback,   5
You can't laugh off their capacity to take it.
The mammoth rests between his cyclonic dramas.

The people so often sleepy, weary, enigmatic,
is a vast huddle with many units saying:
'I earn my living.   10
I make enough to get by
and it takes all my time.
If I had more time
I could do more for myself
and maybe for others.   15
I could read and study
and talk things over
and find out about things.
It takes time.
I wish I had the time.'   20

The people is a tragic and comic two-face:
hero and hoodlum: phantom and gorilla twist-
ing to moan with a gargoyle mouth: 'They
buy me and sell me...it's a game...
sometime I'll break loose...'   25

Once having marched
Over the margins of animal necessity,
Over the grim line of sheer subsistence
Then man came

To the deeper rituals of his bones,   30
To the lights lighter than any bones,
To the time for thinking things over,
To the dance, the song, the story,
Or the hours given over to dreaming,
    Once having so marched.   35

Between the finite limitations of the five senses
and the endless yearnings of man for the beyond
the people hold to the humdrum bidding of work and food
while reaching out when it comes their way
for lights beyond the prisms of the five senses,   40
for keepsakes lasting beyond any hunger or death.
    This reaching is alive.
The panderers and liars have violated and smutted it.
    Yet this reaching is alive yet
    for lights and keepsakes.   45

The people know the salt of the sea
and the strength of the winds
lashing the corners of the earth.
The people take the earth
as a tomb of rest and a cradle of hope.   50
Who else speaks for the Family of Man?
They are in tune and step
with constellations of universal law.

The people is a polychrome,
a spectrum and a prism   55
held in a moving monolith,
a console organ of changing themes,
a clavilux of color poems
wherein the sea offers fog
and the fog moves off in rain   60
and the labrador sunset shortens
to a nocturne of clear stars
serene over the shot spray
of northern lights.

The steel mill sky is alive.   65
The fire breaks white and zigzag
shot on a gun-metal gloaming.
Man is a long time coming.

Man will yet win.
Brother may yet line up with brother: 70

This old anvil laughs at many broken hammers.
  There are men who can't be bought.
  The fireborn are at home in fire.
  The stars make no noise.
  You can't hinder the wind from blowing.   75
  Time is a great teacher.
  Who can live without hope?

In the darkness with a great bundle of grief
  the people march.
In the night, and overhead a shovel of stars for   80
  keeps, the people march:
                    'Where to? what next?'

Waiting for the Chariot

Can bare fact make the cloth of a shining poem?
In Sangamon County, Illinois, they remembered how
The aged widow walked a mile from home to Bethel Chapel
Where she heard the services and was called on
'To give her testimony,' rising to speak freely, ending: 5
  'The past three weeks have been the happiest
  of all my life; I am waiting for the chariot.'
The pastor spoke the benediction; the members rose and moved
Into the aisles toward the door, and looking back
They saw the widow of the famous circuit rider   10
Sitting quiet and pale in an inviolable dignity
And they heard the pastor: 'The chariot has arrived.'

WALLACE STEVENS

Wallace Stevens was born in 1879 in Reading, Pennsylvania. His father was a lawyer, who enjoyed writing in his spare time. His mother, according to Stevens, was of Dutch ancestry. In 1897, after graduating with distinction from the local high school, Stevens enrolled as a special student at Harvard University, where he read English. The next three years were very full ones: quite apart from his academic work, Stevens found time to edit one college magazine and to contribute prose and verse to several others. He also came into contact with George Santayana; a philosopher who, together with another philosopher Henri Bergson and several writers in the Romantic-Symbolist tradition, was to exercise a major influence upon Stevens in his later life, when the poet was trying to shape his own theory of the imagination. For the moment, however, just after he had left Harvard, Stevens was more intent upon making a career for himself in law than on formulating any aesthetic theories; and to this end he enrolled in New York Law School in 1901.

After he was admitted to the Bar in 1904, Stevens engaged in general practice in New York. There he continued to compose verse and eventually, in 1914, had four of his poems accepted by the magazine *Poetry*. He was also becoming acquainted with many of the other writers living in New York at this time, among them Marianne Moore, E. E. Cummings, and William Carlos Williams. 'He was always the well-dressed one,' Williams recalled of him later, 'diffident about letting his hair down. Precise when we were sloppy. But we all knew, liked, and admired him. He really was felt to be part of the gang.' During this period just as later in his life, in fact, Stevens managed to lead a double life: to be at once a poet and a lawyer, a man of letters and a family man (he had married in 1909). It was not that the one career ever impinged upon or limited the other: it was rather that Stevens appeared able, with very little effort, to keep his allegiances scrupulously divided.

In 1916 Stevens moved to Hartford, Connecticut, to join the legal staff of the Hartford Accident and Indemnity Company. There he was to remain until his death, becoming vice-president of the company in 1934. More of his poetry, meanwhile, was appearing in the periodicals and his literary friends, whom he continued to visit whenever he could, began urging him to publish a complete book. Finally, in 1923, he did prepare a volume, called *Harmonium*, for publication in New York. It was warmly praised by one or two reviewers, including Marianne Moore, but in general the critical reception was poor and other interest virtually negligible: the edition sold fewer than a hundred copies. Perhaps this, along with Stevens' desire to consolidate his career in business, helps to account for the long creative drought which followed. No new poems appeared for the next seven years.

New verse began at last to show up in the periodicals in 1930 and then, in 1931, a second edition of *Harmonium* was issued. Several fresh volumes followed quickly upon one another after that. *Ideas of Order* was published in 1935, and subseqently re-published as *Owl's Clover* in 1936. *The Man With the Blue Guitar and Other Poems* appeared in 1937; *Parts of a World* and *Notes Toward a Supreme Fiction* in 1942; *Esthétique du Mal* in 1944 and *Transport to Summer*, a larger collection including both *Notes* and *Esthétique du Mal*, three years later. By this time Stevens was also acquiring an enthusiastic, if still fairly small, audience for his work. He began to receive invitations to read his own poetry, and to lecture at universities. He was made a member of the National Institute of Arts and Letters; and in 1950 a new volume of poetry, *The Auroras of Autumn*, was awarded the Bollingen prize.

In the last five years of his life, interest in Stevens' work continued to increase, although still rather slowly. He received several more literary prizes, including two National Book Awards and a Pulitzer Prize, and he was given an honorary degree by his old university. His creative work continued unabated too, with *The Necessary Angel: Essays in Reality and the Imagination* appearing in 1951 and the *Collected Poems*, containing an entirely new section entitled 'The Rock', in 1954. Nor did Stevens' death bring any abrupt halt to the growth either of his oeuvre or of his reputation. There was enough unpublished prose and poetry still remaining for a further distinguished volume, *Opus Posthumous*, to be issued in 1957, two years after Stevens died; and in the years subsequent to this he was acknowledged, with tardy justice, as one of the greatest of twentieth-century American poets.

FURTHER READING

Beckett, Lucy. *Wallace Stevens*. Cambridge, 1974.

Blessing, Richard Allen. *Wallace Stevens' 'Whole Harmonium'*. Syracuse, N.Y., 1970.

Fuchs, Daniel. *The Comic Spirit of Wallace Stevens*. Durham, N.C., 1963.

Kermode, Frank. *Wallace Stevens*. Edinburgh, 1960.

Litz, A. Walton. *Introspective Voyager: the Poetic Development of Wallace Stevens*. New York, 1972.

Pearce, Roy Harvey and Miller, J. Hillis (eds.). *The Act of the Mind: Essays on the Poetry of Wallace Stevens*. Baltimore, Md., 1965.

The Snow Man

One must have a mind of winter
To regard the frost and the boughs
Of the pine-trees crusted with snow;

And have been cold a long time
To behold the junipers shagged with ice,   5
The spruces rough in the distant glitter

Of the January sun; and not to think
Of any misery in the sound of the wind,
In the sound of a few leaves,

Which is the sound of the land   10
Full of the same wind
That is blowing in the same bare place

For the listener, who listens in the snow
And, nothing himself, beholds
Nothing that is not there and the nothing that is.   15

A High-Toned Old Christian Woman

Poetry is the supreme fiction, madame.
Take the moral law and make a nave of it
And from the nave build haunted heaven. Thus,
The conscience is converted into palms,
Like windy citherns hankering for hymns.   5
We agree in principle. That's clear. But take
The opposing law and make a peristyle,

And from the peristyle project a masque
Beyond the planets. Thus, our bawdiness,
Unpurged by epitaph, indulged at last,   10
Is equally converted into palms,
Squiggling like saxophones. And palm for palm,
Madame, we are where we began. Allow,
Therefore, that in the planetary scene
Your disaffected flagellants, well-stuffed,   15
Smacking their muzzy bellies in parade,
Proud of such novelties of the sublime,
Such tink and tank and tunk-a-tunk-tunk,
May, merely may, madame, whip from themselves
A jovial hullabaloo among the spheres.   20
This will make widows wince. But fictive things
Wink as they will. Wink most when widows wince.

Sunday Morning

I

Complacencies of the peignoir, and late
Coffee and oranges in a sunny chair,
And the green freedom of a cockatoo
Upon a rug mingle to dissipate
The holy hush of ancient sacrifice.   5
She dreams a little, and she feels the dark
Encroachment of that old catastrophe,
As a calm darkens among water-lights.
The pungent oranges and bright, green wings
Seem things in some procession of the dead,   10
Winding across wide water, without sound.
The day is like wide water, without sound,
Stilled for the passing of her dreaming feet
Over the seas, to silent Palestine,
Dominion of the blood and sepulchre.   15

II

Why should she give her bounty to the dead?
What is divinity if it can come
Only in silent shadows and in dreams?

Shall she not find in comforts of the sun,
In pungent fruit and bright, green wings, or else   5
In any balm or beauty of the earth,
Things to be cherished like the thought of heaven?
Divinity must live within herself:
Passions of rain, or moods in falling snow;
Grievings in loneliness, or unsubdued   10
Elations when the forest blooms; gusty
Emotions on wet roads on autumn nights;
All pleasures and all pains, remembering
The bough of summer and the winter branch.
These are the measures destined for her soul.   15

III

Jove in the clouds had his inhuman birth.
No mother suckled him, no sweet land gave
Large-mannered motions to his mythy mind
He moved among us, as a muttering king,
Magnificent, would move among his hinds,   5
Until our blood, commingling, virginal,
With heaven, brought such requital to desire
The very hinds discerned it, in a star.
Shall our blood fail? Or shall it come to be
The blood of paradise? And shall the earth   10
Seem all of paradise that we shall know?
The sky will be much friendlier then than now,
A part of labor and a part of pain,
And next in glory to enduring love,
Not this dividing and indifferent blue.   15

IV

She says, 'I am content when wakened birds,
Before they fly, test the reality
Of misty fields, by their sweet questionings;
But when the birds are gone, and their warm fields
Return no more, where, then, is paradise?'   5
There is not any haunt of prophecy,
Nor any old chimera of the grave,
Neither the golden underground, nor isle
Melodious, where spirits gat them home,
Nor visionary south, nor cloudy palm   10

Remote on heaven's hill, that has endured
As April's green endures; or will endure
Like her remembrance of awakened birds,
Or her desire for June and evening, tipped
By the consummation of the swallow's wings.   15

V

She says, 'But in contentment I still feel
The need of some imperishable bliss.'
Death is the mother of beauty; hence from her,
Alone, shall come fulfilment to our dreams
And our desires. Although she strews the leaves   5
Of sure obliteration on our paths,
The path sick sorrow took, the many paths
Where triumph rang its brassy phrase, or love
Whispered a little out of tenderness,
She makes the willow shiver in the sun   10
For maidens who were wont to sit and gaze
Upon the grass, relinquished to their feet.
She causes boys to pile new plums and pears
On disregarded plate. The maidens taste
And stray impassioned in the littering leaves.   15

VI

Is there no change of death in paradise?
Does ripe fruit never fall? Or do the boughs
Hang always heavy in that perfect sky,
Unchanging, yet so like our perishing earth,
With rivers like our own that seek for seas   5
They never find, the same receding shores
That never touch with inarticulate pang?
Why set the pear upon those river-banks
Or spice the shores with odors of the plum?
Alas, that they should wear our colors there,   10
The silken weavings of our afternoons,
And pick the strings of our insipid lutes!
Death is the mother of beauty, mystical,
Within whose burning bosom we devise
Our earthly mothers waiting, sleeplessly.   15

VII

Supple and turbulent, a ring of men
Shall chant in orgy on a summer morn
Their boisterous devotion to the sun,
Not as a god, but as a god might be,
Naked among them, like a savage source.   5
Their chant shall be a chant of paradise,
Out of their blood, returning to the sky;
And in their chant shall enter, voice by voice,
The windy lake wherein their lord delights,
The trees, like serafin, and echoing hills,   10
That choir among themselves long afterward.
They shall know well the heavenly fellowship
Of men that perish and of summer morn.
And whence they came and whither they shall go
The dew upon their feet shall manifest.   15

VIII

She hears, upon that water without sound,
A voice that cries, 'The tomb in Palestine
Is not the porch of spirits lingering.
It is the grave of Jesus, where he lay.'
We live in an old chaos of the sun,   5
Or old dependency of day and night,
Or island solitude, unsponsored, free,
Of that wide water, inescapable.
Deer walk upon our mountains, and the quail
Whistle about us their spontaneous cries;   10
Sweet berries ripen in the wilderness;
And, in the isolation of the sky,
At evening, casual flocks of pigeons make
Ambiguous undulations as they sink,
Downward to darkness, on extended wings.   15

Bantams in Pine-woods

Chieftain Iffucan of Azcan in caftan
Of tan with henna hackles, halt!

Damned universal cock, as if the sun
Was blackamoor to bear your blazing tail.

Fat! Fat! Fat! Fat! I am the personal.   5
Your world is you. I am my world.

You ten-foot poet among inchlings. Fat!
Begone! An inchling bristles in these pines,

Bristles, and points their Appalachian tangs,
And fears not portly Azcan nor his hoos.   10

Anecdote of the Jar

I placed a jar in Tennessee,
And round it was, upon a hill.
It made the slovenly wilderness
Surround that hill.

The wilderness rose up to it,   5
And sprawled around, no longer wild.
The jar was round upon the ground
And tall and of a port in air.

It took dominion everywhere.
The jar was gray and bare.   10
It did not give of bird or bush,
Like nothing else in Tennessee.

Life is Motion

In Oklahoma,
Bonnie and Josie,
Dressed in calico,
Danced around a stump.
They cried,   5

'Ohoyaho,
Ohoo'...
Celebrating the marriage
Of flesh and air.

Thirteen Ways of
Looking at a Blackbird

I

Among twenty snowy mountains,
The only moving thing
Was the eye of the blackbird.

II

I was of three minds,
Like a tree
In which there are three blackbirds.

III

The blackbird whirled in the autumn winds.
It was a small part of the pantomime.

IV

A man and a woman
Are one.
A man and a woman and a blackbird
Are one.

V

I do not know which to prefer,
The beauty of inflections
Or the beauty of innuendoes,
The blackbird whistling
Or just after.

VI

Icicles filled the long window
With barbaric glass.
The shadow of the blackbird

Crossed it, to and fro.
The mood
Traced in the shadow
An indecipherable cause.

VII

O thin men of Haddam,
Why do you imagine golden birds?
Do you not see how the blackbird
Walks around the feet
Of the women about you?

VIII

I know noble accents
And lucid, inescapable rhythms;
But I know, too,
That the blackbird is involved
In what I know.

IX

When the blackbird flew out of sight,
It marked the edge
Of one of many circles.

X

At the sight of blackbirds
Flying in a green light,
Even the bawds of euphony
Would cry out sharply.

XI

He rode over Connecticut
In a glass coach.
Once, a fear pierced him,
In that he mistook
The shadow of his equipage
For blackbirds.

XII

The river is moving.
The blackbird must be flying.

XIII

It was evening all afternoon.
It was snowing
And it was going to snow.
The blackbird sat
In the cedar-limbs.

The Idea of Order at Key West

She sang beyond the genius of the sea.
The water never formed to mind or voice,
Like a body wholly body, fluttering
Its empty sleeves; and yet its mimic motion
Made constant cry, caused constantly a cry,   5
That was not ours although we understood,
Inhuman, of the veritable ocean.

The sea was not a mask. No more was she.
The song and water were not medleyed sound
Even if what she sang was what she heard,   10
Since what she sang was uttered word by word.
It may be that in all her phrases stirred
The grinding water and the gasping wind;
But it was she and not the sea we heard.

For she was the maker of the song she sang.   15
The ever-hooded, tragic-gestured sea
Was merely a place by which she walked to sing.
Whose spirit is this? we said, because we knew
It was the spirit that we sought and knew
That we should ask this often as she sang.   20

If it was only the dark voice of the sea
That rose, or even colored by many waves;
If it was only the outer voice of sky
And cloud, of the sunken coral water-walled,
However clear, it would have been deep air,   25
The heaving speech of air, a summer sound
Repeated in a summer without end
And sound alone. But it was more than that,

More even than her voice, and ours, among
The meaningless plungings of water and the wind,   30
Theatrical distances, bronze shadows heaped
On high horizons, mountainous atmospheres
Of sky and sea.
        It was her voice that made
The sky acutest at its vanishing.
She measured to the hour its solitude.   35
She was the single artificer of the world
In which she sang. And when she sang, the sea,
Whatever self it had, became the self
That was her song, for she was the maker. Then we,
As we beheld her striding there alone,   40
Knew that there never was a world for her
Except the one she sang and, singing, made.

Ramon Fernandez, tell me, if you know,
Why, when the singing ended and we turned
Toward the town, tell why the glassy lights,   45
The lights in the fishing boats at anchor there,
As the night descended, tilting in the air,
Mastered the night and portioned out the sea,
Fixing emblazoned zones and fiery poles,
Arranging, deepening, enchanting night.   50

Oh! Blessed rage for order, pale Ramon,
The maker's rage to order words of the sea,
Words of the fragrant portals, dimly-starred,
And of ourselves and of our origins,
In ghostlier demarcations, keener sounds.   55

from The Man With the Blue Guitar

I

The man bent over his guitar,
A shearsman of sorts. The day was green.

They said, 'You have a blue guitar,
You do not play things as they are.'

The man replied, 'Things as they are   5
Are changed upon the blue guitar.'

And they said then, 'But play, you must,
A tune beyond us, yet ourselves,

A tune upon the blue guitar
Of things exactly as they are.'   10

III

Ah, but to play man number one,
To drive the dagger in his heart,

To lay his brain upon the board
And pick the acrid colors out,

To nail his thought across the door,   5
Its wings spread wide to rain and snow,

To strike his living hi and ho,
To tick it, tock it, turn it true,

To bang it from a savage blue,
Jangling the metal of the strings...   10

IV

So that's life, then: things as they are?
It picks its way on the blue guitar.

A million people on one string?
And all their manner in the thing,

And all their manner, right and wrong,   5
And all their manner, weak and strong?

The feelings crazily, craftily call,
Like a buzzing of flies in autumn air,

And that's life, then: things as they are,
This buzzing of the blue guitar.   10

V

Do not speak to us of the greatness of poetry,
Of the torches wisping in the underground,

Of the structure of vaults upon a point of light.
There are no shadows in our sun,

Day is desire and night is sleep.   5
There are no shadows anywhere.

The earth, for us, is flat and bare.
There are no shadows. Poetry

Exceeding music must take the place
Of empty heaven and its hymns,   10

Ourselves in poetry must take their place,
Even in the chattering of your guitar.

XI

Slowly the ivy on the stones
Becomes the stones. Women become

The cities, children become the fields
And men in waves become the sea.

It is the chord that falsifies.   5
The sea returns upon the men,

The fields entrap the children, brick
Is a weed and all the flies are caught,

Wingless and withered, but living alive.
The discord merely magnifies.   10

Deeper within the belly's dark
Of time, time grows upon the rock.

XIV

First one beam, then another, then
A thousand are radiant in the sky.

Each is both star and orb; and day
Is the riches of their atmosphere.

The sea appends its tattery hues.   5
The shores are banks of muffling mist.

One says a German chandelier—
A candle is enough to light the world.

It makes it clear. Even at noon
It glistens in essential dark.   10

At night, it lights the fruit and wine,
The book and bread, things as they are,

In a chiaroscuro where
One sits and plays the blue guitar.

XXXII

Throw away the lights, the definitions,
And say of what you see in the dark

That it is this or that it is that,
But do not use the rotted names.

How should you walk in that space and know   5
Nothing of the madness of space,

Nothing of its jocular procreations?
Throw the lights away. Nothing must stand

Between you and the shapes you take
When the crust of shape has been destroyed.   10

You as you are? You are yourself.
The blue guitar surprises you.

from ' Notes Toward a Supreme Fiction'

It Must Be Abstract

I

Begin, ephebe, by perceiving the idea
Of this invention, this invented world,
The inconceivable idea of the sun.

You must become an ignorant man again
And see the sun again with an ignorant eye   5
And see it clearly in the idea of it.

Never suppose an inventing mind as source
Of this idea nor for that mind compose
A voluminous master folded in his fire.

How clean the sun when seen in its idea,   10
Washed in the remotest cleanliness of a heaven
That has expelled us and our images...

The death of one god is the death of all.
Let purple Phoebus lie in umber harvest,
Let Phoebus slumber and die in autumn umber,   15

Phoebus is dead, ephebe. But Phoebus was
A name for something that never could be named.
There was a project for the sun and is.

There is a project for the sun. The sun
Must bear no name, gold flourisher, but be   20
In the difficulty of what it is to be.

IV

The first idea was not our own. Adam
In Eden was the father of Descartes
And Eve made air the mirror of herself,

Of her sons and of her daughters. They found
themselves
In heaven as in a glass; a second earth;   5
And in the earth itself they found a green—

The inhabitants of a very varnished green.
But the first idea was not to shape the clouds
In imitation. The clouds preceded us

There was a muddy centre before we breathed.   10
There was a myth before the myth began,
Venerable and articulate and complete.

From this the poem springs: that we live in a place
That is not our own and, much more, not ourselves
And hard it is in spite of blazoned days.   15

We are the mimics. Clouds are pedagogues
The air is not a mirror but bare board,
Coulisse bright-dark, tragic chiaroscuro

And comic color of the rose, in which
Abysmal instruments make sounds like pips   20
Of the weeping meanings that we add to them.

It Must Change

IV

Two things of opposite natures seem to depend
On one another, as a man depends
On a woman, day on night, the imagined

On the real. This is the origin of change.
Winter and spring, cold copulars, embrace   5
And forth the particulars of rapture come.

Music falls on the silence like a sense,
A passion that we feel, not understand.
Morning and afternoon are clasped together

And North and South are an intrinsic couple   10
And sun and rain a plural, like two lovers
That walk away as one in the greenest body.

In solitude the trumpets of solitude
Are not of another solitude resounding;
A little string speaks for a crowd of voices.   15

The partaker partakes of that which changes him.
The child that touches takes character from the thing,
The body, it touches. The captain and his men

Are one and the sailor and the sea are one.
Follow after, O my companion, my fellow, my self,   20
Sister and solace, brother and delight.

X

A bench was his catalepsy, Theatre
Of Trope. He sat in the park. The water of
The lake was full of artificial things,

Like a page of music, like an upper air,
Like a momentary color, in which swans   5
Were seraphs, were saints, were changing essences.

The west wind was the music, the motion, the force
To which the swans curveted, a will to change,
A will to make iris frettings on the blank.

There was a will to change, a necessitous   10
And present way, a presentation, a kind
Of volatile world, too constant to be denied,

The eye of a vagabond in metaphor
That catches our own. The casual is not
Enough. The freshness of transformation is   15

The freshness of a world. It is our own,
It is ourselves, the freshness of ourselves,
And that necessity and that presentation

Are rubbings of a glass in which we peer.
Of these beginnings, gay and green, propose   20
The suitable amours. Time will write them down.

It Must Give Pleasure

VIII

What am I to believe? If the angel in his cloud,
Serenely gazing at the violent abyss,
Plucks on his strings to pluck abysmal glory,

Leaps downward through evening's revelations, and
On his spredden wings, needs nothing but deep space,   5
Forgets the gold centre, the golden destiny,

Grows warm in the motionless motion of his flight,
Am I that imagine this angel less satisfied?
Are the wings his, the lapis-haunted air?

Is it he or is it I that experience this?   10
Is it I then that keep saying there is an hour
Filled with expressible bliss, in which I have

No need, am happy, forget need's golden hand,
Am satisfied without solacing majesty,
And if there is an hour there is a day,   15

There is a month, a year, there is a time
In which majesty is a mirror of the self:
I have not but I am and as I am, I am.

These external regions, what do we fill them with
Except reflections, the escapades of death,   20
Cinderella fulfilling herself beneath the roof?

X

Fat girl, terrestrial, my summer, my night,
How is it I find you in difference, see you there
In a moving contour, a change not quite completed?

You are familiar yet an aberration.
Civil, madam, I am, but underneath   5
A tree, this unprovoked sensation requires

That I should name you flatly, waste no words,
Check your evasions, hold you to yourself.
Even so when I think of you as strong or tired,

Bent over work, anxious, content, alone,   10
You remain the more than natural figure. You
Become the soft-footed phantom, the irrational

Distortion, however fragrant, however dear.
That's it: the more than rational distortion,
The fiction that results from feeling. Yes, that.   15

They will get it straight one day at the Sorbonne.
We shall return at twilight from the lecture
Pleased that the irrational is rational,

Until flicked by feeling, in a gildered street,
I call you by name, my green, my fluent mundo.   20
You will have stopped revolving except in crystal.

Final Soliloquy of
the Interior Paramour

Light the first light of evening, as in a room
In which we rest and, for small reason, think
The world imagined is the ultimate good.

This is, therefore, the intense rendezvous.
It is in that thought that we collect ourselves,   5
Out of all the indifferences, into one thing:

Within a single thing, a single shawl
Wrapped tightly round us, since we are poor, a
    warmth,
A light, a power, the miraculous influence.

Here, now, we forget each other and ourselves.   10
We feel the obscurity of an order, a whole,
A knowledge, that which arranged the rendezvous.

Within its vital boundary, in the mind.
We say God and the imagination are one...
How high that highest candle lights the dark.   15

Out of this same light, out of the central mind,
We make a dwelling in the evening air,
In which being there together is enough.

WILLIAM CARLOS
WILLIAMS

William Carlos Williams was born in 1883, in Rutherford, New Jersey. His parents were both immigrants, his father from England and his mother from Puerto Rico. After attending school both in America and France he entered the University of Pennsylvania Medical School in 1902 and, while studying in Philadelphia, met Ezra Pound, who became a life-long friend. He received his M.D. in 1906 and then began his internship in New York: but it was in Rutherford that his first volume of *Poems*, a series of pale imitations of Keats, was published in 1909.

After studying pediatrics in Leipzig and visiting Pound in London, Williams returned to become a general practitioner in Rutherford and there, in 1912, he married a local girl, Florence Herman. His poetic activities continued, meanwhile, with the publication of a second volume under the auspices of Pound, and contributions to little magazines like *Poetry* and *The Dial*. By now he was also acquainted with many other American poets, among them Marianne Moore and Wallace Stevens.

The year 1913 was a crucial one for Williams. He became acquainted with a group of painters centred in New York, who were largely responsible for introducing the severe, sharp-edged images of Cubism to the American public. His mentor Ezra Pound published the credo of a new poetic movement, called Imagism (for which, see Introduction); and Williams himself began to read Walt Whitman, the 'poet of American democracy', with renewed enthusiasm. The result of all this was a fresh direction for his verse, towards a greater concern with the hard lines of objects, and the discovery of a language and rhythms more appropriate to the American experience. Williams' contributions to an Imagist anthology and *Al Que Quiere!*, a collection published in 1917, witnessed the change.

Many more volumes of prose and poetry followed in the next few years, among them *In the American Grain*, which argued that American writers should interest themselves more in their native culture, turning away from European models; and Williams still contributed to a wide variety of magazines. The rest of his time was taken up with his medical practice and his work as a pediatrician at the local hospital; or trips with his wife abroad, where he met such celebrated literary exiles as Gertrude Stein and James Joyce.

During the thirties Williams was associated with another poetic movement, called Objectivism, the aims of which were roughly the same as those of Imagism, and he also began work on a trilogy of novels based on the life of his wife's family. It was not until the forties, though, that he began to receive widespread recognition. True, he had been awarded a prize by *The Dial* magazine as early as 1926, and the Guarantor's Prize in 1931. But he had to wait until 1946 for his first honorary degree, and it was another two years before he was given a literary award of any national standing. Almost immediately after this, in 1950 and 1951 respectively, *The Collected Earlier Poems* and *The Collected Later Poems* appeared, to become the standard texts for the verse written up until that time.

Early in 1951, a stroke forced Williams to retire from his medical practice. His creative energy continued unabated, however. During the next twelve years he published three more volumes of poetry, one novel, two books of plays, book V of his epic poem *Paterson*, and selected letters and essays. Given his often stated belief that 'without change there is nothing' it seems appropriate that he should continue writing at this feverish pace, and developing, right up until the moment of his death; and equally appropriate, perhaps, that he should die where he had spent most of his life, in Rutherford.

FURTHER READING

Breslin, James. *William Carlos Williams: an American Artist*. Oxford, 1970.

Koch, Vivienne. *William Carlos Williams*. Norfolk, Conn., 1950.

Miller, J. Hillis (ed.). *William Carlos Williams: a Collection of Critical Essays*. Englewood Cliffs, N.J., 1966.

Tomlinson, Charles (ed.). *William Carlos Williams: a Critical Anthology*. London, 1972.

Wagner, Linda W. *The Poems of William Carlos Williams: a Critical Study*. Middletown, Conn., 1964.

Weaver, Mike. *William Carlos Williams: the American Background*. Cambridge, 1972.

The Revelation

I awoke happy, the house
Was strange, voices
Were across a gap
Through which a girl
Came and paused,   5
Reaching out to me—

Then I remembered
What I had dreamed—
A girl
One whom I knew well   10
Leaned on the door of my car
And stroked my hand—

I shall pass her on the street
We shall say trivial things
To each other   15
But I shall never cease
To search her eyes
For that quiet look—

Sea-Trout and Butterfish

The contours and the shine
hold the eye—caught and lying

orange-finned and the two
half its size, pout-mouthed

beside it on the white dish—   5
Silver scales, the weight

quick tails
whipping the streams aslant

The eye comes down eagerly
unravelled of the sea   10

separates this from that
and the fine fins' sharp spines

Proletarian Portrait

A big young bareheaded woman
in an apron

Her hair slicked back standing
on the street

One stockinged foot toeing   5
the sidewalk

Her shoe in her hand. Looking
intently into it

She pulls out the paper insole
to find the nail   10

That has been hurting her

Tract

I will teach you my townspeople
how to perform a funeral
for you have it over a troop
of artists—
unless one should scour the world—   5
you have the ground sense necessary.

See! the hearse leads.
I begin with a design for a hearse.
For Christ's sake not black—
nor white either—and not polished!   10
Let it be weathered—like a farm wagon—
with gilt wheels (this could be
applied fresh at small expense)
or no wheels at all:
a rough dray to drag over the ground.   15

Knock the glass out!
My God—glass, my townspeople!
For what purpose? Is it for the dead
to look out or for us to see

how well he is housed or to see   20
the flowers or the lack of them—
or what?
To keep the rain and snow from him?
He will have a heavier rain soon:
pebbles and dirt and what not.   25
Let there be no glass—
and no upholstery, phew!
and no little brass rollers
and small easy wheels on the bottom—
my townspeople what are you thinking of?   30

A rough plain hearse then
with gilt wheels and no top at all.
On this the coffin lies
by its own weight.

          No wreaths please—   35
especially no hot house flowers.
Some common memento is better,
something he prized and is known by:
his old clothes—a few books perhaps—
God knows what! You realize   40
how we are about these things
my townspeople—
something will be found—anything
even flowers if he had come to that.
So much for the hearse.   45

For heaven's sake though see to the driver!
Take off the silk hat! In fact
that's no place at all for him—
up there unceremoniously
dragging our friend out to his own dignity!   50
Bring him down—bring him down!
Low and inconspicuous! I'd not have him ride
on the wagon at all—damn him—
the undertaker's understrapper!
Let him hold the reins   55
and walk at the side
and inconspicuously too!

Then briefly as to yourselves:
Walk behind—as they do in France,
seventh class, or if you ride   60
Hell take curtains! Go with some show
of inconvenience; sit openly—
to the weather as to grief.
Or do you think you can shut grief in?
What—from us? We who have perhaps   65
nothing to lose? Share with us
share with us—it will be money
in your pockets.
                          Go now
I think you are ready.   70

The Widow's Lament in Springtime

Sorrow is my own yard
where the new grass
flames as it has flamed
often before but not
with the cold fire   5
that closes round me this year.
Thirtyfive years
I lived with my husband.
The plumtree is white today
with masses of flowers.   10

Masses of flowers
load the cherry branches
and color some bushes
yellow and some red
but the grief in my heart   15
is stronger than they
for though they were my joy
formerly, today I notice them
and turned away forgetting.
Today my son told me   20
that in the meadows,
at the edge of the heavy woods
in the distance, he saw

trees of white flowers.
I feel that I would like 25
to go there
and fall into those flowers
and sink into the marsh near them.

from 'Spring and All'

I

By the road to the contagious hospital
under the surge of the blue
mottled clouds driven from the
northeast—a cold wind. Beyond, the
waste of broad, muddy fields 5
brown with dried weeds, standing and fallen

patches of standing water
the scattering of tall trees

All along the road the reddish
purplish, forked, upstanding, twiggy 10
stuff of bushes and small trees
with dead, brown leaves under them
leafless vines—

Lifeless in appearance, sluggish
dazed spring approaches— 15

They enter the new world naked,
cold, uncertain of all
save that they enter. All about them
the cold, familiar wind—

Now the grass, tomorrow 20
the stiff curl of wildcarrot leaf
One by one objects are defined—
It quickens: clarity, outline of leaf

But now the stark dignity of
entrance—Still, the profound change 25
has come upon them: rooted, they
grip down and begin to awaken

II

Pink confused with white
flowers and flowers reversed
take and spill the shaded flame
darting it back
into the lamp's horn   5

petals aslant darkened with mauve

red where in whorls
petal lays its glow upon petal
round flamegreen throats

petals radiant with transpiercing light   10
contending
        above
the leaves
reaching up their modest green
from the pot's rim   15

and there, wholly dark, the pot
gay with rough moss.

III

The farmer in deep thought
is pacing through the rain
among his blank fields, with
hands in pockets,
in his head   5
the harvest already planted.
A cold wind ruffles the water
among the browned weeds.
On all sides
the world rolls coldly away: 10
black orchards
darkened by the March clouds—
leaving room for thought.
Down past the brushwood
bristling by   15
the rainsluiced wagonroad
looms the artist figure of
the farmer—composing
—antagonist

XXI

so much depends
upon

a red wheel
barrow

glazed with rain   5
water

beside the white
chickens.

Young Sycamore

I must tell you
this young tree
whose round and firm trunk
between the wet

pavement and the gutter   5
(where water
is trickling) rises
bodily

into the air with
one undulant   10
thrust half its height—
and then

dividing and waning
sending out
young branches on   15
all sides—

hung with cocoons
it thins
till nothing is left of it
but two   20

eccentric knotted
twigs
bending forward
hornlike at the top

Raleigh Was Right

We cannot go to the country
for the country will bring us
    no peace
What can the small violets tell us
that grow on furry stems in   5
the long grass among lance shaped
    leaves?

Though you praise us
and call to mind the poets
who sung of our loveliness   10
it was long ago!
long ago! when country people
would plow and sow with
flowering minds and pockets
    at ease—   15
if ever this were true.

Not now. Love itself a flower
with roots in a parched ground.
Empty pockets make empty heads.
Cure it if you can but   20
do not believe that we can live
today in the country
for the country will bring us
    no peace.

The Night Rider

Scoured like a conch
or the moon's shell
I ride from my love
through the damp night.

there are lights   5
through the trees,
falling leaves,
the air and the blood

an even mood
warm with summer dwindling,   10
relic of heat:
Ruin dearly bought

smoothed to a round
carved by the sand
the pulse a remembered pulse   15
of full-tide gone

Preface to 'Paterson': Book One

'Rigor of beauty is the quest. But how will you find beauty   1
when it is locked in the mind past all remonstrance?'

To make a start,
out of particulars
and make them general, rolling   5
up the sum, by defective means—
Sniffing the trees,
just another dog
among a lot of dogs. What
else is there? And to do?   10
The rest have run out—
after the rabbits.
Only the lame stands—on
three legs. Scratch front and back.
Deceive and eat. Dig   15
a musty bone

For the beginning is assuredly
the end—since we know nothing, pure
and simple, beyond
our own complexities.   20
                    Yet there is
no return: rolling up out of chaos,
a nine months' wonder, the city
the man, an identity—it can't be
otherwise—an   25
interpenetration, both ways. Rolling
up! obverse, reverse;

the drunk the sober; the illustrious
the gross; one. In ignorance
a certain knowledge and knowledge,   30
undispersed, its own undoing.

          (The multiple seed,
packed tight with detail, soured,
is lost in the flux and the mind,
distracted, floats off in the same   35
scum)
Rolling up, rolling up heavy with
numbers.

        It is the ignorant sun
rising in the slot of   40
hollow suns risen, so that never in this
world will a man live well in his body
save dying—and not know himself
dying; yet that is
the design. Renews himself   45
thereby, in addition and subtraction,
walking up and down.

      and the craft,
subverted by thought, rolling up, let
him beware lest he turn to no more than   50
the writing of stale poems...
Minds like beds always made up
          (more stony than a shore)
unwilling or unable.

        Rolling in, top up,   55
under, thrust and recoil, a great clatter:
lifted as air, boated, multicolored, a
wash of seas —
from mathematics to particulars—

        divided as the dew,   60
floating mists, to be rained down and
regathered into a river that flows
and encircles:

        shells and animalcules
generally and so to man,   65
        to Paterson.

The Descent

The descent beckons
        as the ascent beckoned.
                Memory is a kind
of accomplishment,
        a sort of renewal
                even
an initiation, since the spaces it opens are new places
        inhabited by hordes
                heretofore unrealized,
of new kinds—
        since their movements
                are toward new objectives
(even though formerly they were abandoned).   5

No defeat is made up entirely of defeat—since
the world it opens is always a place
        formerly
                unsuspected. A
world lost,
        a world unsuspected,
                beckons to new places
and no whiteness (lost) is so white as the memory
of whiteness   .   10

With evening, love wakens
        though its shadows
                which are alive by reason
of the sun shining—
        grow sleepy now and drop away
                from desire
Love without shadows stirs now
        beginning to awaken
                as night
advances.

The descent
        made up of despairs
                and without accomplishment   15
realizes a new awakening:
                which is a reversal
of despair.

        For what we cannot accomplish, what
is denied to love,
           what we have lost in the anticipation—
               a descent follows,
endless and indestructible

The Orchestra

The precise counterpart
        of a cacophony of bird calls
           lifting the sun almighty
into his sphere: wood-winds
        clarinet and violins
           sound a prolonged A!
Ah! the sun, the sun! is about to rise
        and shed his beams
           as he has always done
upon us all,
        drudges and those
           who live at ease,
women and men,
        upon the old,
           upon children and the sick   5
who are about to die and are indeed
        dead in their beds,
           to whom his light
is forever lost. The cello
        raises his bass note
           manfully in the treble din
Ah, ah and ah!
        together, unattuned
           seeking a common tone.
Love is that common tone
        shall raise his fiery head
           and sound his note.

The purpose of an orchestra
        is to organize those sounds
           and hold them   10

to an assembled order
      in spite of the
           'wrong note.' Well, shall we
think or listen? Is there a sound addressed
      not wholly to the ear?
           We half close
our eyes. We do not
      hear it through our eyes.
           It is not
a flute note either, it is the relation
      of a flute note
           to a drum. I am wide
awake. The mind
      is listening. The ear
           is alerted. But the ear   15
in a half-reluctant mood
      stretches
           .   .   and yawns.

And so the banked violins
      in three tiers
           enliven the scene,
pizzicato. For a short
      memory or to
           make the listener listen
the theme is repeated
      stressing a variant:
           it is a principle of music
to repeat the theme. Repeat
      and repeat again,
           as the pace mounts. The   20
theme is difficult
      but no more difficult
           than the facts to be
resolved. Repeat
      and repeat the theme
           and all it develops to be
until thought is dissolved
      in tears.
           Our dreams

have been assaulted
        by a memory that will not
            sleep. The
French horns
        interpose
               .   .   their voices: 25
I love you. My heart
        is innocent. And this
            the first day of the world!

Say to them:
'Man has survived hitherto because he was too ignorant
to know how to realise his wishes. Now that he can realize
them, he must either change them or perish.'   30

Now is the time   .
        in spite of the 'wrong note'
            I love you. My heart is
innocent.
        And this the first
            (and last) day of the world

The birds twitter now anew
        but a design
            surmounts their twittering.
It is a design of a man
        that makes them twitter.
            It is a design.

A Negro Woman

carrying a bunch of marigolds
        wrapped
            in an old newspaper:
She carries them upright,
        bareheaded,
            the bulk
of her thighs
        causing her to waddle
            as she walks

looking into
      the store window which she passes
            on her way.
What is she
      but an ambassador
            from another world   5
a world of pretty marigolds
      of two shades
            which she announces
not knowing what she does
      other
            than walk the streets
holding the flowers upright
      as a torch
            so early in the morning.

from Asphodel, That Greeny Flower

Of asphodel, that greeny flower,
      like a buttercup
            upon its branching stem—
save that it's green and wooden—
      I come, my sweet,
            to sing to you.
We lived long together
      a life filled,
            if you will,
with flowers. So that
      I was cheered
            when I came first to know
that there were flowers also
      in hell.
            Today   5
I'm filled with the fading memory of those flowers
      that we both loved,
            even to this poor
colorless thing—
      I saw it
            when I was a child—

little prized among the living
    but the dead see,
        asking among themselves:
What do I remember
    that was shaped
        as this thing is shaped?
while our eyes fill
    with tears.
        Of love, abiding love   10
it will be telling
    though too weak a wash of crimson
        colors it
to make it wholly credible.
    There is something
        something urgent
I have to say to you
    and you alone
        but it must wait
while I drink in
    the joy of your approach,
        perhaps for the last time.
And so
    with fear in my heart
        I drag it out   15
and keep on talking
    for I dare not stop.
        Listen while I talk on
against time.
    It will not be
        for long.
I have forgot
    and yet I see clearly enough
        something
central to the sky
    which ranges round it.
        An odor
springs from it!
    A sweetest odor!
        Honeysuckle! And now   20

there comes the buzzing of a bee!
      and a whole flood
           of sister memories!
Only give me time,
      time to recall them
           before I shall speak out.
Give me time,
      time.
When I was a boy
      I kept a book
           to which, from time
to time,
      I added pressed flowers
           until, after a time,   25
I had a good collection.
      The asphodel,
           forebodingly,
among them.
      I bring you,
           reawakened,
a memory of those flowers.
      They were sweet
           when I pressed them
and retained
      something of their sweetness
           a long time.
It is a curious odor,
      a moral odor,
           that brings me   30
near to you.
      The color
           was the first to go.
There had come to me
      a challenge,
           your dear self,
mortal as I was,
      the lily's throat
           to the hummingbird!
Endless wealth,
      I thought,
           held out its arms to me.

A thousand topics
      in an apple blossom.
            The generous earth itself   35
gave us lief.
      The whole world
            became my garden!
But the sea
      which no one tends
            is also a garden
when the sun strikes it
      and the waves
            are wakened.
I have seen it
      and so have you
            when it puts all flowers
to shame.
      Too, there are the starfish
            stiffened by the sun   40
and other sea wrack
      and weeds. We knew that
            along with the rest of it
for we were born by the sea,
      knew its rose hedges
            to the very water's brink.
There the pink mallow grows
      and in their season
            strawberries
and there, later,
      we went to gather
            the wild plum.
I cannot say
      that I have gone to hell
            for your love   45
but often
      found myself there
            in your pursuit.
I do not like it
      and wanted to be
            in heaven. Hear me out.
Do not turn away.

I have learned much in my life
        from books
               and out of them
about love.
        Death
               is not the end of it.   50
There is a hierarchy
        which can be attained,
             I think,
in its service.
        Its guerdon
               is a fairy flower;
a cat of twenty lives.
        If no one came to try it
             the world
would be the loser.
        It has been
               for you and me
as one who watches a storm
        come in over the water.
               We have stood   55
from year to year
        before the spectacle of our lives
             with joined hands.
The storm unfolds.
        Lightning
               plays about the edges of the clouds.
The sky to the north
        is placid,
             blue in the afterglow
as the storm piles up.
        It is a flower
               that will soon reach
the apex of its bloom. . .

from Pictures from Brueghel

I

In a red winter hat blue
eyes smiling
just the head and shoulders

crowded on the canvas
arms folded one   5
big ear the right showing

the face slightly tilted
a heavy wool coat
with broad buttons

gathered at the neck reveals   10
a bulbous nose
but the eyes red-rimmed

from over-use he must have
driven them hard
but the delicate wrists   15

show him to have been a
man unused to
manual labor unshaved his

blond beard half trimmed
no time for any-   20
thing but his painting

II

According to Brueghel
when Icarus fell
it was spring

a farmer was ploughing
his field   5
the whole pageantry

of the year was
awake tingling
near

the edge of the sea 10
concerned
with itself

sweating in the sun
that melted
the wings' wax 15

unsignificantly
off the coast
there was

a splash quite unnoticed
this was 20
Icarus drowning

MARIANNE MOORE

Born in St Louis, Missouri, in 1887, Marianne Moore scarcely knew her father. He suffered a nervous breakdown while she was still young, and the rest of the family then went to live with Moore's maternal grandfather, the Reverend John Warner, a pastor in the local Presbyterian church. In 1894 the Reverend Warner died, and the family moved soon afterwards to Carlisle, Pennsylvania, where Moore was to spend the rest of her childhood. She attended the local high school and, after graduating, enrolled at Bryn Mawr. It was here that she first began to write poetry: academic imitations, mostly, of various late Victorian writers, some of which were published in the college magazine.

Moore graduated from Bryn Mawr in 1909 and returned to Carlisle, to take a secretarial course at the local commercial college. She then spent nearly four years teaching stenography, book-keeping, and commercial law at the United States Indian School in Carlisle. Much of her spare time was devoted to verse, both reading and writing it, and in 1915 she had her first success when two of her poems were published, one in the London magazine *The Egoist* and one in *Poetry*.

In 1916 Marianne Moore moved with her mother to Chatham, New Jersey, to keep house for her brother, who had been assigned there as a Presbyterian minister. Chatham was not far from New York, and she began travelling to the city quite frequently. There, she became acquainted with the group of poets associated with the magazine *Others*, among them William Carlos Williams, Wallace Stevens, and Kenneth Burke; and within a short time her work was appearing both in the magazine and in its annual anthology. Her contacts with the group were made easier, and the more frequent, when in 1918 her brother became a chaplain in the Navy. There was no reason why she and Mrs Moore should remain in Chatham any longer, and so they moved to Greenwich Village near the centre of the city. She has continued to live in the New York area ever since; working for a while during the early years as a secretary, a private tutor, and as an assistant in the New York Public Library.

As a permanent resident of the city, Moore's acquaintanceship with other writers and literary circles steadily grew, and in the meantime her work began to appear regularly in *The Dial*. Then in 1921 her first volume, entitled simply *Poems*, was published in London: a selection compiled without her knowledge by two of her friends. Three years later *Observations*, a volume which she had prepared herself, appeared under the imprint of the Dial Press in New York and received the Dial Award for that year. Shortly after that, in 1925, she became editor of *The Dial* and retained the post until the demise of the magazine in 1929. The responsibilities of this post left her very little time for her own work: but as soon as she was free again, new volumes began to follow one another in quick succession. *Selected Poems* was published in New York and London in 1935, with an introduction by T. S. Eliot; *The Pangolin and Other Verse* in 1936; *What Are Years?* in 1941; *Nevertheless* in 1944; and *Collected Poems* in 1951. This last collection was awarded not only the Pulitzer Prize, but the National Book Award, and the Bollingen Prize as well.

Moore devoted the next few years to her verse translations of *The Fables of La Fontaine*, which were published in 1954. *Predilections*, a collection of her essays, followed a year later; and a new volume of poetry, *Like a Bulwark*, a year after that. By now she had become something of a national institution, instantly recognisable because of the black cape and black tricorn hat that she habitually wore. A measure of her celebrity was that, in 1955, the Ford Motor Company asked her to assist them in devising a name for their new model; and that, as recently as 1969, she was invited to open the baseball season by throwing the first ball at the Yankee Stadium. Despite these new demands on her time and attention, though, Moore has continued to be as prolific as ever. She produced three more volumes between 1959 and 1966, and in 1967 the appearance of her *Collected Poems* confirmed her status as one of the major American poets of this century.

FURTHER READING

Engel, Bernard F. *Marianne Moore.* New York, 1964.
Hall, Donald. *Marianne Moore: the Cage and the Animal.* New York, 1970.
Nitchie, George W. *Marianne Moore: an Introduction to the Poetry.* New York, 1969.
Tomlinson, Charles (ed.). *Marianne Moore: a Collection of Critical Essays.* Englewood Cliffs, N.J., 1969.

The Steeple-Jack

Dürer would have seen a reason for living
    in a town like this, with eight stranded whales
to look at; with the sweet sea air coming into your house
on a fine day, from water etched
    with waves as formal as the scales   5
on a fish.

One by one in two's and three's, the seagulls keep
    flying back and forth over the town clock,
or sailing around the lighthouse without moving their wings—
rising steadily with a slight   10
    quiver of the body—or flock
mewing where

a sea the purple of the peacock's neck is
    paled to greenish azure as Dürer changed
the pine green of the Tyrol to peacock blue and guinea   15
gray. You can see a twenty-five-
    pound lobster; and fish nets arranged
to dry. The

whirlwind fife-and-drum of the storm bends the salt
    marsh grass, disturbs stars in the sky and the   20
star on the steeple; it is a privilege to see so
much confusion. Disguised by what
    might seem the opposite, the sea-
side flowers and

trees are favored by the fog so that you have   25
    the tropics at first hand: the trumpet vine,
foxglove, giant snapdragon, a salpigloss is that has
spots and stripes; morning-glories, gourds,
    or moon-vines trained on fishing twine
at the back door: 30

cattails, flags, blueberries and spiderwort,
    striped grass, lichens, sunflowers, asters, daisies—
yellow and crab-claw ragged sailors with green bracts—toad-
    plant,

petunias, ferns; pink lilies, blue
   ones, tigers; poppies; black sweet-peas.   35
The climate

is not right for the banyan, frangipani, or
   jack-fruit trees; or for exotic serpent
life. Ring lizard and snakeskin for the foot, if you see fit;
but here they've cats, not cobras, to   40
   keep down the rats. The diffident
little newt

with white pin-dots on black horizontal spaced-
   out bands lives here; yet there is nothing that
ambition can buy or take away. The college student   45
named Ambrose sits on the hillside
   with his not-native books and hat
and sees boats

at sea progress white and rigid as if in
   a groove. Liking an elegance of which   50
the source is not bravado, he knows by heart the antique
sugar-bowl shaped summerhouse of
   interlacing slats, and the pitch
of the church

spire, not true, from which a man in scarlet lets   55
   down a rope as a spider spins a thread;
he might be part of a novel, but on the sidewalk a
sign says C. J. Poole, Steeple Jack,
   in black and white; and one in red
and white says   60

Danger. The church portico has four fluted
   columns, each a single piece of stone, made
modester by whitewash. This would be a fit haven for
waifs, children, animals, prisoners,
   and presidents who have repaid   65
sin-driven

senators by not thinking about them. The
   place has a schoolhouse, a post-office in a
store, fish-houses, hen-houses, a three-masted
   schooner on   70

the stocks. The hero, the student,
  the steeple jack, each in his way,
is at home.

It could not be dangerous to be living
  in a town like this, of simple people,   75
who have a steeple-jack placing danger signs by the church
while he is gilding the solid-
  pointed star, which on a steeple
stands for hope.

No Swan So Fine

'No water so still as the
  dead fountains of Versailles.' No swan,
with swart blind look askance
and gondoliering legs, so fine
  as the chintz china one with fawn-   5
brown eyes and toothed gold
collar on to show whose bird it was.

Lodged in the Louis Fifteenth
  candelabrum-tree of cockscomb-
tinted buttons, dahlias,   10
sea urchins, and everlastings,
  it perches on the branching foam
of polished sculptured
flowers—at ease and tall. The king is dead.

The Frigate Pelican

Rapidly cruising or lying on the air there is a bird
  that realizes Rasselas's friend's project
of wings uniting levity with strength. This
  hell-diver, frigate bird, hurricane-
bird; unless swift is the proper word   5
  for him, the storm omen when
he flies close to the waves, should be seen
  fishing, although oftener
  he appears to prefer

to take, on the wing, from industrious crude-winged species, 10
  the fish they have caught, and is seldom successless.
  A marvel of grace, no matter how fast his
    victim may fly or how often may
turn. The others with similar ease,
  slowly rising once more,   15
    move out to the top
    of the circle and stop

and blow back, allowing the wind to reverse their direction—
  unlike the more stalwart swan that can ferry the
  woodcutter's two children home. Make hay; keep   20
    the shop; I have one sheep; were a less
limber animal's mottoes. This one
    finds sticks for the swan's-down dress
of his child to rest upon and would
    not know Gretel from Hänsel.   25
    As impassioned Handel—

meant for a lawyer and a masculine German domestic
  career—clandestinely studied the harpsichord
  and never was known to have fallen in love,
    the unconfiding frigate bird hides   30
in the height and in the majestic
    display of his art. He glides
a hundred feet or quivers about
    as charred paper behaves—full
    of feints; and an eagle   35

of vigilance.... *Festina lente*. Be gay
  civilly? How so? 'If I do well I am blessed
  whether any bless me or not, and if I do
    ill I am cursed.' We watch the moon rise
on the Susquehanna. In his way,   40
    this most romantic bird flies
to a more mundane place, the mangrove
    swamp to sleep. He wastes the moon
    But he, and others, soon

rise from the bough and though flying, are able to foil the tired 45
  moment of danger that lays on heart and lungs the
  weight of the python that crushes to powder.

Poetry

I, too, dislike it: there are things that are important beyond all
           this fiddle.
   Reading it, however, with a perfect contempt for it, one
           discovers in
     it after all, a place for the genuine.
       Hands that can grasp, eyes
        that can dilate, hair that can rise   5
          if it must, these things are important not because a
high-sounding interpretation can be put upon them but because
           they are
    useful. When they become so derivative as to become
           unintelligible,
    the same thing may be said for all of us, that we
       do not admire what   10
       we cannot understand: the bat
         holding on upside down or in quest of something to
eat, elephants pushing, a wild horse taking a roll, a tireless wolf
           under
    a tree, the immovable critic twitching his skin like a horse
           that feels a flea, the base-
    ball fan, the statistician—   15
       nor is it valid
         to discriminate against 'business documents and
school-books'; all these phenomena are important. One must
           make a distinction
    however; when dragged into prominence by half poets, the
           result is not poetry,
    nor till the poets among us can be   20
       'literalists of
        the imagination'—above
         insolence and triviality and can present
for inspection, 'imaginary gardens with real toads in them',
           shall we have
    it. In the meantime, if you demand on the one hand,   25
    the raw material of poetry in
       all its rawness and
       that which is on the other hand
        genuine, you are interested in poetry.

When I Buy Pictures

or what is closer to the truth,
when I look at that of which I may regard myself as the
                                    imaginary possessor,
I fix upon what would give me pleasure in my average moments:
the satire upon curiosity in which no more is discernible
than the intensity of the mood;   5
or quite the opposite—the old thing, the medieval decorated
                                        hatbox,
in which there are hounds with waists diminishing like the
                                    waist of the hourglass,
and deer and birds and seated people;
it may be no more than a square of parquetry; the literal
                                  biography perhaps,
in letters standing well apart upon a parchment-like expanse;   10
an artichoke in six varieties of blue; the snipe-legged
                                hieroglyphic in three parts;
the silver fence protecting Adam's grave, or Michael taking
                                Adam by the wrist.
Too stern an intellectual emphasis upon this quality or that
                              detracts from one's enjoyment.
It must not wish to disarm anything; nor may the approved
                          triumph easily be honored—
that which is great because something else is small.   15
It comes to this: of whatever sort it is,
it must be 'lit with piercing glances into the life of things';
it must acknowledge the spiritual forces which have made it.

A Grave

Man looking into the sea,
taking the view from those who have as much right to it as
                              you have to it yourself,
it is human nature to stand in the middle of a thing,
but you cannot stand in the middle of this;
the sea has nothing to give but a well excavated grave.   5
The firs stand in a procession, each with an emerald turkey
                                foot at the top,

reserved as their contours, saying nothing;
repression, however, is not the most obvious characteristic of
                                                    the sea;
the sea is a collector, quick to return a rapacious look.
There are others besides you who have worn that look—   10
whose expression is no longer a protest; the fish no longer
                                    investigate them
for their bones have not lasted:
men lower nets, unconscious of the fact that they are
                                    desecrating a grave,
and row quickly away—the blades of the oars
moving together like the feet of water spiders as if there were
                        no such thing as death.   15
The wrinkles progress among themselves in a phalanx—
                        beautiful under networks of foam,
and fade breathlessly while the sea rustles in and out of the
                                                seaweed;
the birds swim through the air at top speed, emitting catcalls
                                    as heretofore—
the tortoise shell scourges about the feet of the cliffs, in motion
                                    beneath them;
and the ocean, under the pulsation of lighthouses and noise of
                            bell buoys,   20
advances as usual, looking as if it were not that ocean in which
                        dropped things are bound to sink—
in which if they turn and twist, it is neither with volition nor
                                    consciousness.

An Egyptian Pulled Glass Bottle
in the Shape of a Fish

Here we have thirst
and patience, from the first,
   and art, as in a wave held up for us to see
   in its essential perpendicularity;

not brittle but   5
intense—the spectrum, that
      pectacular and nimble animal the fish,
      whose scales turn aside the sun's sword by their polish.

To a Snail

If 'compression is the first grace of style,'
you have it. Contractility is a virtue
as modesty is a virtue.
It is not the acquisition of any one thing
that is able to adorn,   5
or the incidental quality that occurs
as a concomitant of something well said,
that we value in style,
but the principle that is hid:
in the absence of feet, 'a method of conclusions';   10
'a knowledge of principles,'
in the curious phenomenon of your occipital horn.

What are Years?

What is our innocence,
what is our guilt? All are
   naked, none is safe. And whence
is courage: the unanswered question,
the resolute doubt—   5
dumbly calling, deafly listening—that
in misfortune, even death,
   encourages others
   and in its defeat, stirs

   the soul to be strong? He   10
sees deep and is glad, who
   accedes to mortality
and in his imprisonment rises
upon himself as
the sea in a chasm, struggling to be   15
free and unable to be,
   in its surrendering
   finds its continuing.

   So he who strongly feels,
behaves. The very bird,   20
   grown taller as he sings, steels

his form straight up. Though he is captive,
his mighty singing
says, satisfaction is a lowly
thing, how pure a thing is joy.   25
    This is mortality,
    this is eternity.

Melchior Vulpius

c. 1560–1615

a contrapuntalist—
              composer of chorales
and wedding-hymns to Latin words
but best of all an anthem:
    'God be praised for conquering faith   5
    which feareth neither pain nor death.'

We have to trust this art—
             this mastery which none
can understand. Yet someone has
acquired it and is able to   10
    direct it. Mouse-skin-bellows'-breath
    expanding into rapture saith

'Hallelujah.' Almost
             utmost absolutist
and fugue-ist, Amen; slowly building   15
from miniature thunder,
    crescendos antidoting death—
    love's signature cementing faith.

ROBINSON JEFFERS

Robinson Jeffers was born in 1887 in Pittsburgh, Pennsylvania. His father was a professor of Biblical languages and literature, a student of the classics as well as a stern Calvinist; and for seven years, while Jeffers remained an only child, he supervised the boy's education. After that, parental training was supplemented by tuition at various private schools in the neighbourhood and later, when the family began travelling in Europe a great deal, at a succession of boarding schools in Switzerland and Germany.

At the age of fifteen Jeffers entered the University of Pittsburgh. He did not stay there for long, however: within a year the family moved to California, and he was then enrolled at Occidental College. This move proved to be a momentous one for the poet because in coming West he was, in a sense, coming home. He was to live on the West Coast for the rest of his life. What was more important, he was to find in the West an appropriate spirit of place. Its rugged scenery and way of life, its sense of detachment from the civilised communities of the East, and of Europe: all this was to exercise a potent influence upon Jeffers, helping to determine the subjects of his verse, and to shape his style.

After graduating from Occidental College in 1905, Jeffers then went on to the University of Zurich in Switzerland, the University of California, and the University of Washington. There he studied medicine, forestry, and literature; subjects which nicely combined his intended vocation of poet with the particular interests – in Nature, the human organism and modern science – which were to inform some of his best poetry. It was during this period, as well, that he met Una Kuster, a married woman two years his senior with whom he fell passionately in love. Relatives on both sides tried to break up the relationship, but without success; and in 1913, after Una had finally obtained a divorce, the couple were married. Una, whose own vitality and warmth helped to temper her husband's habits of isolation, then went to live with Jeffers at Carmel on the Californian coast. Carmel was sparsely populated at the time, and Jeffers created further privacy for his wife and himself by building a granite house and a tower on the cliffs facing the sea, and surrounding them with a small forest. The first building, called Tor House, became their home; the second, called Hawk Tower, the place where Jeffers wrote most of his verse.

Jeffers had already had two volumes of poetry published, one of them privately, in 1912 and 1916. Neither of them received much attention, nor really deserved it; consisting as they did, largely, of conventional lyrics and meditative pieces, pale imitations of Victorian verse. Now, however, settled at Tor House with Una, he began to explore new themes and experiment with a new style; harsher, more flexible measures were recruited, and a simpler diction, so as to express his vision of a Nature that was stern and elemental, essentially hostile to human designs. The results, published privately as *Tamar and Other Poems*, appeared in 1924; and so enthusiastic was the reception given to this volume that within a year a commercial edition had been arranged, with fresh poems added. With the new title, *Roan Stallion, Tamar, and Other Poems*, the reissue rapidly became a popular success as well as a critical one, so that within a very short space of time Jeffers found his fame as a poet well established.

More volumes then followed quickly upon one another, most of them containing one or two long narrative pieces together with a series of shorter lyrics. These included *The Women at Point Sur* (1927); *Cawdor and Other Poems* (1928); *Thurso's Landing and Other Poems* (1932); *Give Your Heart to the Hawks* (1933); and *Such Counsels You Gave Me* (1937). In 1938, a large volume of *Selected Poetry* was published, and by this time Jeffers' reputation had just about reached its zenith. From then on, the attacks on his verse started to multiply. Critics, in increasing numbers, began to object to his beliefs because they found them too brutal, or to his techniques because they found them monotonous; or they pointed to what was an undoubted deterioration of power in the later work. The American reading public grew hostile too, partly because Jeffers had espoused isolationism, a cause which seemed almost treasonous to many of them after their nation had entered the Second World War. So unpopular did Jeffers' opinions become, in fact, that his publishers felt impelled to introduce his 1948 volume, *The Double Axe*, with a note dissociating themselves from any of the ideas expressed therein.

Jeffers did enjoy a slight recovery of critical esteem and popularity in the last decade of his life: he received several awards,
from the Academy of American Poets among others, and his free
adaptation of the *Medea* by Euripides was a great sucess on
Broadway in 1947. In general, though, attitudes towards his
work continued to vary between the hostile and the indifferent.
His wife died in 1950. His last volume, *Hungerfield and Other
Poems*, was published in 1954; and from then until his own
death in 1962 he lived quietly and alone.

FURTHER READING

Carpenter, Frederic I. *Robinson Jeffers*. New York, 1962.
Coffin, Arthur B. *Robinson Jeffers: Poet of Inhumanism*. Madison, Wisc.,
1971.
Powell, Lawrence C. *Robinson Jeffers: the Man and His Work*. Pasadena,
Calif., 1940.
Squires, Radcliffe. *The Loyalties of Robinson Jeffers*. Ann Arbor, Mich., 1956.
Sterling, George. *Robinson Jeffers: the Man and his Work*. New York, 1926.

Divinely Superfluous Beauty

The storm-dances of gulls, the barking game of seals,
Over and under the ocean...
Divinely superfluous beauty
Rules the games, presides over destinies, makes trees grow
And hills tower, waves fall.   5
The incredible beauty of joy
Stars with fire the joining of lips, O let our loves too
Be joined, there is not a maiden
Burns and thirsts for love
More than my blood for you, by the shore of seals while the
    wings   10
Weave like a web in the air
Divinely superfluous beauty.

To the Stone-Cutters

Stone-cutters fighting time with marble, you foredefeated
Challengers of oblivion
Eat cynical earnings, knowing rock splits, records fall down,

The square-limbed Roman letters
Scale in the thaws, wear in the rain. The poet as well   5
Builds his monument mockingly;
For man will be blotted out, the blithe earth die, the brave sun
Die blind and blacken to the heart:
Yet stones have stood for a thousand years, and pained thoughts
    found
The honey of peace in old poems.   10

Continent's End

At the equinox when the earth was veiled in a late rain, wreathed
    with wet poppies, waiting spring,
The ocean swelled for a far storm and beat its boundary, the
    ground-swell shook the beds of granite.

I gazing at the boundaries of granite and spray, the established
    sea-marks, felt behind me
Mountain and plain, the immense breadth of the continent,
    before me the mass and doubled stretch of water.

I said: You yoke the Aleutian seal-rocks with the lava and coral
    sowings that flower the south,   5
Over your flood the life that sought the sunrise faces ours that
    has followed the evening star.

The long migrations meet across you and it is nothing to you,
    you have forgotten us, mother.
You were much younger when we crawled out of the womb and
    lay in the sun's eye on the tideline.

It was long and long ago: we have grown proud since then and
    you have grown bitter; life retains
Your mobile soft unquiet strength; and envies hardness, the
    insolent quietness of stone.   10

The tides are in our veins, we still mirror the stars, life is your
    child, but there is in me
Older and harder than life and more impartial, the eye that
    watched before there was an ocean.

That watched you fill your beds out of the condensation of thin
    vapor and watched you change them,

That saw you soft and violent wear your boundaries down, eat
  rock, shift places with the continents.

Mother, though my song's measure is like your surf-beat's
  ancient rhythm I never learned it of you.   15
Before there was any water there were tides of fire, both our
  tones flow from the older fountain.

from Roan Stallion

The dog barked; then the woman stood in the doorway, and
  hearing iron strike stone down the steep road
Covered her head with a black shawl and entered the light rain;
  she stood at the turn of the road.
A nobly formed woman; erect and strong as a new tower; the
  features stolid and dark
But sculptured into a strong grace; straight nose with a high
  bridge, firm and wide eyes, full chin,
Red lips; she was only a fourth part Indian; a Scottish
  sailor had planted her in young native earth,   5
Spanish and Indian, twenty-one years before. He had named
  her California when she was born;
That was her name; and had gone north.
                                        She heard the hooves
  and wheels come nearer, up the steep road.
The buckskin mare, leaning against the breastpiece, plodded into
  sight round the wet bank.
The pale face of the driver followed; the burnt-out eyes; they
  had fortune in them. He sat twisted
On the seat of the old buggy, leading a second horse by a
  long halter, a roan, a big one,   10
That stepped daintily; by the swell of the neck, a stallion. 'What
  have you got, Johnny?' 'Maskerel's stallion.
Mine now. I won him last night, I had very good luck.' He was
  quite drunk. 'They bring their mares up here now.
I keep this fellow. I got money besides, but I'll not show you.'
  'Did you buy something, Johnny,
For our Christine? Christmas comes in two days, Johnny.' 'By
  God, forgot,' he answered laughing.

'Don't tell Christine it's Christmas; after while I get her
  something, maybe.' But California: 15
'I shared your luck when you lost: you lost *me* once, Johnny,
  remember? Tom Dell had me two nights
Here in the house: other times we've gone hungry: now that
  you've won, Christine will have her Christmas.
We share your luck, Johnny. You give me money, I go down to
  Monterey to-morrow,
Buy presents for Christine, come back in the evening. Next day
  Christmas.' 'You have wet ride,' he answered
Giggling. 'Here money. Five dollar; ten; twelve dollar. You
  buy two bottles of rye whiskey for Johnny.'   20
'All right. I go to-morrow.'
                                        He was an outcast Hollander; not
  old, but shriveled with bad living.
The child Christine inherited from his race blue eyes, from his
  life a wizened forehead; she watched
From the house-door her father lurch out of the buggy and lead
  with due respect the stallion
To the new corral, the strong one; leaving the wearily breathing
  buckskin mare to his wife to unharness.

Storm in the night; the rain on the thin shakes of the roof
  like the ocean on rock streamed battering; once thunder   25
Walked down the narrow canyon into Carmel valley and wore
  away westward; Christine was wakeful
With fears and wonders; her father lay too deep for storm to
  touch him.

            .   .   .   .   .   .

                                                  Clear daylight
    over the steep hills;
Gray-shining cloud over the tops of the redwoods; the winter
  stream sang loud; the wheels of the buggy
Slipped in deep slime, ground on washed stones at the road-
  edge. Down the hill the wrinkled river smothered the ford.   30
You must keep to the bed of stones: she knew the way by willow
  and alder: the buckskin halted mid-stream,
Shuddering, the water her own color washing up to the traces;
  but California, drawing up

Her feet out of the whirl onto the seat of the buggy swung the
   whip over the yellow water
And drove to the road.
                    All morning the clouds were racing north-
   ward like a river. At noon they thickened.
When California faced the southwind home from Monterey
   it was heavy with level rainfall.   35
She looked seaward from the foot of the valley; red rays cried
   sunset from a trumpet of streaming
Cloud over Lobos, the southwest occident of the solstice. Twilight came soon, but the tired mare
Feared the road more than the whip. Mile after mile of slow
   gray twilight.
                 Then, quite suddenly, darkness.
'Christine will be asleep. It is Christmas Eve. The ford. That
   hour of daylight wasted this morning!'
She could see nothing; she let the reins lie on the dashboard
   and knew at length by the cramp of the wheels   40
And the pitch down, they had reached it. Noise of wheels on
   stones, plashing of hooves in water; a world
Of sounds; no sight; the gentle thunder of water; the mare
   snorting, dipping her head, one knew,
To look for footing, in the blackness, under the stream. The
   hushing and creaking of the sea-wind
In the passion of invisible willows.
                  The mare stood still; the woman
   shouted to her; spared whip,
For a false leap would lose the track of the ford.   45

       .   .   .   .   .   .

                 The mare stood still as if asleep in the midst
   of the water. Then California
Reached out a hand over the stream and fingered her rump; the
   solid wet convexity of it
Shook like the beat of a great heart. 'What are you waiting for?'
   But the feel of the animal surface
Had wakened a dream, obscured real danger with a dream of
   danger. 'What for? For the water-stallion
To break out of the stream, that is what the rump strains for,
   him to come up flinging foam sidewise,   50

Fore-hooves in air, crush me and the rig and curl over his
   woman.' She flung out with the whip then,
The mare plunged forward. The buggy drifted sidelong: was
   she off ground? Swimming? No: by the splashes.
The driver, a mere prehensile instinct, clung to the side-irons
   of the seat and felt the force
But not the coldness of the water, curling over her knees, breaking up to the waist
Over her body. They'd turned. The mare had turned up
   stream and was wallowing back into shoal water.   55
Then California dropped her forehead to her knees, having seen
   nothing, feeling a danger,
And felt the brute weight of a branch of alder, the pendulous
   light leaves brush her bent neck
Like a child's fingers. The mare burst out of water and stopped
   on the slope to the ford. The woman climbed down
Between the wheels and went to her head. 'Poor Dora,' she
   called her by her name, 'there, Dora. Quietly,'
And led her around, there was room to turn on the margin,
   the head to the gentle thunder of the water.   60
She crawled on hands and knees, felt for the ruts, and shifted
   the wheels into them. 'You can see, Dora.
I can't. But this time you'll go through it.' She climbed into the
   seat and shouted angrily. The mare
Stopped, her two forefeet in the water. She touched with the
   whip. The mare plodded ahead and halted.
Then California thought of prayer: 'Dear little Jesus,
Dear baby Jesus born to-night, your head was shining   65
Like silver candles. I've got a baby too, only a girl. You had light
   wherever you walked.
Dear baby Jesus give me light.' Light streamed: rose, gold, rich
   purple, hiding the ford like a curtain.
The gentle thunder of water was a noise of wing-feathers, the
   fans of paradise lifting softly.
The child afloat on radiance had a baby face, but the angels had
   birds' heads, hawks' heads,
Bending over the baby, weaving a web of wings about him.
   He held in the small fat hand   70
A little snake with golden eyes, and California could see clearly
   on the under radiance

The mare's pricked ears, a sharp black fork against the shining
    light-fall. But it dropped; the light of heaven
Frightened poor Dora. She backed; swung up the water,
And nearly oversetting the buggy turned and scrambled back-
    ward; the iron wheel-tires rang on boulders.

Then California weeping climbed between the wheels. Her
    wet clothes and the toys packed under   75
Dragged her down with their weight: she stripped off cloak and
    dress and laid the baby's things in the buggy;
Brought Johnny's whiskey out from under the seat; wrapped all
    in the dress, bottles and toys, and tied them
Into a bundle that would sling over her back. She unharnessed
    the mare, hurting her fingers
Against the swollen straps and the wet buckles. She tied the
    pack over her shoulders, the cords
Crossing her breasts, and mounted. She drew up her shift
    about her waist and knotted it, naked thighs   80
Clutching the sides of the mare, bare flesh to the wet withers, and
    caught the mane with her right hand,
The looped-up bridle reins in the other. 'Dora, the baby gives
    you light.' The blinding radiance
Hovered the ford. 'Sweet baby Jesus give us light.' Cataracts of
    light and Latin singing
Fell through the willows; the mare snorted and reared: the roar
    and thunder of the invisible water;
The night shaking open like a flag, shot with the flashes;
    the baby face hovering; the water   85
Beating over her shoes and stockings up to the bare thighs; and
    over them, like a beast
Lapping her belly; the wriggle and pitch of the mare swimming;
    the drift, the sucking water; the blinding
Light above and behind with not a gleam before, in the throat
    of darkness; the shock of the fore-hooves
Striking bottom, the struggle and surging lift of the haunches.
    She felt the water streaming off her
From the shoulders down; heard the great strain and sob of
    the mare's breathing, heard the horseshoes grind on gravel.   90
When California came home the dog at the door snuffed at her
    without barking; Christine and Johnny

Both were asleep; she did not sleep for hours, but kindled fire
and knelt patiently over it,
Shaping and drying the dear-bought gifts for Christmas morning.

She hated (she thought) the proud-necked stallion.
He'd lean the big twin masses of his breast on the rail, his red-
brown eyes flash the white crescents,
She admired him then, she hated him for his uselessness,
serving nothing   95
But Johnny's vanity. Horses were too cheap to breed. She
thought, if he could range in freedom,
Shaking the red-roan mane for a flag on the bare hills.
                                              A man
brought up a mare in April;
Then California, though she wanted to watch, stayed with
Christine indoors. When the child fretted
The mother told her once more about the miracle of the ford;
her prayer to the little Jesus
The Christmas Eve when she was bringing the gifts home;
the appearance, the lights, the Latin singing,   100
The thunder of wing-feathers and water, the shining child, the
cataracts of splendor down the darkness.
'A little baby,' Christine asked, 'the God is a baby?' 'The child
of God. That was his birthday.
His mother was named Mary: we pray to her too: God came to
her. He was not the child of a man
Like you or me. God was his father: she was the stallion's wife—
what did I say—God's wife,'
She said with a cry, lifting Christine aside, pacing the planks
of the floor. 'She is called more blessed   105
Than any woman. She was so good, she was more loved.' 'Did
God live near her house?' 'He lives
Up high, over the stars; he ranges on the bare blue hill of the
sky.' In her mind a picture
Flashed, of the red-roan mane shaken out for a flag on the bare
hills, and she said quickly, 'He's more
Like a great man holding the sun in his hand.' Her mind giving
her words the lie, 'But no one
Knows, only the shining and the power. The power, the
terror, the burning fire covered her over...'   110

'Was she burnt up, mother?' 'She was so good and lovely, she
    was the mother of the little Jesus.
If you are good nothing will hurt you.' 'What did she think?'
    'She loved, she was not afraid of the hooves—
Hands that had made the hills and sun and moon, and the sea
    and the great redwoods, the terrible strength,
She gave herself without thinking.'

       .   .   .   .   .   .

                        Johnny came in, his
    face reddened as if he had stood   115
Near fire, his eyes triumphing. 'Finished,' he said, and looked
    with malice at Christine. 'I go
Down valley with Jim Carrier; owes me five dollar, fifteen I
    charge him, he brought ten in his pocket.
Has grapes on the ranch, maybe I take a barrel red wine instead
    of money. Be back to-morrow.
To-morrow night I tell you— Eh, Jim,' he laughed over his
    shoulder, 'I say to-morrow evening
I show her how the red fellow act, the big fellow. When I
    come home.' She answered nothing, but stood   120
In front of the door, holding the little hand of her daughter, in
    the path of sun between the redwoods,
While Johnny tied the buckskin mare behind Carrier's buggy,
    and bringing saddle and bridle tossed them
Under the seat. Jim Carrier's mare, the bay, stood with dropped
    head and started slowly, the men
Laughing and shouting at her; their voices could be heard down
    the steep road, after the noise
Of the iron-hooped wheels died from the stone. Then one might
    hear the hush of the wind in the tall redwoods,   125
The tinkle of the April brook, deep in its hollow.

                          Humanity is
    the start of the race; I say
Humanity is the mould to break away from, the crust to break
    through, the coal to break into fire,
The atom to be split.
                  Tragedy that breaks man's face and a white
fire flies out of it; vision that fools him

Out of his limits, desire that fools him out of his limits, unnatural
crime, inhuman science,
Slit eyes in the mask; wild loves that leap over the walls of
nature, the wild fence-vaulter science,   130
Useless intelligence of far stars, dim knowledge of the spinning
demons that make an atom,
These break, these pierce, these deify, praising their God shrilly
with fierce voices: not in a man's shape
He approves the praise, he that walks lightning-naked on the
Pacific, that laces the suns with planets,
The heart of the atom with electrons: what is humanity in this
cosmos? For him, the last
Least taint of a trace in the dregs of the solution; for itself, the
mould to break away from, the coal   135
To break into fire, the atom to be split.

After the child slept, after
the leopard-footed evening
Had glided oceanward, California turned the lamp to its least
flame and glided from the house.

.   .   .   .   .   .

It was like daylight
Outdoors and she hastened without faltering down the foot-
path, through the dark fringe of twisted oak-brush,
To the open place in a bay of the hill. The dark strength of
the stallion had heard her coming; she heard him   140
Blow the shining air out of his nostrils, she saw him in the white
lake of moonlight
Move like a lion along the timbers of the fence, shaking the
nightfall
Of the great mane; his fragrance came to her; she leaned on the
fence;
He drew away from it, the hooves making soft thunder in the
trodden soil.
Wild love had trodden it, his wrestling with the stranger, the
shame of the day   145
Had stamped it into mire and powder when the heavy fetlocks
Strained the soft flanks. 'Oh, if I could bear you!
If I had the strength. O great God that came down to Mary,
gently you came. But I will ride him

Up into the hill, if he throws me, if he tramples me, is it not
    my desire
To endure death?' She climbed the fence, pressing her
    body against the rail, shaking like fever,   150
And dropped inside to the soft ground. He neither threatened
    her with his teeth nor fled from her coming,
And lifting her hand gently to the upflung head she caught
    the strap of the headstall,
That hung under the quivering chin. She unlooped the halter
    from the high strength of the neck
And the arch the storm-cloud mane hung with live darkness. He
    stood; she crushed her breasts
On the hard shoulder, an arm over the withers, the other
    under the mass of his throat, and murmuring   155
Like a mountain dove, 'If I could bear you.' No way, no help,
    a gulf in nature. She murmured, 'Come,
We will run on the hill. O beautiful, O beautiful,' and led him
To the gate and flung the bars on the ground. He threw his head
    downward
To snuff at the bars; and while he stood, she catching mane and
    withers with all sudden contracture
And strength of her lithe body, leaped, clung hard, and was
    mounted. He had been ridden before; he did not   160
Fight the weight but ran like a stone falling;
Broke down the slope into the moon-glass of the stream, and
    flattened to his neck
She felt the branches of a buckeye tree fly over her, saw the wall
    of the oak-scrub
End her world: but he turned there, the matted branches
Scraped her right knee, the great slant shoulders   165
Laboring the hill-slope, up, up, the clear hill. Desire had died
    in her
At the first rush, the falling like death, but now it revived,
She feeling between her thighs the labor of the great engine, the
    running muscles, the hard swiftness,
She riding the savage and exultant strength of the world. Having
    topped the thicket he turned eastward,
Running less wildly; and now at length he felt the halter
    when she drew on it; she guided him upward;   170
He stopped and grazed on the great arch and pride of the hill,
    the silent calvary. A dwarfish oakwood

Climbed the other slope out of the dark of the unknown canyon
    beyond; the last wind-beaten bush of it
Crawled up to the height, and California slipping from her
    mount tethered him to it. She stood then,
Shaking. Enormous films of moonlight
Trailed down from the height. Space, anxious whiteness,
    vastness. Distant beyond conception the shining ocean   175
Lay light like a haze along the ledge and doubtful world's end.
    Little vapors gleaming, and little
Darknesses on the far chart underfoot symbolized wood and
    valley; but the air was the element, the moon-
Saturate arcs and spires of the air.
                           Here is solitude, here on the
    calvary, nothing conscious
But the possible God and the cropped grass, no witness, no eye
    but that misformed one, the moon's past fullness.
Two figures on the shining hill, woman and stallion, she
    kneeling to him, brokenly adoring.   180
He cropping the grass, shifting his hooves, or lifting the long
    head to gaze over the world.
Tranquil and powerful. She prayed aloud, 'O God, I am not
    good enough, O fear, O strength, I am draggled.
Johnny and other men have had me, and O clean power! Here
    am I,' she said, falling before him,
And crawled to his hooves. She lay a long while, as if asleep, in
    reach of the fore-hooves, weeping. He avoided
Her head and the prone body. He backed at first; but
    later plucked the grass that grew by her shoulder.   185
The small dark head under his nostrils: a small round stone, that
    smelt human, black hair growing from it:
The skull shut the light in: it was not possible for any eyes
To know what throbbed and shone under the sutures of the
    skull, or a shell full of lightning
Had scared the roan strength, and he'd have broken tether,
    screaming, and run for the valley.
                        The atom bounds-breaking,
Nucleus to sun, electrons to planets, with recognition   190
Not praying, self-equaling, the whole to the whole, the
    microcosm
Not entering nor accepting entrance, more equally, more
    utterly, more incredibly conjugate

With the other extreme and greatness; passionately perceptive of
    identity...
                    The fire threw up figures
And symbols meanwhile, racial myths formed and dissolved in
    it, the phantom rulers of humanity
That without being are yet more real than what they are born
    of, and without shape, shape that which makes them: 195
The nerves and the flesh go by shadowlike, the limbs and the
    lives shadowlike, these shadows remain, these shadows
To whom temples, to whom churches, to whom labors and wars,
    visions and dreams are dedicate:
Out of the fire in the small round stone that black moss covered,
    a crucified man writhed up in anguish;
A woman covered by a huge beast in whose mane the stars were
    netted, sun and moon were his eyeballs,
Smiled under the unendurable violation, her throat swollen
    with the storm and blood-flecks gleaming   200
On the stretched lips; a woman—no, a dark water, split by jets
    of lightning, and after a season
What floated up out of the furrowed water, a boat, a fish, a fire-
    globe?
                It had wings, the creature,
And flew against the fountain of lightning, fell burnt out of the
    cloud back to the bottomless water...
Figures and symbols, castlings of the fire, played in her brain;
    but the white fire was the essence,
The burning in the small round shell of bone that black hair
    covered, that lay by the hooves on the hilltop.   205

She rose at length, she unknotted the halter; she walked and
    led the stallion; two figures, woman and stallion,
Came down the silent emptiness of the dome of the hill, under
    the cataract of the moonlight.

The next night there was moon through cloud. Johnny had re-
    turned half drunk toward evening, and California
Who had known him for years with neither love nor loathing
    to-night hating him had let the child Christine
Play in the light of the lamp for hours after her bedtime; who
    fell asleep at length on the floor   210

Beside the dog; then Johnny: 'Put her to bed.' She gathered the
  child against her breasts, she laid her
In the next room, and covered her with a blanket. The window
  was white, the moon had risen. The mother
Lay down by the child, but after a moment Johnny stood in the
  doorway. 'Come drink.' He had brought home
Two jugs of wine slung from the saddle, part payment for the
  stallion's service...

.   .   .   .   .   .

...'We have a good evening,' he laughed, pouring it.   215
'One glass yet then I show you what the red fellow did.' She
  moving toward the house-door his eyes
Followed her, the glass filled and the red juice ran over the table.
  When it struck the floor-planks
He heard and looked. 'Who stuck the pig?' he muttered stupidly,
  'here's blood, here's blood,' and trailed his fingers
In the red lake under the lamplight. While he was looking down
  the door creaked, she had slipped outdoors,
And he, his mouth curving like a faun's imagined the chase
  under the solemn redwoods, the panting   220
And unresistant victim caught in a dark corner. He emptied the
  glass and went outdoors
Into the dappled lanes of moonlight. No sound but the April
  brook's. 'Hey Bruno,' he called, 'find her.'

.   .   .   .   .   .

                            She ran down to the new corral, she saw
  the stallion
Move like a lion along the timbers of the fence, the dark arched
  neck shaking the nightfall
Of the great mane; she threw herself prone and writhed
  under the bars, his hooves backing away from her   225
Made muffled thunder in the soft soil. She stood in the midst of
  the corral, panting, but Johnny
Paused at the fence. The dog ran under it, and seeing the stallion
  move, the woman standing quiet,
Danced after the beast, with white-tooth feints and dashes. When
  Johnny saw the formidable dark strength
Recoil from the dog, he climbed up over the fence.

    The child Christine waked when her mother left her...   230

.   .   .   .   .   .

And crept toward light, where it gleamed under the crack of the
   door. She opened the door, the room was empty,
The table-top was a red lake under the lamplight. The color of
   it was terrible to her...

      ·   ·   ·   ·   ·   ·

...the color frightened her, the empty house frightened her,
   she followed down hill in the white lane of moonlight
The friendly noise of the dog. She saw in the big horse's corral,
   on the level shoulder of the hill,
Black on white, the dark strength of the beast, the dancing
   fury of the dog, and the two others.   235
One fled, one followed; the big one charged, rearing; one fell
   under his fore-hooves. She heard her mother
Scream: without thought she ran to the house, she dragged a
   chair past the red pool and climbed to the rifle,
Got it down from the wall and lugged it somehow through the
   door and down the hillside, under the hard weight
Sobbing. Her mother stood by the rails of the corral, she gave
   it to her. On the far side
The dog flashed at the plunging stallion; in the midst of
   the space the man, slow-moving, like a hurt worm   240
Crawling, dragged his body by inches toward the fence-line.
   Then California, resting the rifle
On the top rail, without doubting, without hesitance,
Aimed for the leaping body of the dog, and when it stood, fired.
   It snapped, rolled over, lay quiet.
'O mother you've hit Bruno!' 'I couldn't see the sights in the
   moonlight,' she answered quietly. She stood
And watched, resting the rifle-butt on the ground. The
   stallion wheeled, freed from his torment, the man   245
Lurched up to his knees, wailing a thin and bitter bird's cry, and
   the roan thunder
Struck; hooves left nothing alive but teeth tore up the remnant.
   'O mother, shoot, shoot!' Yet California
Stood carefully watching, till the beast having fed all his fury
   stretched neck to utmost, head high,
And wrinkled back the upper lip from the teeth, yawning
   obscene disgust over—not a man—
A smear on the moon-like earth: then California moved by
   some obscure human fidelity   250

Lifted the rifle. Each separate nerve-cell of her brain flaming the
    stars fell from their places
Crying in her mind: she fired three times before the haunches
    crumpled sidewise, the forelegs stiffening,
And the beautiful strength settled to earth: she turned then on
    her little daughter the mask of a woman
Who has killed God. The night-wind veering, the smell of the
    spilt wine drifted down hill from the house.

Hurt Hawks

I

The broken pillar of the wing jags from the clotted shoulder,
The wing trails like a banner in defeat,
No more to use the sky forever but live with famine
And pain a few days: cat nor coyote
Will shorten the week of waiting for death, there is game with-
    out talons.   5
He stands under the oak-bush and waits
The lame feet of salvation; at night he remembers freedom
And flies in a dream, the dawns ruin it.
He is strong and pain is worse to the strong, incapacity is worse.
The curs of the day come and torment him   10
At distance, no one but death the redeemer will humble that
    head,
The intrepid readiness, the terrible eyes.
The wild God of the world is sometimes merciful to those
That ask mercy, not often to the arrogant.
You do not know him, you communal people, or you have for-
    gotten him;   15
Intemperate and savage, the hawk remembers him;
Beautiful and wild, the hawks, and men that are dying, remember
    him.

II

I'd sooner, except the penalties, kill a man than a hawk; but the
    great redtail
Had nothing left but unable misery
From the bone too shattered for mending, the wing that trailed
    under his talons when he moved.   20

We had fed him six weeks, I gave him freedom,
He wandered over the foreland hill and returned in the evening,
    asking for death,
Not like a beggar, still eyed with the old
Implacable arrogance. I gave him the lead gift in the twilight.
    What fell was relaxed,
Owl-downy, soft feminine feathers; but what   25
Soared: the fierce rush: the night-herons by the flooded river
    cried fear at its rising
Before it was quite unsheathed from reality.

The Eye

The Atlantic is a stormy moat; and the Mediterranean,
The blue pool in the old garden,
More than five thousand years has drunk sacrifice
Of ships and blood, and shines in the sun; but here the Pacific—
Our ships, planes, wars are perfectly irrelevant.   5
Neither our present blood-feud with the brave dwarfs
Nor any future world-quarrel of westering
And eastering man, the bloody migrations, greed of power,
    clash of faiths—
Is a speck of dust on the great scale-pan.
Here from this mountain shore, headland beyond stormy head-
    land plunging like dolphins through the blue sea-smoke   10
Into pale sea—look west at the hill of water: it is half the planet:
    this dome, this half-globe, this bulging
Eyeball of water, arched over to Asia,
Australia and white Antarctica: those are the eyelids that never
    close; this is the staring unsleeping
Eye of the earth; and what it watches is not our wars.

My Burial Place

I have told you in another poem, whether you've read it or not,
About a beautiful place the hard-wounded
Deer go to die in; their bones lie mixed in their little
    graveyard
Under leaves by a flashing cliff-brook, and if

They have ghosts they like it, the bones and mixed antlers are
     well content.   5
Now comes for me the time to engage
My burial place: put me in a beautiful place far off from men
No cemetery, no necropolis,
And for God's sake no columbarium, nor yet no funeral.

But if the human animal were precious   10
As the quick deer or that hunter in the night the lonely puma
I should be pleased to lie in one grave with 'em.

JOHN CROWE RANSOM

John Crowe Ransom was born in Pulaski, Tennessee, in 1888 and spent his boyhood in various small towns in the central region of the state. His father was a Methodist minister but, far from accepting the family pieties, Ransom himself soon became an inveterate agnostic. At the age of fifteen he was enrolled at Vanderbilt University in Nashville, Tennessee, where he read classics and philosophy. He proved to be an outstanding student and was awarded a Rhodes scholarship to Oxford. There he met another American student, Christopher Morley, who introduced him to contemporary poetry, and it was as a consequence of this that Ransom began to have serious doubts about his choice of specialisation. He returned to the United States and, after teaching Latin at a preparatory school for a year, was appointed an instructor in English at Vanderbilt.

Ransom now began to write verse seriously. Within a short while he had enough poems completed for a small volume, and this Morley arranged to have published in 1919 with the title *Poems About God*. They excited little attention outside Ransom's immediate circle and, since they are clearly apprentice work, Ransom has excluded them from subsequent collections of his verse. Meanwhile, new interests and friendships were forming: Ransom became acquainted with a local eccentric called Sidney Mttron Hirsch, and a group of Hirsch's friends who met regularly in Nashville to discuss problems of philosophy and ethics. Gradually, under Ransom's guidance, the group turned its attention from philosophy to poetry; and then decided to publish its own magazine of verse. The first edition of the magazine, *The Fugitive*, appeared in 1922, the last three years later, and it was during the period of its publication that nearly all of Ransom's mature poetry was written. Much of this poetry, which appeared for the first time in the pages of *The Fugitive*, was collected in two, roughly contemporaneous, volumes: *Chills and Fever*, published in 1924, and *Two Gentlemen in Bonds*, published in 1927.

After 1927 Ransom committed only four new poems to print. One reason for this was simple. He had become much more interested in other activities, chiefly in public affairs and aesthetics – so interested in fact that in the next fifteen years he published three separate books on the subjects: *God Without Thunder*, which appeared in 1929, *The World's Body*, a collection of critical essays published in 1938, and *The New Criticism* published in 1941. In these, Ransom defended the world of myth, ritual, and above all art against what he saw as the overweening assumptions of the world of science. Science, he argued, is partial because it supplies us with abstract knowledge only: it, and its language, satisfy no more than the rational man. Myth and the fine arts, on the other hand, bring order and meaning into life without ever denying the charm of contingency and the particular – or the mystery and ultimate intractability of the universe. Combining and qualifying abstractions with a firm sense of the concrete, they satisfy the *whole* man: his intellect, his emotions, *and* his senses. These ideas had been implicit in Ransom's mature poetry (see the Notes on the poems). But formulated now in polemical, or even philosophical, terms they began to exercise a new and enormous influence, which was extended in 1937 when Ransom became a professor at Kenyon College, Ohio, and editor of the *Kenyon Review*. The *Review* swiftly established itself as one of the most important organs of scholarship in the country; and the 'New Criticism' practised in it by Ransom and his associates, with its emphasis on the concrete, or close reading of the text, and on the poem as a separate thing in itself – this soon became, and to some extent still is, the ruling critical orthodoxy.

Although Ransom retired in 1958 from full-time academic life, he never ceased revising and rearranging his earlier work for different editions: principally, for the volumes of *Selected Poems* published in 1945, 1963 and 1970 and the *Poems and Essays* which appeared in 1955. That work alone, for which he received a National Book Award in 1963, is enough to assure him of a place among the major American poets. Ransom died in 1974 at the age of eighty-six.

FURTHER READING

Buffington, Robert. *The Equilibrists : John Crowe Ransom's Poems, 1916–1963*. Nashville, Tenn., 1967.

Knight, Karl F. *The Poetry of John Crowe Ransom*. The Hague, 1964.

Magner, James E. *John Crowe Ransom : Critical Principles and Preoccupations*. The Hague, 1971.

Parsons, Thornton H. *John Crowe Ransom*. New York, 1967.
Stewart, John L. *John Crowe Ransom*. Minneapolis, Minn., 1962.
Young, Thomas D. (ed.). *John Crowe Ransom: Critical Essays and a Biblio-graphy*. Nashville, Tenn., 1968.

Winter Remembered

Two evils, monstrous either one apart,
Possessed me, and were long and loath at going:
A cry of Absence, Absence, in the heart,
And in the wood the furious winter blowing.

Think not, when fire was bright upon my bricks,   5
And past the tight boards hardly a wind could enter,
I glowed like them, the simple burning sticks,
Far from my cause, my proper heat and center.

Better to walk forth in the frozen air
And wash my wound in the snows; that would be healing; 10
Because my heart would throb less painful there,
Being caked with cold, and past the smart of feeling.

And where I walked, the murderous winter blast
Would have this body bowed, these eyeballs streaming,
And though I think this heart's blood froze not fast   15
It ran too small to spare one drop for dreaming.

Dear love, these fingers that had known your touch,
And tied our separate forces first together,
Were ten poor idiot fingers not worth much,
Ten frozen parsnips hanging in the weather.   20

Dead Boy

The little cousin is dead, by foul subtraction,
A green bough from Virginia's aged tree,
And none of the county kin like the transaction,
Nor some of the world of outer dark, like me.

A boy not beautiful, nor good, nor clever,   5
A black cloud full of storms too hot for keeping,

A sword beneath his mother's heart—yet never
Woman bewept her babe as this is weeping.

A pig with a pasty face, so I had said,
Squealing for cookies, kinned by poor pretense   10
With a noble house. But the little man quite dead,
I see the forbears' antique lineaments.

The elder men have strode by the box of death
To the wide flag porch, and muttering low send round
The bruit of the day. O friendly waste of breath!   15
Their hearts are hurt with a deep dynastic wound.

He was pale and little, the foolish neighbors say;
The first-fruits saith the Preacher, the Lord hath taken;
But this was the old tree's late branch wrenched away,
Grieving the sapless limbs, the shorn and shaken.   20

Bells for John Whiteside's Daughter

There was such speed in her little body,
And such lightness in her footfall,
It is no wonder her brown study
Astonishes us all.

Her wars were bruited in our high window.   5
We looked among orchard trees and beyond
Where she took arms against her shadow,
Or harried unto the pond

The lazy geese, like a snow cloud
Dripping their snow on the green grass,   10
Tricking and stopping, sleepy and proud,
Who cried in goose, Alas,

For the tireless heart within the little
Lady with rod that made them rise
From their noon apple-dreams and scuttle   15
Goose-fashion under the skies!

But now go the bells, and we are ready,
In one house we are sternly stopped
To say we are vexed at her brown study,
Lying so primly propped.   20

Parting at Dawn

If there was a broken whispering by night
It was an image of the coward heart,
But the white dawn assures them how to part—
Stoics are born on the cold glitter of light,
And with the morning star lovers take flight.   5
Say then your parting; and most dry should you drain
Your lips of their wine, your eyes of the frantic rain,
Till these be as the barren cenobite.

And then? O dear Sir, stumbling down the street,
Continue, till you come to wars and wounds;   10
Beat the air, Madam, till your house-clock sounds;
And if no Lethe flows beneath your casement,
And when ten years have not brought full effacement,
Philosophy was wrong, and you may meet.

Blue Girls

Twirling your blue skirts, travelling the sward
Under the towers of your seminary,
Go listen to your teachers old and contrary
Without believing a word.

Tie the white fillets then about your hair   5
And think no more of what will come to pass
Than bluebirds that go walking on the grass
And chattering on the air.

Practise your beauty, blue girls, before it fail;
And I will cry with my loud lips and publish   10
Beauty which all our power shall ever establish,
It is so frail.

For I could tell you a story which is true;
I know a lady with a terrible tongue,
Blear eyes fallen from blue,   15
All her perfections tarnished—yet it is not long
Since she was lovelier than any of you.

Captain Carpenter

Captain Carpenter rose up in his prime
Put on his pistols and went riding out
But had got wellnigh nowhere at that time
Till he fell in with ladies in a rout.

It was a pretty lady and all her train   5
That played with him so sweetly but before
An hour she'd taken a sword with all her main
And twined him of his nose for evermore.

Captain Carpenter mounted up one day
And rode straightway into a stranger rogue   10
That looked unchristian but be that as may
The Captain did not wait upon prologue.

But drew upon him out of his great heart
The other swung against him with a club
And cracked his two legs at the shinny part   15
And let him roll and stick like any tub.

Captain Carpenter rode many a time
From male and female took he sundry harms
He met the wife of Satan crying 'I'm
The she-wolf bids you shall bear no more arms.'   20

Their strokes and counters whistled in the wind
I wish he had delivered half his blows
But where she should have made off like a hind
The bitch bit off his arms at the elbows.

And Captain Carpenter parted with his ears   25
To a black devil that used him in this wise
O Jesus ere his threescore and ten years
Another had plucked out his sweet blue eyes.

Captain Carpenter got up on his roan
And sailed from the gate in hell's despite   30
I heard him asking in the grimmest tone
If any enemy yet there was to fight?

'To any adversary it is fame
If he risk to be wounded by my tongue

Or burnt in two beneath my red heart's flame   35
Such are the perils he is cast among.

'But if he can he has a pretty choice
From an anatomy with little to lose
Whether he cut my tongue and take my voice
Or whether it be my round red heart he choose.'   40

It was the neatest knave that ever was seen
Stepping in perfume from his lady's bower
Who at this word put in his merry mien
And fell on Captain Carpenter like a tower.

I would not knock old fellows in the dust   45
But there lay Captain Carpenter on his back
His weapons were the old heart in his bust
And a blade shook between rotten teeth alack.

The rogue in scarlet and grey soon knew his mind
He wished to get his trophy and depart   50
With gentle apology and touch refined
He pierced him and produced the Captain's heart.

God's mercy rest on Captain Carpenter now
I thought him Sirs an honest gentleman
Citizen husband soldier and scholar enow   55
Let jangling kites eat of him if they can.

But God's deep curses follow after those
That shore him of his goodly nose and ears
His legs and strong arms at the two elbows
And eyes that had not watered seventy years.   60

The curse of hell upon the sleek upstart
That got the Captain finally on his back
And took the red red vitals of his heart
And made the kites to whet their beaks clack clack.

Vision by Sweetwater

Go and ask Robin to bring the girls over
To Sweetwater, said my Aunt; and that was why
It was like a dream of ladies sweeping by
The willows, clouds, deep meadowgrass, and the river.

Robin's sisters and my Aunt's lily daughter   5
Laughed and talked, and tinkled light as wrens
If there were a little colony all hens
To go walking by the steep turn of Sweetwater.

Let them alone, dear Aunt, just for one minute
Till I go fishing in the dark of my mind: 10
Where have I seen before, against the wind,
These bright virgins, robed and bare of bonnet,

Flowing with music of their strange quick tongue
And adventuring with delicate paces by the stream,—
Myself a child, old suddenly at the scream   15
From one of the white thoats which it hid among?

Antique Harvesters

(SCENE: *Of the Mississippi the bank sinister, and of the
Ohio the bank sinister.*)

Tawny are the leaves turned but they still hold,
And it is harvest; what shall this land produce?
A meager hill of kernels, a runnel of juice;
Declension looks from our land, it is old.
Therefore let us assemble, dry, grey, spare,   5
And mild as yellow air.

'I hear the croak of a raven's funeral wing.'
The young men would be joying in the song
Of passionate birds; their memories are not long.
What is it thus rehearsed in sable? 'Nothing.'   10
Trust not but the old endure, and shall be older
Than the scornful beholder.

We pluck the spindling ears and gather the corn.
One spot has special yield? 'On this spot stood
Heroes and drenched it with their only blood.'   15
And talk meets talk, as echoes from the horn
Of the hunter—echoes are the old men's arts,
Ample are the chambers of their hearts.

Here come the hunters, keepers of a rite;
The horn, the hounds, the lank mares coursing by   20
Straddled with archetypes of chivalry;

And the fox, lovely ritualist, in flight
Offering his unearthly ghost to quarry;
And the fields, themselves to harry.

Resume, harvesters. The treasure is full bronze   25
Which you will garner for the Lady, and the moon
Could tinge it no yellower than does this noon;
But grey will quench it shortly—the field, men, stones.
Pluck fast, dreamers; prove as you amble slowly
Not less than men, not wholly.   30

Bare the arm, dainty youths, bend the knees
Under bronze burdens. And by an autumn tone
As by a grey, as by a green, you will have known
Your famous Lady's image; for so have these;
And if one say that easily will your hands   35
More prosper in other lands,

Angry as wasp-music be your cry then:
'Forsake the Proud Lady, of the heart of fire,
The look of snow, to the praise of a dwindled choir,
Song of degenerate specters that were men?   40
The sons of the fathers shall keep her, worthy of
What these have done in love.'

True, it is said of our Lady, she ageth.
But see, if you peep shrewdly, she hath not stooped
Take no thought of her servitors that have drooped,   45
For we are nothing; and if one talk of death—
Why, the ribs of the earth subsist frail as a breath
If but God wearieth.

Painted Head

By dark severance the apparition head
Smiles from the air a capital on no
Column or a Platonic perhaps head
On a canvas sky depending from nothing;

Stirs up an old illusion of grandeur   5
By tickling the instinct of heads to be
Absolute and to try decapitation
And to play truant from the body bush;

But too happy and beautiful for those sorts
Of head (homekeeping heads are happiest)   10
Discovers maybe thirty unwidowed years
Of not dishonoring the faithful stem;

Is nameless and has authored for the evil
Historian headhunters neither book
Nor state and is therefore distinct from tart   15
Heads with crowns and guilty gallery heads;

So that the extravagant device of art
Unhousing by abstraction this once head
Was capital irony by a loving hand
That knew the no treason of a head like this;   20

Makes repentance in an unlovely head
For having vinegarly traduced the flesh
Till, the hurt flesh recusing, the hard egg
Is shrunken to its own deathlike surface;

And an image thus. The body bears the head   25
(So hardly one they terribly are two)
Feeds and obeys and unto please what end?
Not to the glory of tyrant head but to

The increase of body. Beauty is of body.
The flesh contouring shallowly on a head   30
Is a rock-garden needing body's love
And best bodiness to colorify

The big blue birds sitting and sea-shell flats
And caves, and on the iron acropolis
To spread the hyacinthine hair and rear   35
The olive garden for the nightingales.

E. E. CUMMINGS

Edward Estlin Cummings was born in 1894 in Cambridge, Massachusetts. His father was then teaching at Harvard University and later served as minister of Old South Church, a famous Unitarian establishment in Boston. In 1911 Cummings was enrolled at Harvard and there contributed verse to the college magazines, most of it showing the influence of the Pre-Raphaelite school of poetry. He also helped organise the Harvard Poetry Society. After receiving his B.A. in English and Classics in 1915 and his M.A. in 1916, he left college to work for a mail order firm in New York; and it was while he was in New York that *Eight Harvard Poets* appeared, a collection of verse which included some of Cummings' own apprentice work.

Shortly after this, in the same year of 1917, Cummings joined the Norton-Harjes Ambulance Unit and was sent to France on active duty. A censor's error led to his imprisonment for three months: an experience on which he later based his first book, *The Enormous Room* (1922), a fragment of autobiography that can nevertheless stand on its own as a masterpiece of radical individualism and one of the most memorable prose records of the First World War. Almost as soon as he was released from prison, Cummings was inducted into the United States Army, but the war ended even before he had left the training camp. So Cummings was left free to return to New York where he could devote himself to his paintings and his poetry. That city and Paris were to be his two principal bases for the remainder of his life: there he mingled with other painters and writers of the day – and there, too, he shared a series of different homes with three successive wives.

Cummings' work began to appear in *The Dial* when that magazine started in 1920 and it was only a few years subsequent to this, in 1923, that his first book of verse entitled *Tulips and Chimneys* was published. This was followed in 1925 by *XLI Poems* and *&* which, together with *Tulips and Chimneys*, quickly established him as one of the most controversial and important of the contemporary American poets. It was in 1925, in fact, that he received his first major award for his work, *The Dial* prize for poetry. Many more volumes of Cummings' verse appeared over the next thirty years, to be brought together eventually in *Poems 1923–1954* (1954), and a further two were to be published even after this collected edition: *95 Poems* in 1958, and *73 Poems* in 1963.

Although Cummings was primarily interested in poetry he experimented in other forms as well. His play, *HIM*, was produced by the Provincetown Players in 1927; to be followed by *Tom*, a satirical ballet, in 1935, and *Santa Claus*, in 1946, which like *HIM* mixed fantasy, comedy, and symbolism. In 1931 he visited Russia and out of this came *EIMI* (1933) a highly idiosyncratic account of his travels which attacked the Soviet idea of state supremacy from the standpoint of Cummings' own individualistic beliefs. There was, too, the series of *Six Non-lectures* (1953) which Cummings gave while he was Charles Eliot Norton Professor of Poetry at Harvard; and throughout his life, in addition to his literary work, he continued to devote much of his time and attention to his painting – holding several exhibitions in New York and Paris, and collecting some of his best work in *CIOPW* published in 1931.

FURTHER READING

Baum, S. V. (ed.). ΕΣΤΙ :*eec* : *E. E. Cummings and the Critics*. East Lansing, Mich., 1962.

Friedman, Norman. *E. E. Cummings: the Art of His Poetry*. New York, 1962.

Friedman, Norman. *E. E. Cummings: the Growth of a Writer*. Carbondale, Ill., 1964.

Norman, Charles. *The Magic-Maker: E. E. Cummings*. New York, 1969.

in Just-
spring   when the world is mud-
luscious the little
lame balloonman

whistles   far   and wee   5

and eddieandbill come
running from marbles and
piracies and it's
spring

when the world is puddle-wonderful   10

the queer
old balloonman whistles
far   and   wee
and bettyandisbel come dancing

from hop-scotch and jump-rope and   15

it's
spring
and
    the

        goat-footed   20

balloonMan   whistles
far
and
wee

Buffalo Bill's
defunct
        who used to
        ride a watersmooth-silver
                                stallion
and break onetwothreefourfive pigeonsjustlikethat
                                                Jesus

he was a handsome man
                        and what i want to know is
how do you like your blueeyed boy   5
Mister Death

Dick Mid's large bluish face without eyebrows

sits in the kitchen nights and chews a two-bit
cigar
        waiting for the bulls to pull his joint.
Jimmie was a dude. Dark hair and nice hands.

with a little eye that rolled and made its point   5

Jimmie's sister worked for Dick. And had some rows
over percent. The gang got shot up twice, it
operated in the hundred ands

All the chips would kid Jimmie to give them a kiss
but Jimmie lived regular. stewed three times a week.　　　10
and slept twice a week with a big toothless girl
in Yonkers.
　　　　　　　Dick Mid's green large three teeth leak

smoke:remembering, two pink big lips curl. . . .

how Jimmie was framed and got his

　　　'next to of course god america i
　　　love you land of the pilgrims' and so forth oh
　　　say can you see by the dawn's early my
　　　country 'tis of centuries come and go
　　　and are no more what of it we should worry　　　5
　　　in every language even deafanddumb
　　　thy sons acclaim your glorious name by gorry
　　　by jingo by gee by gosh by gum
　　　why talk of beauty what could be more beaut-
　　　iful than these heroic happy dead　　　10
　　　who rushed like lions to the roaring slaughter;
　　　they did not stop to think they died instead
　　　then shall the voice of liberty be mute?'

He spoke. And drank rapidly a glass of water

　　　　　since feeling is first
　　　　　who pays any attention
　　　　　to the syntax of things
　　　　　will never wholly kiss you;

　　　　　wholly to be a fool　　　5
　　　　　while Spring is in the world

　　　　　my blood approves,
　　　　　and kisses are a better fate
　　　　　than wisdom

lady i swear by all flowers. Don't cry   10
—the best gesture of my brain is less than
your eyelid's flutter which says

we are for each other: then
laugh, leaning back in my arms
for life's not a paragraph   15

And death i think is no parenthesis

somewhere i have never travelled, gladly beyond
any experience,your eyes have their silence:
in your most frail gesture are things which enclose me,
or which i cannot touch because they are too near

your slightest look easily will unclose me   5
though i have closed myself as fingers,
you open always petal by petal myself as Spring opens
(touching skilfully,mysteriously)her first rose

or if your wish be to close me,i and
my life will shut very beautifully,suddenly,   10
as when the heart of this flower imagines
the snow carefully everywhere descending;

nothing which we are to perceive in this world equals
the power of your intense fragility:whose texture
compels me with the colour of its countries,   15
rendering death and forever with each breathing

(i do not know what it is about you that closes
and opens;only something in me understands
the voice of your eyes is deeper than all roses)
nobody,not even the rain,has such small hands   20

    IN)
        all those who got
        athlete's mouth jumping
        on&off bandwaggons
                            (MEMORIAM

my father moved through dooms of love
through sames of am through haves of give,
singing each morning out of each night
my father moved through depths of height

this motionless forgetful where   5
turned at his glance to shining here;
that if(so timid air is firm)
under his eyes would stir and squirm

newly as from unburied which
floats the first who,his april touch   10
drove sleeping selves to swarm their fates
woke dreamers to their ghostly roots

and should some why completely weep
my father's fingers brought her sleep:
vainly no smallest voice might cry   15
for he could feel the mountains grow.

Lifting the valleys of the sea
my father moved through griefs of joy;
praising a forehead called the moon
singing desire into begin   20

joy was his song and joy so pure
a heart of star by him could steer
and pure so now and now so yes
the wrists of twilight would rejoice

keen as midsummer's keen beyond   25
conceiving mind of sun will stand,
so strictly(over utmost him
so hugely)stood my father's dream

his flesh was flesh his blood was blood:
no hungry man but wished him food;   30
no cripple wouldn't creep one mile
uphill to only see him smile.

Scorning the pomp of must and shall
my father moved through dooms of feel;
his anger was as right as rain   35
his pity was as green as grain

septembering arms of year extend
less humbly wealth to foe and friend
than he to foolish and to wise
offered immeasurable is   40

proudly and(by octobering flame
beckoned)as earth will downward climb,
so naked for immortal work
his shoulders marched against the dark

his sorrow was as true as bread: 45
no liar looked him in the head;
if every friend became his foe
he'd laugh and build a world with snow.

My father moved through theys of we,
singing each new leaf out of each tree   50
(and every child was sure that spring
danced when she heard my father sing)

then let men kill which cannot share,
let blood and flesh be mud and mire,
scheming imagine,passion willed,   55
freedom a drug that's bought and sold

giving to steal and cruel kind,
a heart to fear,to doubt a mind,
to differ a disease of same,
conform the pinnacle of am   60

though dull were all we taste as bright,
bitter all utterly things sweet,
maggoty minus and dumb death
all we inherit,all bequeath

and nothing quite so least as truth   65
—i say though hate were why men breathe—
because my father lived his soul
love is the whole and more than all

a–

float on some
?
i call twilight you

'll see   5

an in
-ch
of an if

&

who   10
is
the

)

more
dream than become   15
more

am than imagine

enter no(silence is the blood whose flesh
is singing)silence:but unsinging. In
spectral such hugest how hush,one

dead leaf stirring makes a crash
—far away(as far as alive)lies   5
april;and i breathe-move-and-seem some
perpetually roaming whylessness—

autumn has gone:will winter never come?

o come,terrible anonymity;enfold
phantom me with the murdering minus of cold   10
—open this ghost with millionary knives of wind—
scatter his nothing all over what angry skies and

gently
            (very whiteness:absolute peace,
never imaginable mystery)   15
                        descend

HART CRANE

Harold Hart Crane was born in 1899 in Garrettsville, Ohio, and grew up in the neighbouring city of Cleveland. His father, a prosperous sweet manufacturer, was determined to prepare him for a career in business. Crane, however, who began writing verse at a very early age and had his first work published when he was only fifteen, was quite as determined to become a writer. This necessarily created a large number of tensions in the family: tensions given a sharper edge by the fact that an equally uneasy relationship existed between husband and wife. Crane's parents quarrelled incessantly, about their son's education among other things, and finally separated when he was still young. Crane then went to live with his grandparents, while his mother, who suffered from nervous disorders throughout her life, was admitted to a sanatorium. The 'curse of sundered parenthood', as Crane was later to call it, was to leave a marked effect on the poet's character, confirming him in his sense of rootlessness – and perhaps contributing to the homosexuality of his adult years as well.

At the age of sixteen, Crane refreshed childhood memories of the Caribbean by staying, with his mother, at his grandparents' fruit plantation on the Isle of Pines, Cuba: an experience of exotic nature which was to inform his subsequent work. Then he set out for New York where he found employment, first in his father's business and afterwards as a labourer, munitions worker, and advertising agent. The jobs gave him some financial support while he pursued his chosen vocation of poet. During this period he also became acquainted with other writers living in the city, among whom were a group contributing to *The Little Review*: and it was in this periodical that some of his poems were first published. Other poems appeared in *Pagan*, *Poetry*, and *The Dial*. In general, Crane found the tasks of writing and of shaping his poetic gifts quite exhausting. Worn down by them as he was, and often depressed, he became increasingly dependent upon alcohol.

In 1926 Crane's first volume of poetry, *White Buildings*, was published to appreciative reviews from critics and fellow poets alike. Before it had appeared, however, Crane already had another enterprise in hand, a 'Myth of America' as he described it, which he was subsequently to entitle *The Bridge*. He had conceived of the work while living in a rented room overlooking Brooklyn Bridge and now, with the financial help of the philanthropist Otto Kahn, he set about preparing it in earnest. But by this time Crane was finding his creative periods ever more difficult to maintain and, despite Kahn's help, it took him several years of moving restlessly between New York, the Isle of Pines, and Europe to complete his projected epic.

Eventually *The Bridge* was published, in a limited edition inscribed to Otto Kahn in 1929, and in a general edition in 1930. The praise for it was lukewarm, even from many of Crane's friends; and this reception, based largely on a misunderstanding of the poet's real aims, naturally disappointed and unnerved him. Still, he continued with his plans for an even more grandiose epic, concerned this time with Mexican history, and in 1931 he was awarded a Guggenheim Fellowship to go to Mexico to begin writing it.

The next few months were a period of increasing unhappiness for the poet. He could make little progress with his Mexican epic. He became dogged with a sense of failure, and with the notion that his own irregular habits were responsible for this failure. His personal life too was, as he believed, in ruins. His father was dead and he had fallen out, not only with his mother but with many of his closest friends as well. So it was in a mood of profound despondency that he boarded the steamship *Orizaba*, to travel back from Vera Cruz to New York; and it was while still in this mood, presumably, that on 27 April 1932 he took his life by leaping overboard into the sea.

FURTHER READING

Butterfield, R. W. *The Broken Arc: a Study of Hart Crane*. Edinburgh, 1969.
Leibowitz. H. A. *Hart Crane: an Introduction to the Poetry*. New York, 1968.
Lewis, R .W. B. *The Poetry of Hart Crane*. New York, 1967.
Spears, Monroe K. *Hart Crane*. Minneapolis, Minn., 1965.
Unterecker, John. *Voyager: a Life of Hart Crane*. London, 1970.
Weber, Brom. *Hart Crane: a Biographical and Critical Study*. New York, 1948.

Black Tambourine

The interests of a black man in a cellar
Mark tardy judgment on the world's closed door.
Gnats toss in the shadow of a bottle,
And a roach spans a crevice in the floor.

Aesop, driven to pondering, found   5
Heaven with the tortoise and the hare;
Fox brush and sow ear top his grave
And mingling incantations on the air.

The black man, forlorn in the cellar,
Wanders in some mid-kingdom, dark, that lies,   10
Between his tambourine, stuck on the wall,
And, in Africa, a carcass quick with flies.

Chaplinesque

We make our meek adjustments,
Contented with such random consolations
As the wind deposits
In slithered and too ample pockets.

For we can still love the world, who find   5
A famished kitten on the step, and know
Recesses for it from the fury of the street,
Or warm torn elbow coverts.

We will sidestep, and to the final smirk
Dally the doom of that inevitable thumb   10
That slowly chafes its puckered index toward us,
Facing the dull squint with what innocence
And what surprise!

And yet these fine collapses are not lies
More than the pirouettes of any pliant cane;   15
Our obsequies are, in a way, no enterprise.
We can evade you, and all else but the heart:
What blame to us if the heart live on.

The game enforces smirks; but we have seen
The moon in lonely alleys make   20
A grail of laughter of an empty ash can,
And through all sound of gaiety and quest
Have heard a kitten in the wilderness.

from For the Marriage of Faustus and Helen

Capped arbiter of beauty in this street
That narrows darkly into motor dawn,—
You, here beside me, delicate ambassador
Of intricate slain numbers that arise
In whispers, naked of steel;

                        religious gunman!   5
Who faithfully, yourself, will fall too soon,
And in other ways than as the wind settles
On the sixteen thrifty bridges of the city:
Let us unbind our throats of fear and pity.

                             We even,   10
Who drove speediest destruction
In corymbulous formations of mechanics,—
Who hurried the hill breezes, spouting malice
Plangent over meadows, and looked down
On rifts of torn and empty houses   15
Like old women with teeth unjubilant
That waited faintly, briefly and in vain:

We know, eternal gunman, our flesh remembers
The tensile boughs, the nimble blue plateaus,
The mounted, yielding cities of the air!   20

That saddled sky that shook down vertical
Repeated play of fire—no hypogeum
Of wave or rock was good against one hour.

We did not ask for that, but have survived,
And will persist to speak again before   25
All stubble streets that have not curved
To memory, or known the ominous lifted arm
That lowers down the arc of Helen's brow
To saturate with blessing and dismay.

A goose, tobacco and cologne— 30
Three-winged and gold-shod prophecies of heaven,
The lavish heart shall always have to leaven
And spread with bells and voices, and atone
The abating shadows of our conscript dust.

Anchises' navel, dripping of the sea,— 35
The hands Erasmus dipped in gleaming tides,
Gathered the voltage of blown blood and vine;
Delve upward for the new and scattered wine,
O brother-thief of time, that we recall.
Laugh out the meager penance of their days 40
Who dare not share with us the breath released,
The substance drilled and spent beyond repair
For golden, or the shadow of gold hair.

Distinctly praise the years, whose volatile
Blamed bleeding hands extend and thresh the height 45
The imagination spans beyond despair,
Outpacing bargain, vocable and prayer.

At Melville's Tomb

Often beneath the wave, wide from this ledge
The dice of drowned men's bones he saw bequeath
An embassy. Their numbers as he watched,
Beat on the dusty shore and were obscured.

And wrecks passed without sound of bells, 5
The calyx of death's bounty giving back
A scattered chapter, livid hieroglyph,
The portent wound in corridors of shells.

Then in the circuit calm of one vast coil,
Its lashings charmed and malice reconciled, 10
Frosted eyes there were that lifted altars;
And silent answers crept across the stars.

Compass, quadrant and sextant contrive
No farther tides...High in the azure steeps
Monody shall not wake the mariner. 15
This fabulous shadow only the sea keeps.

from Voyages

I

Above the fresh ruffles of the surf
Bright striped urchins flay each other with sand.
They have contrived a conquest for shell shucks,
And their fingers crumble fragments of baked weed
Gaily digging and scattering.   5

And in answer to their treble interjections
The sun beats lightning on the waves,
The waves fold thunder on the sand;
And could they hear me I would tell them:

O brilliant kids, frisk with your dog,   10
Fondle your shells and sticks, bleached
By time and the elements; but there is a line
You must not cross nor ever trust beyond it
Spry cordage of your bodies to caresses
Too lichen-faithful from too wide a breast.   15
The bottom of the sea is cruel.

II

—And yet this great wink of eternity,
Of rimless floods, unfettered leewardings,
Samite sheeted and processioned where
Her undinal vast belly moonward bends,
Laughing the wrapt inflections of our love;   5

Take this Sea, whose diapason knells
On scrolls of silver snowy sentences,
The sceptred terror of whose sessions rends
As her demeanors motion well or ill,
All but the pieties of lovers' hands.   10

And onward, as bells off San Salvador
Salute the crocus lustres of the stars,
In these poinsettia meadows of her tides,—
Adagios of islands, O my Prodigal,
Complete the dark confessions her veins spell.   15

Mark how her turning shoulders wind the hours,
And hasten while her penniless rich palms

Pass superscription of bent foam and wave,—
Hasten, while they are true,—sleep, death, desire,
Close round one instant in one floating flower.   20

Bind us in time, O Seasons clear, and awe.
O minstrel galleons of Carib fire,
Bequeath us to no earthly shore until
Is answered in the vortex of our grave
The seal's wide spindrift gaze toward paradise.   25

III

Infinite consanguinity it bears—
This tendered theme of you that light
Retrieves from sea plains where the sky
Resigns a breast that every wave enthrones;
While ribboned water lanes I wind   5
Are laved and scattered with no stroke
Wide from your side, whereto this hour
The sea lifts, also, reliquary hands.

And so, admitted through black swollen gates
That must arrest all distance otherwise,—   10
Past whirling pillars and lithe pediments,
Light wrestling there incessantly with light,
Star kissing star through wave on wave unto
Your body rocking!
              and where death, if shed,
Presumes no carnage, but this single change,—   15
Upon the steep floor flung from dawn to dawn
The silken skilled transmemberment of song;

Permit me voyage, love, into your hands...

VI

Where icy and bright dungeons lift
Of swimmers their lost morning eyes,
And ocean rivers, churning, shift
Green borders under stranger skies,

Steadily as a shell secretes   5
Its beating leagues of monotone,
Or as many waters trough the sun's
Red kelson past the cape's wet stone;

O rivers mingling toward the sky
And harbor of the phoenix' breast—   10
My eyes pressed black against the prow,
—Thy derelict and blinded guest

Waiting, afire, what name, unspoke,
I cannot claim: let thy waves rear
More savage than the death of kings,   15
Some splintered garland for the seer.

Beyond siroccos harvesting
The solstice thunders, crept away,
Like a cliff swinging or a sail
Flung into April's inmost day—   20

Creation's blithe and petalled word
To the lounged goddess when she rose
Conceding dialogue with eyes
That smile unsearchable repose—

Still fervid covenant, Belle Isle,   25
—Unfolded floating dais before
Which rainbows twine continual hair—
Belle Isle, white echo of the oar!

The imaged Word, it is, that holds
Hushed willows anchored in its glow.   30
It is the unbetrayable reply
Whose accent no farewell can know.

from 'The Bridge'

Proem: To Brooklyn Bridge

How many dawns, chill from his rippling rest
The seagull's wings shall dip and pivot him,
Shedding white rings of tumult, building high
Over the chained bay waters Liberty—

Then, with inviolate curve, forsake our eyes   5
As apparitional as sails that cross
Some page of figures to be filed away;
—Till elevators drop us from our day...

I think of cinemas, panoramic sleights
With multitudes bent toward some flashing scene   10
Never disclosed, but hastened to again,
Foretold to other eyes on the same screen;

And Thee, across the harbor, silver-paced
As though the sun took step of thee, yet left
Some motion ever unspent in thy stride,—   15
Implicitly thy freedom staying thee!

Out of some subway scuttle, cell or loft
A bedlamite speeds to thy parapets,
Tilting there momently, shrill shirt ballooning,
A jest falls from the speechless caravan.   20

Down Wall, from girder into street noon leaks,
A rip-tooth of the sky's acetylene;
All afternoon the cloud-flown derricks turn...
Thy cables breathe the North Atlantic still.

And obscure as that heaven of the Jews,   25
Thy guerdon...Accolade thou dost bestow
Of anonymity time cannot raise:
Vibrant reprieve and pardon thou dost show.

O harp and altar, of the fury fused,
(How could mere toil align thy choiring strings!)   30
Terrific threshold of the prophet's pledge,
Prayer of pariah, and the lover's cry,—

Again the traffic lights that skim thy swift
Unfractioned idiom, immaculate sigh of stars,
Beading thy path—condense eternity: 35
And we have seen night lifted in thine arms.

Under thy shadow by the piers I waited;
Only in darkness is thy shadow clear.
The City's fiery parcels all undone,
Already snow submerges an iron year...   40

O Sleepless as the river under thee,
Vaulting the sea, the prairies' dreaming sod,
Unto us lowliest sometime sweep, descend
And of the curveship lend a myth to God.

Royal Palm

Green rustlings, more-than-regal charities
Drift coolly from that tower of whispered light.
Amid the noontide's blazed asperities
I watched the sun's most gracious anchorite

Climb up as by communings, year on year   5
Uneaten of the earth or aught earth holds,
And the grey trunk, that's elephantine, rear
Its frondings sighing in aetherial folds.

Forever fruitless, and beyond that yield
Of sweat the jungle presses with hot love   10
And tendril till our deathward breath is sealed—
It grazes the horizons, launched above

Mortality—ascending emerald-bright,
A fountain at salute, a crown in view—
Unshackled, casual of its azured height   15
As though it soared suchwise through heaven too.

THEODORE ROETHKE

Theodore Roethke was born in 1908 in Michigan, where his family had a successful business as florists. Between them his father and his uncle owned twenty-five acres of greenhouses and it was in and around these that the boy grew up: working among them, playing beside them, and eventually finding in them a potent symbolic landscape for his verse. Upon graduating from high school, Roethke attended the University of Michigan where he received his B.A. in 1929 and then spent a brief period at Harvard before returning to Michigan to study for his M.A. By the time he had received his higher degree he had abandoned his former plans of working in the law or advertising and decided to dedicate himself to poetry; a decision that seemed well justified when he found his work gaining an immediate and regular acceptance with several eminent journals.

In 1931 Roethke was appointed an Instructor in English at Lafayette College, Pennsylvania. He worked there for four years before moving on to become an assistant professor at Pennsylvania State College. Other academic posts followed, at Bennington College in Vermont from 1943 until 1946, and then at the University of Washington where he stayed until his death, first as an associate professor and later as poet in residence. While he was teaching at the University of Washington he met one of his former students from Bennington again, Beatrice O'Connell, and in 1953 after a brief courtship they were married. His constant companion both at home and on his occasional trips to Europe, it was Beatrice who subsequently helped nurse Roethke through the fits of manic depressiveness to which he remained subject throughout his adult life.

Roethke's first volume of poetry, *Open House*, was not published until 1941 when he was already thirty-three. Its relative conventionality, the dependence Roethke showed on traditional forms and on the currently fashionable mode of tough intellectualism, virtually guaranteed that it should be well received; and in the event it was accorded a warmer reception than many of his later and better collections. His second volume, *The Lost Son and Other Poems* (1948), met with a distinctly mixed response. The looser, more varied rhythms he chose to employ here, his reliance on development by association, above all his interest in the prerational world of plants and animals and in the possible connections between that world and the sub-conscious: all this made the book seem startlingly new and, to some reviewers at least, disorganised and unintelligible. The impression was compounded with the appearance of *Praise to the End!* some three years later, a sequence of poems in which Roethke used fractured rhythms and syntax, elliptical imagery and a primitive mode of speech, to chart the journey into the deepest recesses of the self. Several eminent critics, and English commentators in particular, began to express severe misgivings or even outright disapproval.

But by now, despite all the hostile criticism, Roethke was becoming recognised and honoured as a major poet. He had received a Fellowship from the Guggenheim Foundation as early as 1945, and an award from *Poetry* magazine in 1947. Then in 1953 his fourth volume, *The Waking*, was awarded a Pulitzer Prize. Other national prizes quickly followed – most notably the Bollingen and National Book Awards which he earned for *Words for the Wind* (1958) – and Roethke seemed to be just about at the height of his fame when he died suddenly, of a heart attack, in 1963. His fame has in no way diminished since his death, however: if anything, it has continued to grow, helped along by books like *The Far Field*, an impressive collec-tion of new verse published in 1964, and the *Collected Poems*, which appeared two years later.

FURTHER READING

Malkoff, Karl. *Theodore Roethke: an Introduction to the Poetry*. New York, 1966.

Mills, Jr, Ralph J. *Theodore Roethke*. Minneapolis, Minn., 1963.

Seager, Allan. *The Glass House: the Life of Theodore Roethke*. New York, 1968.

Stein, Arnold (ed.). *Theodore Roethke: Essays on the Poetry*. Seattle, Wash., 1965.

Open House

My secrets cry aloud.
I have no need for tongue.
My heart keeps open house,

My doors are widely swung.
An epic of the eyes   5
My love, with no disguise.

My truths are all foreknown,
This anguish self-revealed.
I'm naked to the bone,
With nakedness my shield.   10
Myself is what I wear:
I keep the spirit spare.

The anger will endure,
The deed will speak the truth
In language strict and pure.   15
I stop the lying mouth:
Rage warps my clearest cry
To witless agony.

Cuttings

Sticks-in-a-drowse droop over sugary loam,
Their intricate stem-fur dries;
But still the delicate slips keep coaxing up water;
The small cells bulge;

One nub of growth   5
Nudges a sand-crumb loose,
Pokes through a musty sheath
Its pale tendrilous horn.

Cuttings
(later)

This urge, wrestle, resurrection of dry sticks,
Cut stems struggling to put down feet,
What saint strained so much,
Rose on such lopped limbs to a new life?

I can hear, underground, that sucking and sobbing,   5
In my veins, in my bones I feel it,—
The small waters seeping upward,

The tight grains parting at last.
When sprouts break out,
Slippery as fish,   10
I quail, lean to beginnings, sheath-wet.

Night Crow

When I saw that clumsy crow
Flap from a wasted tree,
A shape in the mind rose up:
Over the gulfs of dream
Flew a tremendous bird   5
Further and further away
Into a moonless black,
Deep in the brain, far back.

Unfold! Unfold!

I

By snails, by leaps of frog, I came here, spirit.
Tell me, body without skin, does a fish sweat?
I can't crawl back through those veins,
I ache for another choice.
The cliffs! The cliffs! They fling me back.   5
Eternity howls in the last crags,
The field is no longer simple:
It's a soul's crossing time.
The dead speak noise.

II

It's time you stood up and asked
            —Or sat down and did.   10
A tongue without song
            —Can still whistle in a jug.
You're blistered all over
            —Who cares? The old owl?
When you find the wind
            —Look for the white fire.

III

What a whelm of proverbs, Mr. Pinch!
Are the entrails clear, immaculate cabbage?   15
The last time I nearly whispered myself away.
I was far back, farther than anybody else.
On the jackpine plains I hunted the bird nobody knows;
Fishing, I caught myself behind the ears.
Alone, in a sleep-daze, I stared at billboards;   20

I was privy to oily fungus and the algae of standing waters;
Honored, on my return, by the ancient fellowship of rotten
                                                           stems.
I was pure as a worm on a leaf; I cherished the mold's children.
Beetles sweetened my breath.
I slept like an insect.   25

I met a collector of string, a shepherd of slow forms.
My mission became the salvation of minnows.
I stretched like a board, almost a tree.
Even thread had a speech.

Later, I did and I danced in the simple wood.   30
A mouse taught me how, I was a happy asker.
Quite-by-chance brought me many cookies.
I jumped in butter.
Hair had kisses.

IV

Easy the life of the mouth. What a lust for ripeness!   35
All openings praise us, even oily holes.
The bulb unravels. Who's floating? Not me.
The eye perishes in the small vision.
What else has the vine loosened?
I hear a dead tongue halloo.   40

V

Sing, sing, you symbols! All simple creatures,
All small shapes, willow-shy,
In the obscure haze, sing!

A light song comes from the leaves.
A slow sigh says yes. And light sighs;   45

6   G A P

A low voice, summer-sad.
Is it you, cold father? Father,
For whom the minnows sang?

A house for wisdom; a field for revelation.
Speak to the stones, and the stars answer.   50
At first the visible obscures:
Go where light is.

This fat can't laugh.
Only my salt has a chance.
I'll seek my own meekness.   55
What grace I have is enough.
The lost have their own pace.
The stalks ask something else.
What the grave says,
The nest denies.   60

In their harsh thickets
The dead thrash.
They help.

Memory

I

In the slow world of dream,
We breathe in unison.
The outside dies within,
And she knows all I am.

II

She turns, as if to go,   5
Half-bird, half-animal.
The wind dies on the hill.
Love's all. Love's all I know.

III

A doe drinks by a stream,
A doe and its fawn.   10
When I follow after them,
The grass changes to stone.

from Meditations of an Old Woman

First Meditation

I

On love's worst ugly day,
The weeds hiss at the edge of the field,
The small winds make their chilly indictments.
Elsewhere, in houses, even pails can be sad;
While stones loosen on the obscure hillside,   5
And a tree tilts from its roots,
Toppling down an embankment.

The spirit moves, but not always upward,
While animals eat to the north,
And the shale slides an inch in the talus,   10
The bleak wind eats at the weak plateau,
And the sun brings joy to some.
But the rind, often, hates the life within.

How can I rest in the days of my slowness?
I've become a strange piece of flesh,   15
Nervous and cold, bird-furtive, whiskery,
With a cheek soft as a hound's ear.
What's left is light as a seed;
I need an old crone's knowing.

II

Often I think of myself as riding—   20
Alone, on a bus through western country.
I sit above the back wheels, where the jolts are hardest,
And we bounce and sway along toward the midnight,
The lights tilting up, skyward, as we come over a little rise,
Then down, as we roll like a boat from a wave-crest.   25

All journeys, I think, are the same:
The movement is forward, after a few wavers,
And for a while we are all alone,
Busy, obvious with ourselves,
The drunken soldier, the old lady with her peppermints;   30
And we ride, we ride, taking the curves
Somewhat closer, the trucks coming

6-2

Down from behind the last ranges,
Their black shapes breaking past;
And the air claps between us,   35
Blasting the frosted windows,
And I seem to go backward,
Backward in time:

    Two song sparrows, one within a greenhouse,
    Shuttling its throat while perched on a wind-vent,   40
    And another, outside, in the bright day,
    With a wind from the west and the trees all in motion.
    One sang, then the other,
    The songs tumbling over and under the glass,
    And the men beneath them wheeling in dirt to the cement
                                         benches,   45
    The laden wheelbarrows creaking and swaying,
    And the up-spring of the plank when a foot left the runway.

Journey within a journey:
The ticket mislaid or lost, the gate
Inaccessible, the boat always pulling out   50
From the rickety wooden dock,
The children waving;
Or two horses plunging in snow, their lines tangled,
A great wooden sleigh careening behind them,
Swerving up a steep embankment.   55
For a moment they stand above me,
Their black skins shuddering:
Then they lurch forward,
Lunging down a hillside.

III

As when silt drifts and sifts down through muddy pond-
                                    water,   60
Settling in small beads around weeds and sunken branches,
And one crab, tentative, hunches himself before moving along
   the bottom,
Grotesque, awkward, his extended eyes looking at nothing in
   particular,
Only a few bubbles loosening from the ill-matched tentacles,

The tail and smaller legs slipping and sliding slowly
   backward—   65
So the spirit tries for another life,
Another way and place in which to continue;
Or a salmon, tired, moving up a shallow stream,
Nudges into a back-eddy, a sandy inlet,
Bumping against sticks and bottom-stones, then swinging   70
Around, back into the tiny maincurrent, the rush of brownish-
   white water,
Still swimming forward—
So, I suppose, the spirit journeys.

IV

I have gone into the waste lonely places
Behind the eye; the lost acres at the edge of smoky cities.   75
What's beyond never crumbles like an embankment,
Explodes like a rose, or thrusts wings over the Caribbean.
There are no pursuing forms, faces on walls:
Only the motes of dust in the immaculate hallways,
The darkness of falling hair, the warnings from lint and
   spiders,   80
The vines graying to a fine powder.
There is no riven tree, or lamb dropped by an eagle.

There are still times, morning and evening:
The cerulean, high in the elm,
Thin and insistent as a cicada,   85
And the far phoebe, singing,
The long plaintive notes floating down,
Drifting through leaves, oak and maple,
Or the whippoorwill, along the smoky ridges,
A single bird calling and calling;   90
A fume reminds me, drifting across wet gravel;
A cold wind comes over stones;
A flame, intense, visible,
Plays over the dry pods,
Runs fitfully along the stubble,   95
Moves over the field,
Without burning.
     In such times, lacking a god,
     I am still happy.

The Moment

We passed the ice of pain,
And came to a dark ravine,
And there we sang with the sea:
The wide, the bleak abyss
Shifted with our slow kiss.   5

Space struggled with time;
The gong of midnight struck
The naked absolute.
Sound, silence sang as one.

All flowed: without, within;   10
Body met body, we
Created what's to be.

What else to say?
We end in joy.

Once More, the Round

What's greater, Pebble or Pond?
What can be known? The Unknown.
My true self runs toward a Hill —
More! O More! visible.

Now I adore my life   5
With the Bird, the abiding Leaf,
With the Fish, the questing Snail,
And the Eye altering all;
And I dance with William Blake
For love, for Love's sake;   10

And everything comes to One,
As we dance on, dance on, dance on.

ROBERT LOWELL

A member of a distinguished New England family, which includes among its earlier generations the poets James Russell Lowell (1819–1891) and Amy Lowell (1874–1925), Robert Lowell was born in Boston, Massachusetts, in 1917. According to his own account of it, his childhood was not a happy one. His mother, a Winslow and a descendant of the first woman to step off the *Mayflower*, was a domineering character who badgered her husband into surrendering the deeds of the house to her, and into leaving the navy for a series of jobs that were as oppressive as they were unrewarding. Lowell was sent to St Mark's School, a wealthy private establishment in Southborough, Massachusetts, where one of the teachers was the poet Richard Eberhart. His initial interest in verse now additionally stimulated by Eberhart, Lowell soon completed a manuscript book of poems (which he presented to his teacher) and achieved his first publication – in the school magazine.

After leaving St Mark's, Lowell enrolled at Harvard University, only to find the academic atmosphere quite stifling. The sole encouragement he received for his writing while he was there was from Robert Frost, who was living in the neighbourhood at the time, and half-way through his second year he decided to leave. He then visited the poet Allen Tate and his wife at their home near Nashville, Tennessee, before enrolling at Kenyon College in Ohio. The years at Kenyon were crucial for Lowell in a number of ways. There, he came under the influence of John Crowe Ransom and other New Critics, whose reverence for the ironic, the ambiguous, and the closely textured was to exercise an enormous influence on his own earlier work. There, also, he was converted to Roman Catholicism; and met Jean Stafford, a writer and a teacher at a neighbouring college, whom he married while he was still an undergraduate.

Almost as soon as Lowell graduated, the couple moved to Louisiana State University, then back to Kenyon for a while; after which they drifted northward to Greenwich Village in New York. When America declared war in 1941, Lowell tried to enlist but he was rejected on the grounds of physical unfitness.

By the time he was drafted, however, he had changed his mind about the conflict (largely because he objected to the Allies' use of the technique of saturation bombing, and to their demand for unconditional surrender), and he refused to serve. He was then sentenced to imprisonment for a year and a day, subsequently commuted to five months, and after serving his sentence he and his wife left New York for Maine.

Shortly before the war ended, in 1944, Lowell's first volume of poetry, *Land of Unlikeness*, was published in a limited edition in Massachusetts. Then in 1946 *Lord Weary's Castle* appeared, containing about a third of the poems from the first volume together with many additions. It was awarded a Pulitzer Prize. At the age of twenty-nine, Lowell found himself acknowledged as a poet of some considerable standing, and his reputation was confirmed with the publication of *Poems, 1938–1949* in 1950. By now, though, his personal life was fraught with difficulties. He was plagued by periodic attacks of mental illness, and by religious doubts which prompted him eventually to leave the Roman Catholic Church. His domestic situation, also, had become intolerable and in 1948 he and Jean Stafford were divorced.

In 1951 Lowell married again, to another writer, Elizabeth Hardwick. The rest of the year he spent teaching at Iowa State University. The couple then travelled in Europe for a time, returning in 1954 to Massachusetts where Lowell bought himself a large house with an inheritance left him by his mother. For the next few years he divided his time between writing, teaching at Boston University, and entertaining a series of guests that included William Carlos Williams and the critic Edmund Wilson. He had already published a third book of verse, *The Mills of the Kavanaughs*, in 1951; and in 1959 *Life Studies* appeared, witnessing a radical change of style and approach. This, together with *For the Union Dead* (1964) and *Near the Ocean* (1967), confirmed his stature as one of the major American poets.

At the same time as writing original verse, Lowell has also composed many free, verse translations of other poets' work, among them the pieces included in *Imitations* (1962) and a version of *Phaedra* (1960) by Racine. He has continued teaching as well, at Harvard and then subsequently in England at the University of Essex. His most recent collections of verse are

Notebook, 1967–1968, published in 1969, *Prometheus Bound* (1970), *The Dolphin* (1973), *For Lizzie and Harriet* (1973) and *History* (1973).

FURTHER READING

Cooper, Philip. *The Autobiographical Myth of Robert Lowell.* Chapel Hill, N.C., 1970.
Cosgrave, Patrick. *The Public Poetry of Robert Lowell.* London, 1970.
Crick, John. *Robert Lowell.* Edinburgh, 1964.
Parkinson, Thomas (ed.). *Robert Lowell: A Collection of Critical Essays.* Englewood Cliffs, N.J., 1968.
Staples, Hugh B. *Robert Lowell: The First Twenty Years.* New York, 1962.
Williamson, Alan. *Pity the Monsters: the Political Vision of Robert Lowell.* New Haven, 1974.

Children of Light

Our fathers wrung their bread from stocks and stones
And fenced their gardens with the Redman's bones;
Embarking from the Nether Land of Holland;
Pilgrims unhouseled by Geneva's night,
They planted here the Serpent's seeds of light;   5
And here the pivoting searchlights probe to shock
The riotous glass houses built on rock,
And candles gutter by an empty altar,
And light is where the landless blood of Cain
Is burning, burning the unburied grain.   10

The Holy Innocents

Listen, the hay-bells tinkle as the cart
Wavers on rubber tires along the tar
And cindered ice below the burlap mill
And ale-wife run. The oxen drool and start
In wonder at the fenders of a car,   5
And blunder hugely up St. Peter's hill.
These are the undefiled by woman—their
Sorrow is not the sorrow of this world:
King Herod shrieking vengeance at the curled
Up knees of Jesus choking in the air,   10

A king of speechless clods and infants. Still
The world out-Herods Herod; and the year,
The nineteen-hundred forty-fifth of grace,
Lumbers with losses up the clinkered hill
Of our purgation; and the oxen near   15
The worn foundations of their resting-place,
The holy manger where their bed is corn
And holly torn for Christmas. If they die,
As Jesus, in the harness, who will mourn?
Lamb of the shepherds, Child how still you lie.   20

Colloquy in Black Rock

Here the jack-hammer jabs into the ocean;
My heart, you race and stagger and demand
More blood-gangs for your nigger-brass percussions,
Till I, the stunned machine of your devotion,
Clanging upon this cymbal of a hand,   5
Am rattled screw and footloose. All discussions

End in low water, slump, and dumps and death.
My heart, beat faster, faster. In Black Mud
Hungarian machinists give their blood
For the martyr Stephen, who was stoned to death.   10

Black Mud, a name to conjure with: O mud
For watermelons gutted to the crust,
Mud for the mole-tide harbour, mud for mouse,
Mud for the armoured Diesel fishing tubs that thud
A year and a day to wind and tidal rust,   15
The heart-skip and the quake that shakes my house

To Jericho, a clay and trumpet death.
My heart, beat faster, faster. In Black Mud
Stephen the martyr was broken down to blood:
Our ransom is the rubble of his death.   20

Christ walks on the black water. In Black Mud
Darts the Kingfisher. On Corpus Christi, heart,
Over the drum-beat of St. Stephen's choir
I hear him, *Stupor Mundi*, and the mud
Flies from his hunching wings and beak—my heart,   25
The blue kingfisher dives on you in fire.

Beyond the Alps

(*On the train from Rome to Paris.* 1950, *the year when Pius XII
defined the dogma of Mary's bodily assumption.*)

Reading how even the Swiss had thrown the sponge
in once again and Everest was still
unscaled, I watched our Paris pullman lunge
mooning across the fallow Alpine snow.
O bella Roma! I saw our stewards go   5
forward on tiptoe banging on their gongs.
Life changed to landscape. Much against my will,
I left the City of God where it belongs.
There the skirt-mad Mussolini unfurled
the eagle of Caesar. He was one of us   10
only, pure prose. I envy the conspicuous
waste of our grandparents on their grand tours—
long-haired Victorian sages accepted the universe,
while breezing on their trust funds through the world.

When the Vatican made Mary's Assumption dogma,   15
the crowds at San Pietro screamed *Papa.*
The Holy Father dropped his shaving glass,
and listened. His electric razor purred,
his pet canary chirped on his left hand.
The lights of science couldn't hold a candle   20
to Mary risen—at one miraculous stroke,
angel-wing'd, gorgeous as a jungle bird!
But who believed this? Who could understand?
Pilgrims still kissed Saint Peter's brazen sandal.
The Duce's lynched, bare, booted skull still spoke.   25
God herded his people to the *coup de grâce*—
the costumed Switzers sloped their pikes to push,
O Pius, through the monstrous human crush. . . .

Our mountain-climbing train had come to earth.
Tired of the querulous hush-hush of the wheels,   30
the blear-eyed ego kicking in my berth
lay still, and saw Apollo plant his heels
on terra firma through the morning's thigh. . .
each backward, wasted Alp, a Parthenon,
fire-branded socket of the Cyclop's eye.   35

There were no tickets for that altitude
once held by Hellas, when the Goddess stood,
prince, pope, philosopher and golden bough,
pure mind and murder at the scything prow—
Minerva, the miscarriage of the brain.   40

Now Paris, our black classic, breaking up
like killer kings on an Etruscan cup.

For Sale

Poor sheepish plaything,
organized with prodigal animosity,
lived in just a year—
my Father's cottage at Beverly Farms
was on the market the month he died.   5
Empty, open, intimate,
its town-house furniture
had an on tiptoe air
of waiting for the mover
on the heels of the undertaker.   10
Ready, afraid
of living alone till eighty,
Mother mooned in a window,
as if she had stayed on a train
one stop past her destination.   15

'To Speak of the Woe that is in Marriage'

'It is the future generation that presses into being by means of these exuberant feelings and supersensible soap bubbles of ours' (Schopenhauer).

'The hot night makes us keep our bedroom windows open.
Our magnolia blossoms. Life begins to happen.
My hopped up husband drops his home disputes,
and hits the streets to cruise for prostitutes,
free-lancing out along the razor's edge.
This screwball might kill his wife, then take the pledge.
Oh the monotonous meanness of his lust....
It's the injustice...he is so unjust—

whiskey-blind, swaggering home at five.
My only thought is how to keep alive.   10
What makes him tick? Each night now I tie
ten dollars and his car key to my thigh. . . .
Gored by the climacteric of his want,
he stalls above me like an elephant.'

Skunk Hour

(*For Elizabeth Bishop*)

Nautilus Island's hermit
heiress still lives through winter in her Spartan cottage;
her sheep still graze above the sea.
Her son's a bishop. Her farmer
is first selectman in our village,   5
she's in her dotage.

Thirsting for
the hierarchic privacy
of Queen Victoria's century,
she buys up all   10
the eyesores facing her shore,
and lets them fall.

The season's ill—
we've lost our summer millionaire,
who seemed to leap from an L. L. Bean   15
catalogue. His nine-knot yawl
was auctioned off to lobstermen.
A red fox stain covers Blue Hill.

And now our fairy
decorator brightens his shop for fall,   20
his fishnet's filled with orange cork,
orange, his cobbler's bench and awl,
there is no money in his work,
he'd rather marry.

One dark night,   25
my Tudor Ford climbed the hill's skull,
I watched for love-cars. Lights turned down,

they lay together, hull to hull,
where the graveyard shelves on the town....
My mind's not right.　　　　　　　　　　30

A car radio bleats,
'Love, O careless Love...' I hear
my ill-spirit sob in each blood cell,
as if my hand were at its throat...
I myself am hell,　　　　　　　　　　35
nobody's here—

only skunks, that search
in the moonlight for a bite to eat.
They march on their soles up Main Street:
white stripes, moonstruck eyes' red fire　　　　40
under the chalk-dry and spar spire
of the Trinitarian Church.

I stand on top
of our back steps and breathe the rich air—
a mother skunk with her column of kittens swills the
　　　garbage pail.
She jabs her wedge head in a cup　　　　45
of sour cream, drops her ostrich tail,
and will not scare.

For the Union Dead

'Relinquunt Omnia Servare Rem Publicam.'

The old South Boston Aquarium stands
in a Sahara of snow now. Its broken windows are boarded.
The bronze weathervane cod has lost half its scales.
The airy tanks are dry.

Once my nose crawled like a snail on the glass;　　　　5
my hand tingled
to burst the bubbles
drifting from the noses of the cowed, compliant fish.

My hand draws back, I often sigh still
for the dark downward and vegetating kingdom　　　　10
of the fish and reptile. One morning last March,
I pressed against the new barbed and galvanized

fence on the Boston Common. Behind their cage,
yellow dinosaur steamshovels were grunting
as they cropped up tons of mush and grass   15
to gouge their underworld garage.

Parking spaces luxuriate like civic
sandpiles in the heart of Boston.
A girdle of orange, Puritan-pumpkin colored girders
braces the tingling Statehouse,   20

shaking over the excavations, as it faces Colonel Shaw
and his bell-cheeked Negro infantry
on St. Gaudens' shaking Civil War relief,
propped by a plank splint against the garage's earthquake.

Two months after marching through Boston,   25
half the regiment was dead;
at the dedication,
William James could almost hear the bronze Negroes
   breathe.

Their monument sticks like a fishbone
in the city's throat.   30
Its Colonel is as lean
as a compass-needle.

He has an angry wrenlike vigilance,
a greyhound's gentle tautness;
he seems to wince at pleasure,   35
and suffocate for privacy.

He is out of bounds now. He rejoices in man's lovely,
peculiar power to choose life and die—
when he leads his black soldiers to death,
he cannot bend his back.   40

On a thousand small town New England greens,
the old white churches hold their air
of sparse, sincere rebellion; frayed flags
quilt the graveyards of the Grand Army of the Republic.

The stone statues of the abstract Union Soldier   45
grow slimmer and younger each year—
wasp-waisted, they doze over muskets
and muse through their sideburns...

Shaw's father wanted no monument
except the ditch,   50
where his son's body was thrown
and lost with his 'niggers.'

The ditch is nearer.
There are no statues for the last war here;
on Boyleston Street, a commercial photograph   55
shows Hiroshima boiling

over a Mosler Safe, the 'Rock of Ages'
that survived the blast. Space is nearer.
When I crouch to my television set,
the drained faces of Negro school-children rise like
        balloons.   60

Colonel Shaw
is riding on his bubble,
he waits
for the blesséd break.

The Aquarium is gone. Everywhere,   65
giant finned cars nose forward like fish;
a savage servility
slides by on grease.

from 'Notebook'

Reading Myself

Like millions, I took just pride and more than just,
first striking matches that brought my blood to boiling;
I memorized tricks to set the river on fire,
somehow never wrote something to go back to.
Even suppose I had finished with wax flowers   5
and earned a pass to the minor slopes of Parnassus....
No honeycomb is built without a bee
adding circle to circle, cell to cell,
the wax and honey of a mausoleum—
this round dome proves its maker is alive,   10
the corpse of such insect lives preserved in honey,
prays that the perishable work live long
enough for the sweet-tooth bear to desecrate—
this open book...my open coffin.

NOTES TO THE POEMS

Edwin Arlington Robinson

Richard Cory

This is one of many poems set in Tilbury Town, a place based on Robinson's boyhood home of Gardiner, Maine. Its irony depends upon the contrast between the serenity of Cory's appearance and the violence of his death; its melancholy, upon our recognising that Cory – for all his privileges – is acutely isolated and spiritually deprived. 'There is more in every person's soul than we think. Even the happy mortals we term ordinary...act their own mental tragedies and live a far deeper and wider life than we are inclined to believe possible in the light of our prejudices' (Robinson).

2–9] Note the contrast here between the poorer townsfolk 'on the pavement' and the regal ('crown', 'imperially') figure of Cory.
5–6] The emphasis here, as throughout the poem, is on Cory's impenetrable *appearance.*
13–14] *light...meat...bread:* All these words have Biblical overtones. Belie in 'the light', in the possible existence of a meaning, is something Cory did not have and, apparently, could not hope for. He had every material advantage, the necessary 'bread' and 'meat', but man does not live by these alone; and this he must instinctively have recognised.
15] *calm:* i.e. for the townsfolk, but certainly not for Cory. The word reaffirms the distance between them and him.

George Crabbe

George Crabbe (1754–1832) described in some detail the problems of rural England; the loneliness of country people, the austerity and sheer poverty of their lives. In this sonnet, Robinson clearly sees him as a spiritual brother, both of them rebelling against the orthodoxies of the pastoral tradition.

14] *flicker...flame:* The flame is an image used frequently by the Romantic poets to describe the transfiguring power of the imagination. A further connection between Crabbe and Robinson lies precisely in this, that traces of this flame are discernible in the verse of both, however flickering and intermittent. Thus, most inhabitants of Tilbury Town may not be capable of transfiguring their environment in the way a Romantic hero would be: but they are not entirely determined by that environment either. At the very least, like Miniver Cheevy and Richard Cory they seem to be dimly aware of the barrenness of their circumstances – and can perhaps dream about better possibilities. And at best, like 'the man against the sky' their imaginations are actively engaged in a quest for meaning.

How Annandale Went Out

This, one of the bleakest of Robinson's poems, sheds its apparent difficulties once we realise that 'Annandale' is the name of a man who has been reduced by some incurable disease, or accident, to the vegetable state; and that the narrator is a doctor who, apparently, has been merciful enough to relieve him of his life.

1] *it:* The person, Annandale, has been deprived of all personality by his illness.

2–3] Note how the austere description captures a whole series of gestures which the speaker has to perform as Annandale's medical attendant.

4–5] Like an emotionally important moment in a Hemingway novel, the power of these lines depends upon the reader recognising just how much emotional pressure there is behind the spare diction.

7] The emphasis placed upon the last four monosyllabic words suggests the narrator's sense of responsibility.

9] *ruin...man:* The opposition registered here, as in 'it...him', 'wreck... him', offers the reasons for the narrator's decision to kill Annandale.

10] This at first sounds as if the narrator is asking his audience to equate the 'ruin' of Annandale with the 'man' he had once been – something that the narrator himself was unable to do. Then, it appears, what he is really asking us to do is put the *situation* together – on the one hand the 'wreck' of Annandale, on the other the doctor with his 'slight kind of engine' and consider whether we would not have done the same.

12] *on the spot:* The poignancy of this phrase, as indeed of the entire sonnet, depends upon the contrast between the enormity of the problem described, an enormity which the narrator fully recognises, and the obviously limited means of expression available to him.

Miniver Cheevy

This poem, combining irony with a touch of sympathetic melancholy, depends for its effect upon a subtle series of comparisons between the unheroic Miniver and his dreams of adventure. These comparisons at first lead us to see no resemblance between the dreamer and his dreams whatsoever and then qualify this impression, just a little, by hinting that a 'flicker' of the heroic impulse is still to be found within Miniver – although much too feeble, perhaps, ever to burst into 'flame'. See the Notes on 'George Crabbe'.

1] *Miniver:* The Christian name, recalling words like 'minim' and 'minute', suggests the relative unimportance of the character and the apparent inappropriateness of his dreams.

2] *seasons:* external circumstances in general.

4] *reasons:* The general feeling of ineffectuality here is reinforced by the deflationary effect of the feminine rhymes.

5–8] The poignancy of these lines stems from the implicit comparison they make between the activities described in Miniver's dreams and the capers of Miniver himself. At this moment, Miniver seems rather like a fool pretending to be king.

11–12] *Thebes...Camelot...Priam's:* respectively, the ancient Greek city, prominent in legend; the site of King Arthur's court; and the King of Troy.

15–16] *On the town* is a slang term for living on charity. This, and 'a vagrant' might refer, respectively, to 'Romance' and 'Art'; or alternatively both phrases might refer to Miniver himself. Perhaps Miniver and the heroic impulse – both of which, it seems, have now fallen on hard times – are not as different as we had been led to assume.

17] *the Medici:* Renaissance merchant-princes, and rulers of Florence for two hundred years. They were renowned for their cruelty and their patronage of the arts.

23–4] Note the ironic contrast between 'grace' and 'iron'. The suggestion is that perhaps no *actual* period could completely satisfy dreamers like Miniver.

27–8] The repetition of 'thought' implies that Miniver is getting nowhere.

30–2] *thinking...drinking:* The rhyming of these two words suggests a link: they are both opiates for Miniver, divine or otherwise.

Eros Turannos

The title means 'the tyrant Love'. This is in many ways a summation of the themes and techniques of Robinson's shorter poems. Its subject is isolation: the distance separating man from man, or man from Nature, and the dreams and illusions to which imprisonment within the self makes one susceptible. Even love, the emotion commonly supposed to bind human beings together, is here seen as a product and symptom of loneliness. The woman in the poem may well be ruled by 'the tyrant Love'; or, at least, by a mixture of need and antagonism which Robinson takes to be a potent illustration of Love's tyranny. But, clearly, what she feels for her husband is limited by the 'mask' he wears before her at all times: what attracts and repels her is much more a matter of appearances than anything else. Both husband and wife, in other words, may well be *dependent* on one another: but they are nevertheless seen as two quite solitary people.

The basic structure of the poem is one Robinson adopted fairly frequently: a series of alternating tetrameter and trimeter lines, more or less regular, which are given an idiosyncratic touch by the extensive use of feminine rhymes.

1] The opening three words are characteristic of the entire poem, in that the apparently simple statement they offer reverberates with further meanings as the narrator continues. The woman, we learn later, 'fears' her husband not just in the obvious sense; but also in the sense that, needing him to protect her against complete loneliness, she *fears for* his departure and *fears* the emotional hold which this gives him over her.

3–4] These lines contain a paradox: the 'mask' worn by the man at once repels his wife and attracts ('engaging') her. The idea, first broached here, of being trapped half-willingly within an illusion will be developed in the following stanzas.

5–8] The woman may be lonely now but, she recognises, she would be lonelier still without her husband; and this is what keeps them together. The image in the last two-and-a-half lines, which suggests the kind of slow and lonely decline the woman is frightened of, is sustained throughout the rest of the poem.

9–10] 'Blurred' continues the imagery of blindness and illusion ('dimmed', 'fades', 'illusion'); while 'sound' takes up the water-imagery of lines 6–8. Note that the latter is also being used now to develop the idea of distance and deception: the man, like the ocean, is supposed to have depths which his wife can no longer penetrate.

17–20] The man finds some comfort in the 'love' of his wife (17–18), and security in the fact that she has a well-established place in the community (19–20). The possibility, registered in 'a sense of ocean', that he is equally deceived adds a new dimension to the argument.

21–4] The woman, in turn, is sensitive to local gossip about her husband, and yet willing to submit to any indignity rather than live alone. 'Secures' is partly ironic: this relationship is anything but secure.

25] *inaugurates:* marks, initiates.

27] *reverberates:* echoes. Note the elaborate series of references to death and decline in these first four lines.

31–2] This may mean either that the locals gossip about the woman's habitual seclusion; or, more simply, that the woman is conspicuous by her absence from the ordinary life of the town. The house, in this and the next stanza, is used as another emblem of isolation.

33–40] A further dimension is added here to the themes of solitude and illusion. The poet, insisting on the 'otherness' of things, now admits that he may not necessarily be telling the whole truth. All he is doing, he says, is describing what *he sees*; and since, being human, he too is isolated he may be as much a victim of appearances and the eccentricities of personal vision as the man and woman who are his subjects. This idea has been implicit from the opening stanza, in Robinson's chosen methods of expression. The marmoreal language, for instance, and the cryptic phrasing make the poem sound rather like an epitaph, dedicated to people whom the narrator hardly knew and whom the reader can never know immediately. And the incessant use of simile, or of images which call attention to themselves, gives the impression, eventually, that the narrator is trying to point to his limitations; that all he can do, in fact, is suggest what his subject *resembles* – not what, in essentials, it *is*.

42] *a god:* Eros.

45–8] A network of metaphor brings the themes of the poem together here: the elusiveness and transience of all our lives (45), the capacity we all share for projecting our own visions on our given circumstances (and so changing them into something 'familiar', a part of our own singular world: 46), and the blindness, loneliness, and death we must all endure (47–8).

from *The Man Against the Sky*

In his later years Robinson tended to concentrate on longer poetic narratives, and became more interested in developing the positive implications of his work. These passages, written at about the midpoint in Robinson's career, offer a partial illustration of the change: they come from a reflective poem over three hundred lines long, which sketches out the mature philosophical attitude implicit in even larger works like *Tristram*.

Briefly, the intention of the poem is to suggest that the simple human will to live, and search for meaning, provides a basis for belief. Despite his isolation, Robinson argues, and the acute limitations imposed on him by his nature and surroundings, man continues to search for order and value; he remains a dreamer. And perhaps his dreams, together with his instinct for survival, bring him closer to the truth than he can ever know. Perhaps they provide him with a source of spiritual 'light', however dim and inadequate that light may appear to be.

1–22] These opening lines establish the basic image of the poem, of a man making the upward climb over the hill of life to death. Note how Robinson manages to suggest at once the diminutiveness of the man, seen from a distance, and his possible grandeur (8–9, 12–13).

2] *world on fire*: This, and all the subsequent references to fire, remind us that the time is the evening – of a particular man's life as well as of the day. Quite probably, they are also an allusion to the First World War which had broken out the year before the poem was written. Robinson saw the war as a symptom of the universal loss of belief and as a reminder that some new vision of order was urgently required.

23] The vision of the man against the sky leads the narrator to speculate on the various attitudes of men as they face death. Representing different philosophies of life as well as death, these attitudes are summarised towards the end of the poem (99–103). They describe a scale of increasing negation, from faith to doubt to denial, and seem to be roughly chronological, moving from primitive religious belief to contemporary materialism.

42] *three in Dura*: the three Jews who refused to worship the idols of Babylon. They were thrown into the 'fiery furnace' as a punishment, but survived unscathed (*Daniel*, 3 and 4).

47–55] Following the discussion of 'A vision answering to a faith unshaken' in 23–46, 'An easy trust assumed of easy trials' is considered here.

56–71] 'A sick negation born of weak denials' is now the subject.

72–81] These few lines come from Robinson's analysis of what he later calls 'A crazed abhorrence of an old condition'.

81] *hierophants*: initiating priests, expounders of mysteries.

82–94] 'A blind attendance on a brief ambition' is now the subject. Included under this heading are the materialism and scientific stoicism which Robinson felt were characteristic of his own times; and which, as he wrote later to a friend, it had become his major purpose to deny, either 'as an explanation or a justification of existence.'

95–108] The narrator lists the different philosophies he has considered, before going on to suggest a further and better alternative.

109–39] The argument is presented tentatively, but it is still clear. The fact that we no longer believe in heaven and hel l('two fond old enormities') is no reason for assuming that life is meaningless and death an annihilation. Perhaps there *is* order in the universe. Admittedly, we can never know for certain whether there is or not because we are limited to the confines of the self. But it is surely *better* to believe that there is such an order, since otherwise life is reduced to a pointless trek ('a blind atomic pigrimage'); better, and *more reasonable*. For our own continued will to survive, Robinson argues, and to perpetuate the race, suggests that we have some intuitive conviction implanted in us, something which tells us that life is worth living. We persist; and that, together with any further glimpses of the truth we may receive by means of dreams, hints and guesses, is the best possible evidence we can have as to the existence of purpose.

145] *Word:* 'In the beginning was the Word, and the Word was with God, and the Word was God' (*John* 1, i).

145–8] Belief in the order of the universe is something so basic to man's nature that it can never be erased: as long as man keeps on living, he is testifying to its continuance. But to perceive the precise nature of this order is something which must always be denied to him. All that is possible is the occasional moment of partial illumination.

149–54] 'The world is not a "prison house" but a kind of spiritual kinder-garten, where millions of bewildered infants are trying to spell "God" with the wrong blocks' (Robinson). Our minds and language, our "words", can never encompass the truth about the order of the universe, the "Word": but that is no proof of its non-existence, only of our limitations.

Mr. Flood's Party

This deserves comparison with 'Miniver Cheevy', published some eleven years earlier. Both poems are about pathetic figures, who retreat from an intolerable present into dreams of the past; both mix irony with sympathy. But whereas in 'Miniver Cheevy' the sympathy is fairly slight and peripheral, in this case it is central to our understanding of the protagonist. Mr Flood may seem merely comic to begin with. By the end of the poem, however, he has become almost heroic as well: a man who comes very close to transfigur-ing his environment with the help of his vivid imagination.

1] *Eben Flood:* The name, a punning equivalent for "ebb and flood", suggests the movement of the tides, the passing of time.

1–5] Note how Robinson uses the rhythm and syntax here to re-create the tortuous passage of his hero.

9] *harvest moon:* an emblem of fulfilment, at first meant ironically.

11–12] 'Come fill the Cup, and in the fire of Spring / Your Winter-garment of Repentance fling: / The Bird of Time has but a little way / To flutter and the Bird is on the Wing" (Edward Fitzgerald, *The Rubáiyát of Omar Khay-yám*, lines 25–8). This allusion serves to recall us to the theme of transience; to prepare us, by virtue of the hedonistic philosophy it announces, for Mr Flood's own 'party'; and, perhaps, to suggest as well a connection between Mr Flood's drunkenness and the divine drunkenness of the poet.

15] At Roncesvalles, in 778, when the battle was lost and most of his friends were gone, Roland, the bravest of Charlemagne's officers, blew on his horn for help and then died. The comparison, which is simultaneously incon-gruous and just, helps to focus Robinson's double-edged attitude towards his protagonist. In some ways, Mr Flood is quite unlike Roland. Thus his 'horn' is not a horn at all, but a jug full of liquor; and he is not so much a bold young adventurer as a tired old man. In other ways, though, the knight and the drunkard turn out to be very much alike. Both, for example, present types of endurance; as men who have lived beyond their due time, and who recall the past while preparing to meet their former companions in another world. And given this covert resemblance between the two, the allusion cannot help but add a touch of pathos and dignity to Robinson's portrait.

25–32] These lines establish Mr Flood's jug as a symbolic object roughly analogous to the 'jar' Wallace Stevens describes in 'Anecdote of the Jar'.

Literally, as Robinson admits, the jug belongs to the world of time and change where 'most things break' (28). But here, just for a moment, it becomes the node around which the entire scene is harmonised (see 48); and therefore seems to belong to the world outside of time – the world of the imagination. Indeed, like the imagination the jug offers a release from mortal cares (see 11–12); like the imagination it contains the past and future as well as the present (the comparison with a 'sleeping child' (25), who can equally be said to contain the past (his parents) and future (his own life) within him, suggests this); and, finally, like the imagination it seems to have access to a type of permanence which 'assuredly' the 'lives of men' do not (30–1).

45] *silver loneliness:* The light of the moon was often used in Romantic poetry as an emblem of the imagination.

47] *two moons:* One belongs to the actual landscape, the other to the 'harmonious landscape' which Flood and his jug have temporarily created.

52] *was again alone:* i.e. Flood returns from a phantom communion with his friends to the world of change and isolation described in the opening lines.

The Sheaves

The change of the wheat from green to gold suggests the mystery of the natural cycle, of which we know the 'how' if not the 'why'. This, in turn, suggests the universal laws governing ourselves and our surroundings which we can sense instinctively (because we live by them) but never properly understand. See Notes to 'The Man Against the Sky'.

4–5] *gold...bought or sold:* Note the ironic reference here to the market-place, the human world of buying and selling. The wheat will be sold eventually but, for the moment, it reminds us of certain fundamental natural laws which make those of the market-place seem trivial and irrelevant.

New England

This is a typically indirect tribute to the region which supplied Robinson with many of his subjects and, perhaps, his tone and philosophy as well. Robinson intended this sonnet, he said, to be 'an oblique attack' on those who ridiculed the 'alleged emotional and moral frigidity' of New Englanders. As much of his own work served to demonstrate, a person need not necessarily wear his emotions on his face; nor need he always 'boil...with...lyric yeast' in order to prove his commitment to a vital principle.

Carl Sandburg

Chicago

This poem is at once a description of the economic centre of the Middle West; a celebration of the common people, its inhabitants; and a song in praise and imitation of American energy, the strength of an emergent culture. Its simple, unanalytical populism is reflected in the style: in which a rhetorical and flexible line, an idiomatic language and bold rhythms, all become part of the attempt to create a poetic equivalent of folk speech.

1] 'His [Sandburg's] rhetoric is really a voice whose rhythms create a basic recurrent form' (R. W. Butterfield and E. Mottram). Note how this introductory series of descriptive phrases is linked together both rhythmically and phonetically (i.e. by the harsh gutturals); and then repeated, in part, at the end of the poem. By devices as simple as this Sandburg evolves the kind of form that Butterfield and Mottram are talking about; which (rudimentary as it is) offers a necessary sense of completeness – of an experience 'placed' and understood as well as recorded – without denying the primary effect of spontaneity.

6–12] The syntax of these lines is characteristically paratactical. Clauses, that is to say, are laid side by side linked only by an 'and', rather than arranged in an elaborate hierarchy of mains and subordinates. The effect of this is to establish a kind of 'democracy of objects'. No particular person or impression, the reader infers, is regarded as any more (or less) important than any other here. Everything has an equal relevance for the innocent, unprejudiced and uninhibited, eye of the poet; who becomes, by reason of this perfect freedom of his, a type of the ideal American.

10–12] At this point the city seems almost transformed into a folk hero, along the lines of Paul Bunyan or Mike Fink; an expression of the best energies of the common people.

13–17] After the slow, accumulative impact of lines 6–12, the speed is suddenly accelerated and the pitch consequently raised by these lines each consisting of one word. Note the habitual use of participles, here and elsewhere in the poem: a symptom of Sandburg's interest in becoming rather than being, in life as a process or activity.

A Fence

Sandburg, as the critic M. L. Rosenthal has pointed out, 'can...be hard as Bertolt Brecht is hard'. That is illustrated clearly enough by this poem, which shows the more critical, aggressive side to the poet's radicalism. Turning now from a celebration of the innate energies of the people to an attack on those who would suppress such energies, or even worse divert them to their own ends, he identifies the rich man with the fence surrounding his house; with the barriers, in other words, behind which he and his special interests prefer to hide.

Ice Handler

This, another poem in which Sandburg voices his partisanship for the working classes, is written in a colloquial or even slangy idiom intended to create the effect of informal conversation.

Fog

Although Sandburg was not active in the Imagist movement (for which see Introduction), this, like many of his shorter pieces, could perhaps be described as an Imagist poem: it re-creates an instant in time with the help of evocative rhythm and a scrupulously exact figure.

1–2] In a manner characteristic of Imagism, the comparison is made as indirectly as possible. As in Eliot's 'Love Song of J. Alfred Prufrok' (15–22), the purpose of this comparison seems to be to emphasise the soft, insinuating nature of the fog, the atmosphere of lethargy or even mystery it brings with it.

5] *silent haunches:* Strictly speaking, the adjective is superfluous, since

'haunches' could hardly be anything other than silent. As far as our emotional response is concerned, however, its very superfluity adds to its impact.
It is as if the poet is trying to describe the quintessence of silence, which is
beyond the compass of anything we have known or had described to us
before.

6] *and then moves on :* The monosyllables, the soft consonants and yawning
vowel-sounds, provide a verbal equivalent of the stealthy movement being
described.

Gone

Poignant and regretful, this poem captures the anonymity of urban life
rather than (as in 'Chicago') its vitality. The girl who is its subject is known
by the narrator, and by us, only as most people in towns and cities are known :
as a fleeting, quite enigmatic presence, whose real personality must remain
lost in the restlessness of her environment.

2] Note the dramatic use of the short line here. The isolated words seem to
echo and recede into the distance, re-enacting the movement of departure.

3] *Everybody loved her :* Acting almost as a refrain to the poem, this statement
gradually assumes ironic proportions. It is a restricted kind of love that
implies no real knowledge of its object's movements or intentions.

8] The broken line is expressive of vacancy, loss.

9–13] This brief, lyrical description assumes a special poignancy when it
is remembered that this, really, is all the 'we' of the poem know about
Chick Lorimer – and all they have ever known.

16–17] These juxtaposed lines re-emphasise the paradox on which the
poem turns. 'Love' in this environment, it seems clear, means no more than
casual intimacy: the studiously nurtured and ephemeral affection of people
who meet occasionally in the crowd.

Sunset from Omaha Hotel Window

Few writers have equalled Sandburg in his portraits of the prairie country.
In this poem, for instance, he does not just describe a Mid-Western sunset,
he makes the reader feel it. The style, hard, spare, almost primitive, charts
the geography of the moment: the desolate quality of 'the long sand', the
stillness and brooding silence – above all, the sense of vast space that hits
the narrator as the last rays of the sun stretch away over an open, scarcely
peopled landscape.

Omaha is in Nebraska.

2] *red sun runners :* the rays of the setting sun.

3] *changes :* i.e. with the changing light of evening.

4] *a goner :* a slang term for something that is over and done with.

7] *gloaming :* evening twilight.

13] *Another yellow plunger...dark :* presumably a reference to a shooting
star.

18] The landscape has disappeared into the darkness.

Still Life

'Like the West itself, Sandburg's poetry is a curious meeting-place of new
and old, of the industrial proletariat and the pioneer farmer...skyscrapers
and prairie' (Henry Wells). This poem, in particular, provides a context

in which the two worlds Wells refers to can meet. As they are presented here, the new (the express train, the city) and the old (the village, the farming land) seem different in many ways, and yet also curiously alike; in that they both reflect the vastness of the American continent – the sense of energy and possibility which an almost unlimited amount of living space can bring with it.

Band Concert

Poems like this one, in which Sandburg records the ordinary life of the poor with sympathy and a good eye for detail, could perhaps be compared to the work of the American realistic painters of the same period; to the urban scenes of Robert Henri (1865–1929), for example, who said of his (mostly working-class) subjects, 'I am looking at each individual with the eager hope of finding something of the dignity of life there, the humour, the humanity, the kindness.'

Sandburg's diction here is the verbal equivalent of a series of bold brush-strokes: simple, abrupt, concrete, deliberately repetitive, and impressionistic.

1] *Livery Stable Blues:* In the recording of the 'Livery Stable Blues' made by the Original Dixieland Jazz Band in 1917, the clarinettist imitates the whinnying noise of a horse on his instrument.

New Feet

'Poetry', Sandburg once said, 'is the harnessing of the paradox of earth cradling life and then entombing it.' Profoundly aware of this paradox, he tends in his work to anticipate the decline of America at the same time as he is describing its ascendancy; to fill his verse with images of ephemerality and decay while he is celebrating life and growth. Sometimes he even goes so far as to give this other, melancholy side of experience a greater emphasis; as in this poem about the battlefields of the American Civil War.

1] *Empty battlefields:* The battlefields provide an effective emblem of decay for several reasons. They were mute witnesses to wholesale carnage. They are an emblem of that moment in the history of America when, for the first time, it was confronted with the challenge of death. And, in their present state of neglect, they are sad proof of the fact that everything passes, even the memory of great battles.

2] *Grass crawls:* This and the ensuing description of the vegetation swallowing up the relics of war reminds us that the processes of life are circular. With nature, as with civilisations, there is a perpetual cycle of growth, decay – and then growth again.

More Country People

In this poetic equivalent of a primitive, abstract portrait, a series of basic colour combinations and strictly proportioned shapes is used to supply a medium through which the creatures of the farm can be seen in a special way: in terms, that is, of a ritual which, although quite familiar and simple, seems every day fresh and new. As the title suggests, by calling these animals 'people' the poem acts in part as a fable, describing a pattern of behaviour which humans would do well to imitate.

6] *Buff:* a pale, yellowish colour.

Cochin: fowls of the Cochin China breed.

10] 'The past', Sandburg said once, 'is a bucket of ashes'; and this line, voiced as it were by the inhabitants of the farm, seems to repeat that message. Each day is lived here, we are told, without any reference to its predecessors – as a unique occasion.

from *The People, Yes*

The People, Yes is Sandburg's ambitious attempt at a populist epic of America, an inventory of all that is best in the folk tradition, its idioms, its customs, its tales and songs; and a declaration of faith in the democratic experiment – taking the word 'democracy' in the most literal sense possible, as a government of the people, by the people, for the people.

7] *The mammoth:* the people. Sandburg's tendency to see the people as a force, lying dormant now but just about to assert its rightful supremacy, is similar to John Steinbeck's descriptions of the common man in the interchapters of *The Grapes of Wrath* (1939). Another point of resemblance between the two writers lies in their equal dependence upon an apocalyptic tone, and an incantatory rhythm and language.

26–35] Characteristically, Sandburg describes a *political* process (the people coming into their own) as a necessary complement to and completion of a *biological* process (the emergence of man from the animal state). There is a strong element of evolutionary determinism behind his commitment to the triumph of the common man.

54] *polychrome:* a work of art in several colours. These and the following lines are meant to remind us that 'the people' are not a dull, uniform mass but rather a collection of individuals each of whom is seeking a separate fulfilment.

58] *clavilux:* an organ which produces music and projects colours on a screen.

59–64] The message ('colour poem') communicated by the people ('clavilux') is that they, combining their individual wills, must eventually come to power, by a process as natural as that by which the stars and sea move, and rain falls.

65–7] Note how Sandburg has proceeded by an association of images: from coloured patterns thrown by a clavilux, to the natural lights in the night sky, to the light cast into that same sky by the steel mills. All of these images bear a common reference to the energy of the people.

71] *old anvil:* the people, who have survived their oppressors. The following six lines use folk sayings, or imitations of them, to develop this idea.

82] The poem ends on a characteristic note of hope.

Waiting for the Chariot

This is one of a number of pieces which Sandburg wrote during his last years about a subject that had always preoccupied him, death. It illustrates some of his best qualities: his use of a fluent, conversational idiom, his interest in ordinary people and the details of their lives – and the ability, which never left him, to create something of permanent significance out of these very simple materials.

Wallace Stevens

The Snow Man

Wallace Stevens believed in the power of the imagination to arrange reality so as to make it adequate to human desires. In a way, he argued, we use the imagination all the time because our senses start to arrange reality almost as soon as they perceive it, and because whenever we think about experience we begin to structure it according to some law (e.g. the scientific law of cause and effect). The supreme example of this structuring capacity, though, is the poetic imagination which composes experience into the durable integrations that are works of art. To be successful, such works have to demonstrate a 'precise equilibrium' between the imagination and reality; they must be neither too ordered nor too chaotic. For the imaginative faculty, in its every operation, does not so much impose designs *on* the world as discovers designs inherent *in* it.

This act of the imagination was something which Stevens saw as continuous. Our given circumstances are always changing, he believed, we and our needs are always changing; so the world, or as he called it the 'mundo', created out of the union between the two must be in a state of continual change as well. We must be continually reassessing our circumstances and our needs so as to create new structures (in our lives, and poems) which do justice to them both. Stevens' analogue for this process was the cycle of the seasons. Winter, in his poems, becomes a figure for the 'pure abstracted reality, a bare icy outline purged clean of all the accretions brought by the human mind to make it possible for us to conceive of reality and live our lives' (Frank Kermode). The arrival of spring, in turn, is used as a metaphor for the mind's producing 'what will suffice' (Stevens) to arrange reality and discover in it meaning. Summer is the period when reality and the imagination exist in a state of pure equilibrium; when, for a time, our 'fictions' satisfy completely. And autumn describes the moment when the fiction no longer satisfies, and the mind experiences the need to purge itself and return to the 'bare, icy outline' of winter again.

This poem is about the 'mind of winter', when we see reality without benefit of any of the structures discovered in it by the human mind. Like much of Stevens' earlier verse, it owes a considerable debt to Imagism (see Introduction); in that it represents an attempt to capture the exact curve of the 'thing' described in the imagery and rhythms. The form of the poem, again characteristic of the period, is a kind of heavily accented free verse. The lines are of varying length, with no rhymes, but with a norm of three beats per line. The only deviations from this norm are lines 1 and 10, which have two beats each, and lines 5 and 15, which have four.

1–11] The heavy accents and the clutter of polysyllables, the repetitions and the harsh vowel sounds, the fact that the entire poem consists of one convoluted sentence: all this helps to decelerate our reading of the verse, and communicates something of the harshness and dourness associated with the 'mind of winter'.

13–15] Reality, as seen by 'the snow man', has no meaning, no sense of law or value, because it is *our* minds working *in conjunction with reality* which create all laws and values. Nor has man any value or meaning in this context either; since any meaning or sense of identity we may discover *in our own lives* equally depends on our sustained powers of imagination.

15] *Nothing that is not...nothing that is:* Nothing which might have been arranged by the imagination; and the nothingness and emptiness of reality when deprived of all 'fictions'. The vision described here is bleak but necessary, as Stevens himself indicated when he described the poem 'an example of the necessity of identifying oneself with reality in order to understand and enjoy it'.

A High-Toned Old Christian Woman

This poem, which is addressed to the kind of woman indicated by its title, argues (i) that the imagination has to structure, and so transform, the here and now, not try to create some better place in another world; and (ii) that the 'mundo' we create out of the engagement between the mind and reality can just as easily be founded on aesthetic values as on moral ones. It can quite as well be a world of pleasure as a world of law. In contrast to 'The Snow Man', Stevens here uses one of the most common of English poetic forms: blank verse. But, it is clear, this is a blank verse 'as idiosyncratic, as rhythmically inexhaustible, as the language is full, coloured, and accurate' (Kermode).

1] Poetry is the supreme example of the power the imagination possesses to create 'fictions' out of the raw material supplied to it by experience.

2-5] These lines describe how the mind, taking certain possibilities latent in experience and arranging them into a series, can endow life with a purely moral reference.

The nave is the main part of the church extending from the inner door to the choir and usually separated from the aisle on each side by a row of pillars. Here Stevens uses the process of building a nave as a figure for the process of building a religion or a religious idea. This in turn leads, via the pun on 'converted' (referring both to physical transformation and to the idea of religious conversion), to the image of the palm, which, as always in Stevens' poetry, represents that other-worldly paradise beloved of the Christian religion (cf. 'Sunday Morning', poem IV, 10).

5] *cithern:* instruments of the guitar kind, much used in the sixteenth and seventeenth centuries.

6-12] These lines describe how the mind, taking certain other possibilities, can endow life with a purely aesthetic or hedonistic reference.

7] *peristyl...masque:* A peristyle is a row of columns surrounding a building, court, or cloister; and, by extension, the court or space surrounded by such columns. This was a common setting for masques: which were a form of theatrical entertainment, involving music, dancing, and dumb shows, very popular in the sixteenth and seventeenth centuries. Stevens is here providing a balance to lines 2-5, by using the process of building a peristyle as a figure for the process of building an *earthly* paradise. This in turn leads, via the pun on 'project' (i.e. both 'imagine' and 'build a projection'), to the figure of the masque, which describes the world of pleasure created by the dreaming imagination.

9-10] *our bawdiness...epitaphs:* our lusts and pleasures uninhibited by any preoccupation with death, or any vision of experience which grows out of that preoccupation (e.g. Christianity).

12–13] The two 'fictions' just described and the infinite number of variations possible upon them, possess a comparable validity. They merely reflect different imaginations working, at different times, on different aspects of raw experience.

13–20] The versions of reality which are founded on the demands of pleasure and taste have as much right to exist, and draw as much support from reality, as those founded on the moral sense: as much and as little, since they all of them depend on a highly selective reading of experience.

16] *muzzy:* colloquialism for blurred, dull, stupid. But here the meaning of the related dialect word, 'mosey' (i.e. stupefied with liquor), seems more applicable. This, like 'bawdiness', 'squiggling', and 'hullabaloo' is characteristic of Stevens' diction, especially during the early period. Apparently precious and finicky, each word turns out in its context to be definitely meant. It is at once accurate and, because of its initial strangeness, suggestive as well.

18] The line captures the noise and colour of this purely hedonistic parade.

21–2] This, the point made by the poem *and* the parade of 'disaffected flagellants', may offend people like the 'high-toned old Christian woman' ('widows' suggests an excessive preoccupation with death and death-centred religions or philosophies): but that is no argument against them. Indeed, it is an argument *for* them, since the world of the imagination, whatever form it may assume, has nothing at all to do with the sort of unearthly paradise that is figured in Christianity.

22] *wink:* a reference to the brightness of the 'fictive things' Stevens is describing (they 'wink' like a brightly polished object in the sunlight); to their gaiety (they 'wink' just as a person in a good mood might); and to their general indifference to the harsh, puritanical, moral world associated with the widows. Note the verbal linking of 'wink', 'will', and 'wince' which helps emphasise the meaning.

Sunday Morning

'The great poems of heaven and hell have been written,' Stevens once claimed, 'and the great poem of earth remains to be written.' He was perhaps being a little disingenuous when he said this because his own 'Sunday Morning', which offers us a statement of personal belief, is clearly a 'great poem of earth'. In it the poet conducts a meditation through the woman whose mind is the scene, which has as its subject the choice between two possible alternatives. One alternative is the vision of paradise proposed to us by the Christian faith; a vision founded upon the belief that since this is a universe of death, never answering to human desires, then we must look for our satisfactions in another place – in another dimension on the other side of life. The other alternative is the vision of an earthly paradise. The universe, the poet admits, may well be a universe of death when looked at in its pristine and unaltered state; but it can perhaps be transformed into a living, ever-changing 'mundo' with the help of the active imagination. It is, of course, the second alternative which is ultimately preferred. Believing, as Coleridge did, that 'we receive but what we give', the poet ends his meditation by celebrating the physical world. We should live 'as and

where we are', he affirms, and all the time use the light of our minds to discover every meaning and satisfaction in our lives that we possibly can.

Poem I] The woman, while enjoying breakfast (her own form of sensual
celebration) on Sunday morning, suddenly remembers the Christian significance of Sunday. In reverie, she returns across the 'wide waters' of space
and time to Palestine and the day of the Crucifixion; and then experiences a
certain nostalgia for the comforts of the ancient faith Christ symbolises.

1–4] The woman is described at her breakfast. Notice how Stevens has
abstracted a few significant lines and colours from the given scene, and then
re-composed them so as to create what is almost a verbal equivalent of a
Cubist painting. This is a good example of the selecting and ordering
activities the poet attributed to the imagination. Note, also, how the
woman scarcely exists for us except as a complex of emotion. The externals
of personality are seldom very central in Stevens' verse because life for him,
as he once said, 'is not people and scene but thought and feeling'.

1] *Complacencies of the peignoir:* This characteristically bizarre phrase brings
together a whole series of appropriate, visual and emotional, impressions:
the opulent surroundings, the laziness of the morning, the complete surrender to a mood of sensuous well-being. 'Peignoir', for house-coat or
dressing-gown, is typical of the Gallicisms which enrich the earlier verse.

2] An 'infallible mastery of pause and tone', Marianne Moore once said,
invariably accompanies Stevens' 'demureness of statement'. Note how the
extra foot placed at the beginning of the line here accelerates our reading of
the blank verse, and gives an extra bounce and ebullience to the description.

3] *green freedom:* Certain colours have a symbolic reference in Stevens'
poetry. In particular, green is associated with reality and blue with the
imagination.

cockatoo: Birds of different kinds appear and reappear throughout the
poem. Here, as elsewhere in Stevens' verse, they act as paradigms of the
physical world; and of the balance between this world and the imagination
which creates our earthly paradise.

4] *dissipate:* scatter. The noun 'dissipation' is perhaps also implied.

5] Note the stately regularity, the hissing sibilants and soft aspirates, of this
line. Christianity, the religion of 'ancient sacrifice', is associated with a
world of calm, silence, and sombre colours; just as the earthly paradise is
identified with movement, noise, and 'green freedom'.

6–8] The woman remembers the death of Christ ('that old catastrophe').

9–15] The woman returns in memory to the time and place of the Crucifixion. Her reverie is described in dream terms; as, quite literally, a journey
back – with her surroundings, now changed by their new context, accompanying her.

15] *blood and sepulchre:* the blood of Christ and the tomb where he was
buried. Both, like most of the concrete details in the poem, are referred to
again and again, acquiring new meanings from their changing contexts.
Words, also, and phrases are constantly being repeated, and the use of
assonance and alliteration is quite elaborate. All this helps to turn the poem
into a kind of mosaic; a pattern in which sounds and objects are constantly
recurring with a difference, and establishing fresh connections. It is as
if Stevens were organising his own special version of the 'mundo' he

celebrates: a self-contained world, in this case a verbal one, which may be abstracted from, and so depend upon, his given world – but which has its own innate structure and system of cross-reference.

Poem II] The woman returns now to her original state of sensuous well-being; and wonders if, in a secular world, this state could replace the idea of heaven.

1] *the dead:* Christ, a major object of Christian worship ('tribute'); and, perhaps, the state of death and life-after-death to which special 'tribute' is paid by the Christian faith.

3] *silent shadows and...dreams:* Compare poem 1, 5, 8, 10–14.

4] *sun:* a major symbol of reality, this physical world, in Stevens' verse.

9] *Passions of rain:* passions either caused by or felt in the rain.

9–15] The seasonal references here introduce another major symbol to the poem; for the significance of which, see the introductory Notes to 'The Snow Man'.

11] *Elations...gusty:* The reversed iambic foot gives an appropriate lift to both of these words. 'Elations' could refer either to the blooming of the flowers or to the expansion of the heart. 'Gusty' could mean either 'windy' or 'exuberant'. Emotion and environment co-exist in these two words, just as they co-exist in Stevens' earthly paradise.

15] *measures:* songs, as opposed to the silence associated with the Christian faith; and measurements or limitations.

Poem III] A brief history of divinity, from the Roman god Jupiter to Jesus Christ, leads the poet to anticipate a new form of belief, in which the idea of god is thoroughly harmonised and paradise is sought for in the here and now.

2–3] No place on earth ('no sweet land') ever devised a myth which translated the divine attributes ('mythy mind') of Jupiter into human terms ('large-mannered motions'). Equally, no place on earth ever served as the home of Jupiter where he could live, move, and act as a model to all men.

3–8] Note how easily the language moves here between high rhetoric and the colloquial. The elaborate verbal music of line 3; conscious archaisms like 'hinds' (for shepherds) or Latinisms like 'commingling' (for mingling or mixing together); and Miltonic effects such as the sandwiching of a noun between two adjectives ('muttering King,/Magnificent') or the accumulative syntactical pattern of lines 12–14 – all of these formal devices are assimilated into the almost casual fluency of the poem as a whole. Speaking of modern verse-rhythm Stevens once said: 'It is like the voice of...some...figure concealed...There is no accompaniment. If occasionally the poet touches the triangle or one of the cymbals, he does it only because he feels like doing it. Instead of a musician we have an orator whose speech sometimes resembles music.' This is a perfect illustration of what he meant.

6] *our blood...virginal:* The mortal blood of the Virgin Mary, mingling with the 'blood' of God, produced Jesus Christ. This history of divinity charts a course in which the godhead is made progressively more human.

7] *requital:* reward. The idea is that the coming of Christ represents one expression of the pervasive human desire to find meaning in the flux of history.

8] *The very hinds:* the three shepherds who followed the star to Bethlehem. This is a witty development of the reference to 'hinds' in line 5.

9–11] Shall our quest after godhead fail? Or shall we recognise, finally, that the true godhead lies within ourselves; and that it is our imaginations alone which can turn earth into a paradise?

12–15] If this happens, and we do try to discover a paradise on earth, then the sky will no longer seem to be a barrier between ourselves and heaven, but a part of our own physical world – sharing in its ordinariness and possible beauty. We shall seek for meaning and a kind of heaven here and now; first, in our relationships with others ('enduring love') and, next, in our relationships with our natural environment.

15] *blue:* As Stevens' colour-symbol for the imagination, it is far from 'indifferent' to our needs. Note the easy modulation between abstract and concrete in this line.

Poem IV] The woman then suggests that an earthly paradise must be a transitory one; to which the reply is that no heavenly paradise ever imagined is as permanent as that of the earth, with its seasonal repetitions. As a possibility, the earthly paradise is always available. The desires of the mind are forever consummating a marriage with the appearances of the world.

1–4] This baroque conceit develops the bird imagery of the first section.

7] *chimera:* a legendary, grotesque monster, with the head of a lion, the body of a goat and the tail of a serpent.

8–9] *golden underground...isle / Melodious:* mythical other-worlds situated beneath the earth like the Kingdom of the Greek god Pluton or on a distant island like the island of Sirens in the *Odyssey*. Compare poem I, 11–15 and poem VIII, 7.

9] *gat:* archaism for 'got'. The entire phrase 'gat them home' is in turn an archaic way of saying 'returned home'.

10] *visionary:* ambiguous. It could mean either spiritual, or illusory.

cloudy palm: a common image in Stevens' verse for traditional religion. Note the beauty of these and the preceding lines: Stevens communicates 'through the feeling of his language a deep nostalgic longing to accept the ideas he is rejecting' (Yvor Winters).

13–15] The memory of the satisfactions we have found in Nature, and the desires which may find continual fulfilment in nature, both describe a type of paradise more permanent than any we may discover in organised religion.

Poem V] The woman repeats her objection, that an earthly paradise cannot last. The poet replies by explaining the function of death. It is precisely our awareness of the imminence of death, he argues, which accentuates our feelings and heightens our perceptions: our knowledge of life's brevity intensifies our search for life's beauty. In this sense, 'Death is the mother of beauty.' It is so in another sense as well: because without death, and the process of change it implies, the unending cycle of desire followed by consummation could never exist.

10] The willow, a traditional emblem of death, shaking in *living* memorial to the maidens who once sat beneath it, reminds us of the permanent existence of the seasonal cycle – and, by extension, the permanent existence of the imaginative process.

13–15] A new generation of boys inherits the plate cast aside by the old, and

GAP

will use it to tempt a new generation of maidens. The maidens tasting the fruit will, in their turn, succumb to the desires of this world; desires which contain within them the seeds of death ('sure obliteration') as well as fulfilment. The description here brings together suggestions of Eden, the fruit mentioned in poems I and II, the earthly paradise celebrated in poems III and IV, the reference to 'the leaves / Of sure obliteration' in lines 5–6, and the dominating symbol of seasonal change.

Poem VI] As a way of demonstrating that change is a condition of fulfilment, the poet describes an hypothetical paradise where change and death do not exist. Without the cycle of desire followed by consummation, and without the special nuance given to our every moment by the knowledge of transience, life is reduced there to a state of ennui. Not only impossible, an other than earthly paradise would be intolerable as well.

2–3] The enforced pause at 'boughs', the reversed iambic foot at the beginning of the next line, the slight pause at the caesura after 'heavy': all help to communicate the sense of an object poised outside of time.

13–15] Death is the mother of beauty because in her bosom is contained both the fire which consumes and the fire which creates: the principle of destruction *and* the principle of change. We may compare death, then, to the creative principle in life ('earthly mothers') as well as the destructive; all the while remembering that, in death, lies a creative principle which never flags – it is always 'waiting, sleeplessly'.

Poem VII] Happiness consists, then, in sharing the common fate of 'men that perish'; and in seeking our only satisfaction in the 'summer morn' and all it symbolises. The poet now anticipates a culture which accepts this.

1] *ring of men :* The ring suggests the cycle of life and of the seasons, both of which these men have accepted.

2] *summer morn :* the time of complete human fulfilment. See the introductory Notes to 'The Snow Man'.

3] *sun :* see Notes to poem II, 4.

4] These men 'worship' the sun, not because they regard it as a god (as, for example, many of the Romans did): but because it is, for them, a *symbol* of the reality with which which their imaginations must deal. Their transformation of this given object into a figurative one is an imaginative act itself and so an index of their commitment.

5] *a savage source :* The sun, as a symbol of reality, is the source of every imaginative endeavour: it figures the raw material in which all men must discover their 'fictions'.

6–7] Compare poem III, 6–7. Their song unites heaven and earth, but definitely not in the same way that Christ and the Virgin Mary did.

6] *chant of paradise :* a song about paradise and, because earth is 'all of paradise that we shall know', a song sung by the inhabitants of paradise too.

7] 'Returning' could refer either to the song or the singers. If the reference is to the song, then the entire phrase describes how the men's voices are carried into the air (compare poem IV, 1–3) and suggests as well how any music, fiction or poem, can reach out to encompass 'heaven' (i.e. the desires of the mind) along with the earth. But if the reference is to the singers, then the phrase emphasises, rather, that the men have become their own 'gods': they have 'returned' themselves to the sky, in preference to other deities, because the only godhead they recognise now lies in their own imaginations.

15] *dew:* like the leaves in poem v, an image for the fugitive and random nature of existence. 'Men do not either come from any direction or disappear in any direction. Life is as meaningless as dew' (Stevens).

Poem VIII] The immortality of Christ is denied and so, by implication, is the immortality of man. Our only possible felicity, the poet affirms, lies in this world and our response to it.

1] *water without sound:* see poem I, 11–12.

2] *tomb in Palestine:* see poem I, 14–15.

3–4] Jesus did not rise again. He was mortal, and remained dead.

5] *chaos:* The world is a 'chaos', and it depends upon us to abstract any order or meaning from it.

6] *dependency of day and night:* two sides of a continuing dialectic, like the imagination and reality.

7] *island solitude:* There is nothing across the 'wide water', no heaven to be reached: only *our* world, existing in isolation.

unsponsored, free: without a god either to support or control it.

8] 'Of that wide water' could refer either to 'island solitude' or 'free'. The meaning is essentially the same in either case. 'Inescapable' refers to 'island solitude': there is nowhere else to go beyond this island.

9–15] In this final stanza, the poet at once celebrates the contact between reality and the imagination; and offers us one more example of the kind of imaginative 'mundo' which can grow out of this contact. As in the opening lines of the poem he so selects from the raw material of experience, and rearranges, as to create his own special vision of an earthly paradise.

9] The two heavy stresses placed at the beginning of the line here make the verse imitate the gesture described, which appears to be poised between motion and rest. 'Mountains' were later to become a major symbol of reality in Stevens' verse.

10] The sibilants and thin 'i' sounds give this line some of the qualities of a fragile bird-song. Compare poem I, 9–14 and poem IV, 1–3. Bird-song is used here, probably, as an analogue of poetry, and of all the other fictions devised by men to give form to their surroundings.

11] *wilderness:* This paradise is situated far from any traditional god, like the one described in poem v, 5–15.

12] *isolation:* There is no god in this 'heaven'.

13–15] The pigeons, avatars of all the other birds which have appeared in the poem, move downward to darkness and death. They cannot help doing that. But even as they go, they seem to weave elaborate patterns in the sky, which give a certain fleeting shapeliness to their fall. Like the 'deer' described in line 9, they appear to be simultaneously in motion and at rest. Like the poet, their limbs and other faculties may be subdued to the element they work in: but they surrender to it in order, somehow, to control it. Like all men, they belong to one particular world of crisis and change: and yet they can still discover in that world the elements which, rearranged, will give their lives a provisional form and meaning.

14] *ambiguous:* because these 'undulations' indicate the birds' 'ambiguous' or double relationship with their environment.

14–15] The rhythm builds, in a series of anapaests, in the penultimate line and then seems to die away, in a series of cascading trochees. The effect of this is to capture something of the activity being described: the gliding rise-and-fall of the pigeons, their poised movements between earth and sky.

Bantams in Pine-Woods

This, one of the most bizarre of Stevens' earlier poems, is as its tone suggests a cry of defiance. The poet, identified with the imaginative faculty, challenges the reality with which he must deal and which he must try, however desperately, to control. The pervasive atmosphere of comedy offers a sly comment on the poet's presumption, as well as his courage.

1–2] Reality is described as a chieftain bristling with feathers: a description which combines mockery with an implicit acknowledgement of power.

1] *Iffucan of Azcan*: If you can give the lie to my fictions: as in fact you can, since in time any fiction becomes obsolete.

caftan: a long robe.

2] *henna*: a plant, used by the American Indians as a dye.

hackles: the long feathers on the nape of a cockerel, which stand up when the bird is angry. The word acts as a means of connecting the image of the first stanza with that of the second.

halt!: The poet is trying to 'stop', to structure and arrange, his gaudy, chaotic world.

3–4] Reality is now compared to a cockerel of enormous dimensions. See the Notes on 'Sunday Morning', poem I, 3.

5–6] Heaping insult upon insult, the poet proudly asserts his power. He can, he claims, abstract his own personal fiction or 'world' from the given reality of the 'world' at large.

5] *Fat!*: The sheer magnitude of reality is described as a ridiculous obesity.

I am the personal: The imagination, in contrast, may construct a small world: but it is at least a personal one – created, in part, out of individual needs.

6] Reality may offer one 'world', or dimension of experience. But the personal imagination, working upon experience, offers us another. In his belief that each man can create his own 'mundo' out of particulars common to us all, Stevens seems occasionally to approach solipsism: 'the world is myself', he once said, 'life is myself'.

7] Reality is described as a universal imagination ('ten-foot poet'), as against the imagination of individuals.

8] *Begone!*: The poet is trying to abstract from reality, and so in a sense to 'dismiss' it, in its fullness and confusion.

inchling: Mockingly, the poet compares himself to a creature only one inch high; and in an attempt to assert this tiny self, it is he now who 'bristles', standing on his toes in a Lilliputian gesture of defiance.

pines: The setting of the poem is identified as somewhere in the Appalachian mountains of the eastern United States. For the significance of mountains, see the Notes on 'Sunday Morning', poem VIII, 9.

9] It is this Appalachian scene, apparently, which the poet is attempting to arrange. Bristling with defiance, he tries to 'point' or give definition to the smells ('tangs') of the pine trees. 'Tangs' can also mean points: the poet is also trying to abstract what he takes to be the more significant aspects of the landscape, and emphasise them – to 'give point to their points'.

10] *hoos :* arrogant cries.

Anecdote of the Jar

The jar here serves as a point which orders all that surrounds it. It performs the imaginative function; just as its surroundings, organised for a while into a series of significant relationships, perform the function of reality. Compare 'Thirteen Ways of Looking at a Blackbird', section 1.

The poem has a characteristic structure. A series of unrhymed couplets leads up to two end-stopped lines (9–10), set off by rhyme. It sounds for a moment as if the argument is completed. In fact it is not, and the premature finality of these lines gives an air of *un*finality to the two lines which follow, and which form another unrhymed couplet. Even this, the feeling that things have not properly been completed, is not left unqualified, however; because the last line then returns us to a word ('Tennessee') used in the first. Joining the end to the beginning the narrator still seems to be trying to round the poem off. So we are brought to feel that the work is at once complete *and* incomplete; that the argument has been concluded – and yet that something has been missed out, left hanging loose. 'Anecdote of the Jar' is, in effect, made to imitate in its form (as well as describe in its content) the continuing act of the imagination; by which worlds are created that are complete in themselves, and yet available to change. Its structure, like the structure of the fiction it celebrates, is at once closed and yet open.

1] *a jar in Tennessee :* We would normally associate a jar in Tennessee with illicitly distilled liquor. There is, perhaps, an implied, comic reference to the divine 'drunkenness' of the poet here. Compare 'Mr. Flood's Party', by Edwin Arlington Robinson.

3] *slovenly :* chaotic.

4] *Surround :* The wilderness is organised into a coherent shape, with the jar at its centre: but it still seems to threaten the jar, and the forms it creates with imminent destruction. Note how the internal rhyming of 'round' and 'surround' helps to emphasise the meaning: the roundness (identified with the arranging power) of the jar makes the wilderness surround it.

6–7] *around...round...ground :* the internal rhymes again emphasise a series of significant relationships.

8] *port :* bearing, demeanour.

a port in air : The jar, as a civilising agency, is comically compared to a teacher of etiquette – a genteel figure prescribing a code of manners to the surrounding wilderness.

9–12] The jar, like the imaginative faculty, is nothing in itself; and it is like nothing in reality. But it engages *with* reality to create, out of this engagement, a fleeting shapeliness.

Life is Motion

The fortuitous, almost 'throwaway', quality of this is intentional. The arbitrary names (1–2), the random descriptive detail (3–4), the anarchic cries of joy (6–7): all point to the purely intuitional nature of the imagination, the fleeting and quite accidental character of many of its creations – and to the spontaneous delight that can spring up sometimes at the union of man with his world (8–9).

Thirteen Ways of Looking at a Blackbird

In this poem, the blackbird acts in each section as a focus, a means of bringing out the meaning of the context in which it is involved. The meaning of the blackbird depends on each context just as the meaning of the context depends on it; with the result that there is exactly that condition of 'interdependence' between the bird and its setting that Stevens believed to be proper to the relationship between the imagination and reality. 'Thirteen Ways' can thus be regarded as a series of examples of how the imagination works, with the blackbird performing the function of the imaginative faculty and its context the function of reality.

Section I] The blackbird provides a focal point for the landscape which it composes, just as a compositional centre composes a landscape painting. This is a paradigm of the way the mind orders reality by discovering significant relations in it.

Section II] Another means of ordering reality is illustrated by the use of the blackbird as a simile; namely, the discovery of connections between apparently unconnected things.

Section III] The blackbird is used as a specific image that represents a general phenomenon. It is a synecdoche for autumn.

Section IV] This assertion that all things are one is given force by the reference to the blackbird.

Section V] Again, the figure of the blackbird reinforces a significance being discovered in reality; this time, by being used as an illustrative metaphor.

Section VI] An ordinary object, the blackbird, creates an extraordinary effect because of the circumstances in which it is placed: it both draws significance from its context and adds significance to it.

Section VII] The point made here is that the ordinary can be turned into the exotic, given the collaboration of the imaginative faculty.

Section VIII] There is something involved in poetry beside language and rhythm: the imagination, represented by the blackbird, working in conjunction with reality.

Section IX] The blackbird becomes a point of reference, defining an intelligible area among many possible but undefined intelligible areas.

Section X] The blackbird of imagination can impress even those who try to evade the real by indulging in the beauty of language alone.

Section XI] It can also impress those who have imprisoned themselves in a world of artifice.

Section XII] This illustrates 'the compulsion frequently back of the things we do' (Stevens). The assumption behind the passage is that if one thing is seen to occur at the same time as another thing often enough, then the mind is likely to establish a causal relationship between the two.

Section XIII] The blackbird is used to create a verbal portrait which has only a literal sense. It is not 'about' anything else. There is only the picture to accept on its surface, as one accepts the surface of a painting. 'A poem need not have a meaning and like most things in nature often does not have' (Stevens).

The Idea of Order at Key West

After his first collection of poetry Stevens gradually turned away from the descriptive and dramatic modes towards the discursive and the more immediately philosophical. The later poems were much more involuted than the earlier ones, their idioms no longer spry and balletic but, on the contrary, spare – or even austere. The change was not a complete one, of course: Stevens was simply developing certain ideas expressed in his first published work, and then investigating their intricacies. Nor was it irreversible: in some ways, a poem like 'The Man With the Blue Guitar' still recalls the witty and idiosyncratic verse of *Harmonium*, as do many of the sections of *Notes Towards a Supreme Fiction*. But as a general tendency it is clear enough; and well illustrated by this meditation, which supplied the centre-piece to Stevens' second volume. In it, the poet describes a woman whom he once heard, singing beside the sea (a traditional figure for raw experience) at Key West, in the Straits of Florida. Slowly, she becomes identified for him with the 'blessed rage for order' (51): the need which singer, poet, and all men alike feel to discover form and meaning in their lives.

1–4] The woman, the poet tells us, sang a song which was beyond the compass of the sea itself, because the sea was without intelligent or articulate forms as we know them. The sea was 'Like a body wholly body': an object possessing neither head nor even hands with which to express itself to us. Note the extraordinary plangency of this verse. The use of alliteration, assonance, and verbal repetition is characteristically elaborate; and each line, a cunning combination of iambs and trochees, seems to roll forward and then fall back like the sea it describes. The entire poem repeats this to-and-fro movement. Words, phrases, and metaphors recur, accumulating meanings; ideas continually reappear; and slowly the poem seems to work its way into our minds, like the sea creeping insidiously up the shore.

4–7] And yet the movements of the sea seemed to offer something that 'we' could interpret after our fashion. The cry of the ocean, its genuine voice, was alien to 'us': but 'we' could abstract from it 'our' own songs and meanings. 'We', here and throughout the rest of the poem, refers to the poet as Everyman: thus including us, his audience, along with himself.

8] This probably means that the sea was not simply being used, in the woman's song, as a means of projecting her own emotions: she was not just trying to impose her own ideas on her circumstances. Nor, on the other hand, was she merely a means by which the reality of the sea could announce *it*self.

9–15] The song did not merely consist of the sound of the woman's voice mingling with the sound of the water. Even if her song was an expression of the ocean-sounds she heard it was different from them because it was an attempt to give articulate form to them. In her song the woman was abstracting from reality, transforming chaotic sound into intelligible words.

16–17] The mysterious ('ever-hooded') sea, tragic because it seemed to deny our 'rage for order', was merely the place where the woman sang: the reality upon which her imagination chose to work.

18–20] It was not the woman but the 'spirit' embodied in her that we sought, the imaginative faculty she possessed and represented.

21–8] If the song had merely been a means by which the reality of the sea, and its surroundings, could announce themselves; then the only sounds to be heard would have been the resonant ('deep') echoes of the waves, pounding against the shore, and other ocean noises in a semi-tropical climate (where it is 'summer without end').

28–33] But her song was more than these alien and meaningless noises; more than just her voice, and ours, mingling wth the chaotic sights and sounds of wind, water, and sea-shadows ('bronze shadows'). Note the accumulative pattern of the syntax here, each clause or phrase 'building' upon its predecessor: the poet is preparing us for the major statement of belief to be made in the next paragraph.

33–42] This is the dramatic climax of the poem. The song sung by the woman, the poet tells us, was an imaginative transformation of her surroundings. It was *her* voice, creating a fiction, which gave special point to the sunset (33–4). It was *she* who, by endowing the moment with an atmosphere of solitude, gave to it a unique emotional tone (35). *She* made the world or 'mundo' in which she sang (36–7); and when she sang the sea, becoming a part of that 'mundo', assumed an identity which *she* had helped to give to it (37–9). Even as we watched, we realised that the world where she lived, and received her satisfactions, was a world that *she* alone had contrived to create.

43] *Ramon Fernandez :* 'I used two everyday names. As I might have expected they turned out to be an actual name.' (Stevens.) The 'actual name' belonged to a French critic, to whose aesthetic theory Stevens' own idea of the imagination bears some resemblance; and of whom, Stevens later admitted, he did have some knowledge.

44–50] The discovery made in the preceding verse paragraph is now gradually generalised. The first stage in this process is to introduce a fresh example of the 'rage for order'. As the poet turned his attention away from the woman by the sea, he tells us, he noticed the lights of the fishing boats in a nearby harbour. These lights seemed to arrange the surrounding night just as the woman's song had seemed to arrange the sea. They endowed the surrounding darkness with a moral ('deepening') and an aesthetic ('enchanting') dimension which it would not otherwise have had.

51–5] The second stage in the generalising process is to move from these two (respectively major and minor) examples of the 'rage for order' to a direct affirmation of belief; of the kind which was to become ever more frequent in Stevens' later verse. It is this, the desire felt by all human beings to give some intelligible form to their lives, which allows them, and us, an entry ('portals') into the kind of pleasurable experience just described. The experience must be an evanescent ('dimly-starred') one, since our fictions quickly die. But it has the value of telling us *something* about ourselves and our environment (because it depends upon both); and giving us finer ('ghostlier') definitions of our world in 'keener', more cruelly sweet, designs (such as those of song and poetry).

from *The Man With the Blue Guitar*

'The general intention of "Blue Guitar" was to say a few things that I felt impelled to say 1. about reality; 2. about the imagination; 3. their inter-relations; and 4. principally, my attitude toward each of these things' (Stevens). Each of the thirty-three poems in 'Blue Guitar' consists of a series of rhymed or unrhymed couplets, the majority of them octosyllabic. The rhythms are driving and angular, the diction crisp and often cryptic; and as a rule Stevens seems to be trying to avoid the more bizarre effects, if not the wit and eccentricity, of his earlier verse. The title figure, inspired by the Picasso painting of an old guitar-player, represents the poet; 'meaning by the poet', as Stevens later explained, 'any man of the imagination'. His guitar, in turn, symbolises the arts – among them music (the guitar player), painting (Picasso), and poetry (Stevens) – and, more generally, the power of the imagination.

The numbers given to the following poems refer to their places in the original sequence.

Poem I] The first poem establishes the major paradox: the imagination must transform reality without denying its power. An equilibrium has to be maintained.

1–2] 'This refers to the posture of the speaker, squatting like a tailor (a shearsman) as he works on his cloth' (Stevens). This is just one example of the extraordinary emphasis on the *visual* in the sequence.

2] *green:* For this, and 'blue' in the next line, see the Notes on 'Sunday Morning', poem 1, line 3.

3–4] The audience objects because the guitar-player does not simply re-produce reality. Note how the rhyming of 'guitar' and 'are' emphasises the opposition between them: on the one hand, the demands of the imagination and, on the other, the exigencies of fact.

5–6] The guitar-player replies that reality is, and must be, transformed by the imagination.

7–8] The audience then demands that the guitarist include this imaginative element. The music must express 'ourselves', in so far as we are a part of reality; *and* that something 'beyond ourselves' which is added by the active mind.

9–10] The music played by the guitar must therefore reproduce the exact character of our world: the fictions we create out of the given particulars of experience. Or as Stevens put it elsewhere, it must 'express people beyond themselves, because that is exactly the way they are'.

Poem III] The imagination must try to discover something significant about reality; and this includes finding out something significant about the individual human nature.

1] *to play man number one:* to create a satisfactory idea of a man, to discover something meaningful about him.

2–4] The violence of the figures used here suggests the difficulties this task involves. This sense of difficulty is further emphasised, in the poem as a whole, by the accumulative pattern of the syntax – and by its lack of a definite ending.

5–6] 'On farms in Pennsylvania a hawk is nailed up, I believe, to frighten off other hawks. Here in New England a bird is more likely to be nailed up merely as an extraordinary object; that is what I had in mind.' (Stevens.)

7–8] 'This means to express man in the liveliness of lively experience, without pose; and to tick it, tock it etc. means to make an exact record of the liveliness of the occasion' (Stevens).

9] *blue:* a synecdoche for the guitar.

Poem IV] The imagination cannot remain static or singular. It must be continually on the move; discovering new and different identities, for different people at different points in time.

1–2] Is 'life' simply our given reality? Perhaps this is what announces itself in the guitar music.

3–6] But can *everyone*, with all their changing versions of experience, be confined to 'life' seen in *these* terms? The answer is already implicit: 'it is not possible to confine all the world (everybody) to reality. They will pick beyond that one string merely by picking it into something different' (Stevens).

7–8] Reality as it 'picks its way' (2) on the blue guitar is transformed by 'feelings', the acts of individual imaginations.

9–10] 'Life', then, things *exactly* as they are (see poem I, 10) is reality in a state of continual and multiple change, transformed by various imaginations. 'In this poem reality changes into the imagination (under one's very eyes) as one experiences it, by reason of one's feelings about it' (Stevens).

Poem V] The imagination, acting upon reality, must supply us with the values and satisfactions which the old mythologies supplied to earlier generations. Its multiple and changing fictions must replace the singular and static fiction of religious belief.

1–3] The old poetry is dead. It moves us, perhaps, as an expression of the 'rage for order': but it can no longer compel belief.

4–8] We live in a secular world, where the added dimensions given to experience by religious faith are no longer possible.

8–10] An important statement: poetry, Stevens declares, and the act of the imagination in general, must now add these dimensions.

10–12] Ourselves and our worlds must be at the centre of these imaginative constructs, replacing the gods and other-worlds of religion (compare 'Sunday Morning'). Stevens himself paraphrased the entire poem thus: 'We live in a world plainly plain. Everything is as you see it. There is no other world. Poetry, then, is the only possible heaven. It must necessarily be the poetry of ourselves; its source is in our imagination (even in the chattering etc.).'

Poem XI] The poet describes two possible ways in which the imagination can fail; and then anticipates a situation in which both are evaded, in favour of a kind of perfect balance.

1–4] Slowly, the mind may be absorbed into its world; just as all these things and people are absorbed into their environment. There then appears to be a harmony ('chord') between the two, but it is a false harmony.

6–10] Alternatively, the world may imprison and debilitate the mind; just as their surroundings entrap the creatures described here. The difference ('discord') between mind and world is thereby acknowledged: but it has been exaggerated out of all justifiable proportions, because the possibility of balance has been denied.

11–12] Contained deep within the womb of time, and the processes of history, is an alternative to both of these; whereby human life is nourished by the world, and the imagination feeds off, and grows out, of reality. 'Time = life, and the rock = the world. As between reality and the imagination, we look forward to an era when there will exist the supreme balance between these two...' (Stevens).

Poem XIV] Not scientific enlightenment, but the light of the imagination, is needed to order and illuminate the world.

1–8] These lines, describing the progressive discoveries of science, have been glossed by Stevens: 'I don't know that one is ever going to get at the secret of the world through the sciences. One after another their discoveries irradiate us and create the view of life that we are now taking, but, after all, this may be just a bit of German laboriousness. It may be that the little candle of the imagination is all we need.'

3] *both star and orb:* both a source of illumination and a world in itself.

5–6] Nature, despite this magnificent series of illuminations, is presented here as half-hidden, still, and inscrutable.

7] 'The German chandelier means an oversized, over-elaborate chandelier' (Stevens).

9–10] The imagination, being a *metaphorical* source of light, illuminates even the day.

11–14] The light of the imagination illuminates and orders the objects of this world; just as the light effects of chiaroscuro help to order the objects in a painting.

Poem XXXII] The imagination must accept the necessity for change, for creating ever fresh definitions of reality. They must be continually making it new, just as the guitar-player and Stevens himself have been doing in this sequence of poems.

1] *the lights, the definitions:* that is, *inherited* lights and *received* definitions.

2] *the dark:* the darkness which occurs when the false light provided by preconceptions and established 'dreams' disappears.

4] *rotted names:* obsolete forms.

5–7] In order to perceive the almost insane diversity of experience, and its riotous fecundity, it is necessary to cast the old fictions aside.

8–10] It is necessary to reject all fictions for a while, the fictions that give form to one's environment and identity to one's self, and confront the nakedness of the real.

11–12] What identity, what definition of yourself and your environment, are you then to adopt? The answer is, the identity which best satisfies you, in your particular time and place. Invariably, the fiction which helps create that identity will startle you because it will be forever new, forever changing in response to changing exigencies. Music, poetry, and their analogues will, and must, always possess this quality of surprise.

from *Notes Toward a Supreme Fiction*

'Poetry must resist the intelligence almost successfully' (Stevens). *Notes Toward a Supreme Fiction* is one of the most difficult of Stevens' works to paraphrase: and also one of the most rewarding and continually pleasurable to read. It consists of a series of thirty-one meditations, divided into three sections, on the power of the imagination in general and the 'supreme fiction' of poetry in particular. Each meditation is made up of seven triadic stanzas, written in a characteristically fluid form of blank verse. Taken all together, they do not present a consecutive argument but are, on the contrary, organised around the 'notes' announced at the beginning of each section. The result, as Frank Kermode happily puts it, 'is a nature, not a physics'. *Notes*, in other words, does what Stevens expected every good poem or sequence of poems to do. It creates its own separate 'mundo' full of noise, colour, and movement; and it is this 'mundo', strange, illogical, and quite unpredictable, which really enables us to see ourselves and our given environment in a new light.

It Must Be Abstract

The meaning of this, the first of the 'notes toward a supreme fiction', will be familiar to readers of the earlier poetry. Man, Stevens argued, must first commit himself to the abstraction *of* reality from all its fictional accretions, the 'rotted names' which surround and partially conceal it. This is the process figured by the season of Winter (see the Notes to 'The Snow Man'). Then, in 'Spring', he must abstract or select *from* reality. He must choose, out of the multiple particulars of experience which come his way, certain details or analogies which appear significant to him, or pleasing, or which simply will not escape his notice. Only after these *two* processes of abstraction are completed can he then move on into 'Summer', and the moment when all that has been abstracted is rearranged into a significant form.

The numbers given to the following poems refer to their places in the original sequence.

Poem I] In this poem Stevens describes the necessity which we all labour under of continually returning to the real. The world, the objects in it, and our selves, must be seen from time to time without benefit of a fiction.

1–3] We should always begin by trying to see what is later called 'the first idea'; that is, the reality which exists underneath all our inventions.

1] *ephebe:* a pupil, a candidate for citizenship in ancient Greece. Stevens is suggesting that he, and we, are learning the rules necessary for citizenship of this world.

3] *inconceivable:* Reality (the sun) is 'inconceivable' in the sense that it exists apart from all our conceptions of it. Stevens is trying to distinguish between *per*ception (by which we see) and *con*ception (by which we know, and evaluate).

4] *ignorant man:* a man without any false preconceptions, who is willing to cast all 'rotted names' aside.

6] We must see reality without any fictions to cover or distort it. The real is seen here as lying at the centre ('in') of a series of layers or skins, given to it by the mind.

7–9] We should never imagine that reality owes its existence to our minds, or to the mind of some superhuman god ('voluminous master'). Pure being does not depend upon knowing.

10–12] Reality, when seen in terms of the 'first idea', without forethought or afterthought, is extraordinarily pure and bare. Naturally so, because it has been purged of our meddling minds and their inventions.

13–14] These lines, which express a certain nostalgia for the very things they reject, return us to a familiar theme. To deny the responsibility of any particular god for the existence of the real, Stevens points out, is to deny the responsibility of all gods. To set aside any one of those anthropomorphic legends by which, traditionally, we have tried to explain life to ourselves is to set them all aside. There is no need for any of those legends now. No story of 'Phoebus' is required any more to explain to us the movements of the sun.

15] *autumn*: the time, in Stevens' poetry, when all fictions die.

umber: the colour of sunset, and of blood.

17] *something that never could be named*: reality (the sun), which exists beyond any of the names or fictions we invent for it (such as 'Phoebus').

18] *There was a project for the sun*: The 'project' is to perceive the sun quite apart from any of our forms or 'projections'; to 'project' ourselves beyond the constructs of the mind.

20] *gold flourishes*: an example of the names we should discard when we are trying to perceive reality.

21] We must perceive reality in its state of pure being. Difficult though it is, we must restrain our minds for a while from any attempts at knowing.

Poem IV] The tone of this poem hovers between the tragic and the comic; like a religious meditation, using both to enforce humility. Reality, we are reminded, exists beyond ourselves, time passes us by with indifference. Consequently, we cannot impose our ideas on the world: we must, rather, accept and abstract our ideas *from* it. Our stance must be that of the attentive pupil rather than the master.

1–4] The opening statement is categorical: reality or the 'first idea' is not an invention of man – does not depend upon him for its existence. Certainly, man would like to think that it did. That is clear enough from the myth of Eden; in which Adam is shown actually imposing his own image upon the world, using his own forms and names to create the real. A story devised to suggest that the world exists *for* man, it also describes how the world was supposedly given being *by* a man.

2] *Descartes*: 'Descartes is used as a symbol of the reason. But we live in a place that is not our own; we do not live in the land of Descartes; we have imposed the reason; Adam imposed it even in Eden' (Stevens). René Descartes (1596–1650) was the French philosopher who based his entire system on the (for him) primary fact of self-consciousness: 'I think, therefore I am' was the ground upon which he built his world. Stevens therefore saw him as a supreme example (like 'Adam') of the tendency to place the human ego at the centre of existence, and see everything as a reflection of it.

4] *her sons and...her daughters*: 'It is not the individual alone who indulges himself in the pathetic fallacy. It is the race' (Stevens).

4–9] Adam and Eve, and their 'descendants', have always tried to create a heaven and an earth in their own images, by mistaking their fictions for reality. But reality is not, and never can be, a matter of shaping the world in imitation of the self, because it exists prior to man.

7] *a very varnished green:* The idea is that man is forever attempting to 'smooth down' reality, by identifying it with his own symmetrical fictions. For 'green', see the Notes on 'Sunday Morning', poem 1, 3.

10–12] The fact existed before we ever perceived it, or tried to form a conception of it. The 'myth' of reality was there before we ever began devising our own 'myths' or fictions. This is not the only time Stevens compares the world to a universal imagination and its products: see 'Bantams in Pine-Woods', line 7.

13–15] These lines add a new sense of urgency and pathos to the argument. We live in an alien world, Stevens reminds us, which exists quite apart from all our conceptions of it and which we cannot, therefore, ever really hope to control. We may achieve the occasional, small triumph, when reality is transfigured for a moment by the mind; but our situation is a generally sad and difficult one, denying all our proud ideas of ourselves.

15] *blazoned:* To 'blazon' means to inscribe with heraldic arms and colours. The idea here is that the imagination can at least give some occasional brightness to our lives; just as the heraldic artist imparts brightness to the instruments of war.

16–21] With characteristic wit, Stevens repeats with a difference a cluster of metaphors used in the opening lines; employing them now to launch a final assault upon our pride. We should not try to shape the 'clouds' in imitation of ourselves, he suggests (see 8–9): but accept, instead, that it is *we* who must imitate the clouds. We must attempt to discover designs inherent *in* experience rather than impose designs on it. Nor should we take reality as a 'mirror' (see 3–5) but as a given fact; a 'bare board', or established setting, which combines the tragic and the comic, the light and the dark, in ways which show a complete indifference to our demands. The world has its own deep music, we must learn, which makes the music of our fictions seem puny, almost laughable, by comparison.

18] *Coulisse:* side-scene on a theatre stage, used here as a synecdoche for theatrical scenery.

20] *abysmal:* bottomless, deep. There is also, probably, a play on the colloquial meaning of 'terrible'.

It Must Change

This, the second of the 'notes', hardly requires any further explanation. It is evident from every one of Stevens' poems that he saw the desires of the mind and the demands of the world as *dynamic* opponents. They change, he argued; and so all the fictions intended to create a balance between them, including the supreme fiction of poetry, must change as well. See the introductory Notes to 'The Snow Man'.

Poem IV] In this, one of the finest pieces in the entire sequence, the poet describes for us 'the origin of change'. All life, we are told, is a matter of intercourse between opposites: between night and day, chaos and order, above all, between reality and the imagination. Life consists of a continuing opposition and union, a *process* in other words, rather than a fixed series of given facts.

1–6] Notice how these lines help to emphasise the passionate and volatile nature of such union. 'Winter' and 'Spring' are 'cold', apparently, until they achieve a sudden contact.

6] *the particulars of rapture :* the new life created at the beginning of the new year (or by coition), and the new fictions created at the beginning of each new imaginative cycle.

7] This seems to mean that it is the interaction of music with silence which produces a certain effect: the 'sense', or complex of thought and feeling, which we associate with a particular musical piece.

11–12] Sunshine and rain together produce the green vegetation of the earth.

13–14] The interaction between a feeling of solitude and a particular way of expressing that feeling helps to give it a certain uniqueness, to distinguish it from all similar feelings.

15] Even a single instrument, united with a whole host of other instruments, plays its part in producing the complete orchestral sound.

16–19] Note how easily Stevens moves here, as elsewhere, between generalisation and the apt example. Opposites engaged in the universal intercourse, he tells us, *take from* each other and so are *changed by* each other; interacting to become one just as, in a sense, the child and the parent, the captain and his men, and the sailor and the sea, all do.

20–1] The poet ends by enjoining the 'ephebe' (see 'It Must Be Abstract', poem 1) to participate in this process as well; and by intimating that he does so, whether he knows it or not, already. For in so far as he exists, he exists as a variety of oppositions and unions – and must be addressed as such all the time.

Poem X] The poet here celebrates change: a world governed by change, and the progressive metamorphoses of reality which our minds create out of that world.

1–3] These lines, and the next two stanzas, describe a man in a park who sits, almost in a state of trance, transforming his environment with the help of his mind. Because he does see the park through the filter of his imagination it becomes, in a sense, a 'Theatre / Of Trope' for him; and the nearby lake can be said to be 'full of artificial things'. It is a fictive environment he transmits to us, not a literal representation.

1] *A bench was his catalepsy :* 'A bench as catalepsy is a place of trance' (Stevens). 'Catalepsy' is a state in which the movements of consciousness, and of the body, are suspended: there is an ironic contrast intended here between the rigidity of the observer and the fluidity of the observed.

2] *Trope :* figurative language.

4–6] This fictive world the man is creating is a world of appearance and alteration: things are constantly assuming fresh identities for him, casting aside one imaginative form in favour of another. Consequently, the lake and its objects can perhaps be compared to a page of music, the notes upon which are interpreted differently at different times. They can be compared, also, to heaven ('an upper air'), which possesses as many characters as there are moods and desires to create them; or to the blankness of our given environment, which depends upon us and our visual sense to give it 'a momentary color.' Any one object or essence the man perceives – the 'swans' for instance – may assume any number of fictive identities, thanks entirely to the 'will to change' shared alike by perceived and perceiver.

7–9] The west wind, a common Romantic emblem for divine energy, is now identified with this 'will to change'; the process of metamorphosis giving different identities to the man, and different colours and patterns ('iris frettings') to the lake.

10–12] The poet now turns from the particular to the general. This will to change, he points out, is an unavoidable fact of experience. It transforms life into a continuous present, and it transforms our given environment into 'a presentation' or Theatre of Trope. It is the one constant in an otherwise inconstant world.

13–14] This double metaphor seems to imply that the world is like a roving eye, which catches our own roving eye and thereby establishes a fleeting contact; and that it is also like a tramp, forever changing clothes or 'metaphors', and so requiring us to see it anew.

14–17] Change, the kind of change celebrated in the opening lines, is not and cannot be left to pure chance. It is a constant in ourselves as well as in our world, and a product of our minds transforming our world. The freshness of our lives depends upon our willingness to engage ourselves with the real, and create new meanings out of it.

18–21] The will to change compels us to discover a series of ever-altering, ever-fresh identities for our world; which like a mirror provide us with a series of ever-altering, ever-fresh identities for ourselves. It creates a situation in which beginning again is the rule; where the mind and the real are forever moving towards new kinds of contact, new metamorphoses that the fullness of time can complete.

It Must Give Pleasure

Stevens used many different terms to describe the function of the imaginative power, and of the fictions it creates. At different times he said that its purpose was to liberate, justify, purify, explain, enrich, order, console, mitigate... and so on. All of these meanings, more or less, are included under the term 'pleasure' which here, as so often in Stevens' work, has a moral as well as an aesthetic reference: to 'give pleasure', in other words, means to gratify our demand for value and significance as well as our demand for joy.

Poem VIII] Pleasure lies in the here and now, in our rediscovery of our own present circumstances rather than in some impossible existence in another world. We must rely on ourselves for bliss, and not on some other being.

1–9] The poem begins with a hypothesis. What, the poet asks, if he were to imagine an angel, a god-like creature who finds bliss in the motions of his flight; one who requires neither the 'gold centre' of a deity nor the 'golden destiny' of heaven in which to find satisfaction, but only the 'deep space' of his own environment? If he imagines this is he not, in effect, creating in the angel a fictive version of his own possibilities? Isn't the angel's joy and fulfilment really an expression of the joy and fulfilment available to himself?

1] *What am I to believe?:* A nicely ambiguous phrase, this could refer either to the following eight-and-a-half lines, or to the question posed by the entire poem.

2] *violent abyss:* the chaos of creation, the world.

3] *abysmal glory:* a pun. The angel makes deep ('abysmal') and mysterious music out of a terrible ('abysmal') environment. Compare 'It Must Be Abstract', poem IV, 20.

9] *lapis-haunted air:* The air is full of angels' wings.

10] The speculation and the questioning continue. Is it, the poet asks, the angel, the fictive expression of possible joy, who has experienced or can experience that joy; or is it the poet himself, the creator of that fiction? The answer, although left implicit, is obvious: it is the creator, who can experience that joy – and *must* have experienced something of it, in order to be able to describe it.

11–18] If he *can* experience that joy and even *has* experienced some small portion of it; if he *can* conceive of an *hour* filled with bliss – then why not a day, a month, or a year? Why not an entire life-time founded upon the belief that happiness, and 'majesty' must be discovered within the self and the individual life, rather than in the supernatural?

13] *need's golden hand:* the 'golden hand' of god created *by* need to *satisfy* need.

14] *solacing majesty:* the idea of god, created by man to give him comfort.

18] The poet has no god or heaven to satisfy his needs: but, being satisfied with himself, with what he is and what he can do, he has no need of them.

19–21] The poem is about the art of the possible and, in a way appropriate to its theme, is developed as a series of questions right to the end. Even so, the questions are by now so framed as to make the poet's own beliefs clear. The heavens, he concludes, and the versions of heavenly pleasure that we create: what are they but reflections of our own desires, a feeble attempt to escape from the reality of death? What are they, in fact, but a series of wish fulfilments which, like the dream of Cinderella for her Prince Charming, betray our frustration rather than offer us a positive step towards bliss?

Poem X] This poem, which is followed in the original sequence by an epilogue, is the nearest thing to a conclusion that Stevens will permit himself. A hymn to the earth, it anticipates a time when the 'notes toward a supreme fiction' will be completed; although, of course, it neither pretends to complete those notes itself nor supposes a time when the fictive *process*, or *making* of supreme fictions, will approach completion.

1–3] The poet addresses the earth in the way that earlier writers addressed their God, or their lover. Why is it, he asks the earth, that she is so fickle; that he can never see her as anything except a teasing, changing shape? Why is she, for him, a figure never quite entire or finished with?

1] *fat girl:* 'the earth' (Stevens).

4] Like a mistress again, or like God, the earth is familiar to the poet and yet strange, departing all the time from what he thinks he knows about her.

5–13] Close to the earth, the love the poet bears towards her requires him to search for words; to pin down her evasiveness to a fixed identity and so, in a special sense, to 'know' her. But he cannot know her in this way, it seems. All he can do is give her a series of provisional identities, which are 'more than natural' in that they owe as much to his own mind as they do to the lady described. So the earth as *he* knows her is the earth imaginatively transformed; 'distorted', as he puts it here, by 'irrational' feeling.

5–6] *underneath/ A tree:* 'There is a double meaning: a. on reflection (a man stretched out at his ease, underneath a tree, thinking;) b. a great tree is a symbol of fixity, permanence, completion, the opposite of "a moving contour"' (Stevens).

14–15] That, the poet suggests suddenly, is the only way in which he – and we – can know: by means of an imaginative transformation. The earth arrives to us via a series of fictions, which are not just 'irrational' but 'more than rational' in that they supply us with a knowledge beyond the scope of reason. In them, the demands of the 'fat girl' and the desires of our own hungering minds are reconciled; and through them we approach much closer to the truth than we could do with the help of abstract thought, or any fixed vocabulary.

16–21] Which is not to deny entirely the value of a fixed vocabulary. We cannot hope to define the earth with the help of it. Still, at the right moment in time we may be able to define the process whereby we know the earth. To speak in figures, we may some day establish exactly how and why we endow our green world with the value of precious crystal, ever bright, attractive, and different. Our fiction-making will not end then, naturally, because it never can: but our note-taking will.

16] *the Sorbonne:* the University of Paris, referred to here as a home of, and consequently a figure for, abstract thought.

Final Soliloquy of the Interior Paramour

This, from the last collection of Stevens' verse to be published during his lifetime, is a hymn to the imagination; a song of love sung, alone, by the poet to the beloved presence within his own mind.

1–3] The opening stanza establishes the controlling metaphor of this poem, and of so many of Stevens' other poems: light, signifying the power of the imagination. The poet invokes the light as if he were officiating at a religious ceremony. His breathless anticipation is registered in the lilt of the opening anapaest; and the ritualistic nature of his address is implied by the association of the light of the mind with the light of Vesper, the evening star.

1] *as in a room | In which we rest:* The light of the imagination provides us with comfort and security against the darkness of deep space, like a temporary resting-place that we might build against the elements.

2] *for small reason:* The light of the imagination is accepted on faith, for reasons which lie beyond the scope of reason.

3] This, the belief stated here, is the belief which prompts us to accept the light of the imagination.

4–9] It is by means of this belief that we discover our closest communion with the world. Thanks to it, we can achieve moments of fullness and harmony, which relieve us from the general indifference of things. It offers us, too, a power or influence which is quite miraculous: in that this power has nothing at all to do with the visible or tangible, and everything to do with the invisible processes of our own minds.

10–13] This, the miraculous power of the imagination, provides us with a condition of beatitude here and now; a strange feeling of coherence, completeness, and knowledge whereby we temporarily lose all awareness of our own weaknesses and our differences. It presents us, in effect, with an idea of order created *by* the mind, *for* the mind, *in* the mind.

14] The numerous religious references draw to a conclusion in this line, where God and the imagination are identified. The initial 'We say' adds a qualifier, though: the statement is only figuratively true. The imagination is not being set up as a God in the traditional sense, nor is the poet suggesting that God manifests Himself through it. The imagination is only *like* the traditional conception of God in that it gives meaning and satisfaction to our lives. It offers us no other world except this one, no possible saviour but ourselves.

15–18] 'The Coleridgean imagination', the critic Marius Bewley once said, became 'the theme of Stevens' poetry as a whole in a way it never became the theme of Coleridge's poetry as a whole.' These beautifully controlled lines recover that theme for us one more time; and remind us, as well, of the kind of tentative affirmation to which, in Stevens' case at least, it usually led. A sudden and high lyric note is caught in line 15, to celebrate the scope of the mind, but it soon dies away; and, more appropriate to its conclusions, the poem then withdraws into a quiet, meditative serenity. The power of the imagination, the poet informs us, that power possessed by all of us in common, it is out of this that we make ourselves a shelter against the surrounding night. It may not provide us with a new heaven, admittedly, nor even a completely new earth: but it does at least, offer 'what will suffice' to enable us to live our lives in peace.

William Carlos Williams

The Revelation

Marianne Moore called Williams a poet who 'is able to fix the atmosphere of a moment'. Here is one such moment when the narrator, awakening from sleep, still feels the memory of an interrupted dream impinging upon him. The form of the poem illustrates Williams' belief that new verse structures and rhythms had to be invented to catch the individual experience and voice of the poet, and the particularity of the moments or objects he described.

1–6] 'Past objects have about them past necessities – like the sonnet – which have conditioned them and from which, as a form itself, they cannot be freed. The poem being an object...it must be the purpose of the poet to make of his words a new form: to invent, that is, an object consonant with his day' (Williams). Verse was not to follow preconceived rules; and it was not, in the purest sense of the word, to be 'free' either. It was to obey, in its rhythms and language, the exigencies of the specific occasion. So here, in the first movement every resource at the poet's disposal – and particularly the rhythm – is used to make us share in the first seconds of the narrator's awakening.

1–2] The meditative pause in the middle and at the end of the first line, the delicate, monosyllabic tread of the second, and the echoing effect of the word 'voices' (the product of placing it before a pause): all help to capture the sense of mystery, and lost bearings, which most of us experience when drowsy.

3–4] The convoluted syntax and purposefully clumsy rhythms imitate the narrator's stumbling attempts to remember his 'revelation' – the girl, just dreamed about, who still seems to be present in the room when he wakes up.

5–6] The 'revelation' returns to him for a moment. As it does so, the lines assume a kind of stillness or breathless wonder and are left unfinished, like an unconsummated wish.

7–12] The detailed memory of the dream returns, but as a memory now – not a moment of transcendent vision.

9] Notice the pause here which makes us linger over the word 'girl', to discover in it an excitement and sense of possibility which it does not usually have. One of Williams' major purposes was to re-vitalise simple words such as this one, and thus avoid what Wordsworth had disparagingly referred to as 'poetic diction'.

11–12] The emphases on 'leaned' and 'stroked' recapture the girl's movements, while the reference to 'my car' suggests how far this dream is from the conventional poetic kind, and how close it is to his readers' (i.e. either as Americans or as people contemporary with Williams).

13–18] The poet returns to the waking world: but with the intention of finding in it the strange beauty of his dreams. The poem turns out to be at once an affirmation and demonstration of the belief that only in ordinary, day-to-day experience can absolutes be discovered. Or as Williams put it: 'This is the poet's business. Not to talk in vague categories but to write particularly, as a physician works upon a patient, upon the thing before him, in the particular to discover the universal.'

13–14] The monotonous rhythms of these lines capture the feelings described.

15] The pause here, at 'other', prepares the reader for the clinching affirmation of the last three lines.

16–18] Characteristically, Williams clings to the specific – the larger, 'universal' meaning of the poem is never separated from the particular occasion – and leaves off on a note of expectancy; with the poem, grammatically speaking, still unfinished. His aim was to capture the movement of things, as well as their individuality: 'living', rather than 'life', was his absolute. So he always tried to communicate to his work a sense of possibility, to leave it 'open' as though it could continue to change like the world it imitated.

Sea-Trout and Butterfish

'Something occurred once when I was about twenty, a sudden resignation to existence...which made everything a unit and at the same time a part of myself' (Williams). For Williams, as for Keats and Whitman, the essential experience is contact, the bridging of the gap between the perceiving subject and the perceived moment or object. Here, for example, the poet is trying through the agency of the poem to live the life of the sea-trout and butterfish he describes, to realise their separate identity; and, of course, he is trying to make the reader do the same.

1–2] Attention is concentrated on the sensuous details of the fish; the aim being, as it is in Keats' verse, to achieve an effort of empathy. 'A thing known passes out of the mind into the muscles' (Williams).

2] The inter-penetration of subject and object is realised, partly, through the use of verbal ambiguity: 'caught' could refer either to the observing eye (i.e. its attention caught by the fish) or the observed sea-trout and butterfish. So, also, could 'unravelled' (10) and 'separates' (11).

5] Each word here seems to stand out, as though it had a separate life of its own, and yet acquires additional force when seen in its context. 'Weight', for instance, has its innate meaning and energy brought out because the rhythm forces us to pause over it, and roll it around our tongues: but it gains further impact when we relate it to the pun on 'scales' (i.e. the scales on a fish *and* weighing-scales), and the feeling for the substance and density of the fish aroused by the entire line. This is symptomatic (i) of the kind of reverence for the individuality of words, as well as objects, that Williams said he learnt from the work of Laurence Sterne and Gertrude Stein, and (ii) of the intense *inner* activity of verse that Williams was thinking of when he declared: 'The poem is made of things – on a field.' Like a series of particles on a magnetic field, the words in a good Williams poem insist on their status as separate entities, engaged in an active relaitonship with their context.

9] In the last four lines of the poem, the grammatical relationship of eye and fish is reversed (i.e. the eye is, in the grammatical sense, the object in the opening lines, but the subject in the closing ones; the fish, vice versa). This further blurs the conventional distinction between subject and object; and increases our sense of the inter-penetration of the two.

10] *the sea :* literally, the matrix from which all individual life derives and, by extension, the mass of undifferentiated matter from which the poetic eye 'separates' its chosen object.

12] The hissing sibilants and fricative 'f' sounds of this line offer us a verbal equivalent for the act of touching.

Proletarian Portrait

This is one of Williams' many American street scenes. Williams considered himself to be a direct poetic descendant of Whitman, in the sense of being dedicated to the recovery of the American experience in verse. He was, he hoped, going to capture American sights and sounds in his 'portraits', and 'the American idiom' was to form his staple language. Clearly, this was not so much a matter of cultural nationalism as a consequence of his commitment to the present moment and the immediate object. To distinguish himself and the realities he described as American, in other words, was simply another way of affirming his and their individuality: both belonged to a particular locale and time.

3] Notice the strong dependence here, and throughout the poem, on verbs. This is part and parcel of Williams' belief that his work is emphatically not just a matter of description. It is meant to re-create the life of the thing or person described; and in order to do this, according to him, it must have 'an intrinsic movement of its own to verify its authenticity' – it must possess its own life and activity and not just be a passive substance. The pattern of verbs, of 'moving' and 'doing' words, helps it to achieve just this.

Tract

Williams was not only an American, he was a native of Rutherford, New Jersey (disguised in many of his poems under the name of 'Paterson'); and his commitment to place led him into the discovery and celebration of this particular town, as well as his country. Again, this was not a matter of simple obscurantism on Williams' part. As he explained: 'Place is the only reality, the true core of the universal. We live in one place at one time, but far from being bound by it, only through it do we realize our freedom..., only if we make ourselves sufficiently aware of it, do we join with others in other places.'

This poem, an example of Williams' public voice, is at once a criticism of the bourgeois habits of his neighbours, and an indication of his sense of fundamental kinship with them. After Whitman, he is probably the finest poet of American democracy.

The Widow's Lament in Springtime

This poem suggests how far Williams' gospel of contact could take him. Contact is now a matter of identifying with the submerged life of the person described, and not just with those aspects of him or her which can be perceived by the senses. The poet *becomes* the widow for the course of the poem. His sympathy allows him – and us – to share in her grief, and as a result the act of identification begins to assume moral overtones of the kind another poet, Thom Gunn, was referring to when he said of Williams: 'His stylistic qualities are governed...by a tenderness and generosity which makes them fully humane.' This, the more obvious moral dimension of the writing, together with the subtle use of flower and tree references, makes 'The Widow's Lament' seem like an anticipation of the verse of Williams' last years.

1–6] The widow tries to speak in short, restrained sentences but her emotion breaks through three times: here, in the initial description, then in lines 15–19, and finally in the last sentence where the two 'and 's imply another surge of feeling.

5–6] The paradox of 'cold fire' foreshadows the conflict outlined by the rest of the poem, between the colours of springtime and the drab grief of the widow, while the idea of this fire closing around her prepares us for the conclusion, where she talks of being smothered near 'white flowers'.

7–8] The general simplicity of the diction adds a touch of poignancy, as if the speaker were searching for the right words.

11–19] Here and elsewhere Williams works with two kinds of statement, emotional and descriptive; and the juxtaposition of the two serves to turn cherry tree, plumtree, and the rest almost, but not quite, into metaphors. They exist at once in the outer world and the inner, as actual objects, and – more tentatively – as stimulants or correlatives for the widow's grief.

19] *turned away forgetting:* This could mean either that the widow forgot the flowers or that she rejected forgetfulness of her late husband. The two meanings, of course, complement and enrich rather than contradict each other. Notice also the sudden change to another tense, as if the flowers have already been pushed into the past before she can tell us they have.

21] *heavy:* The word, strange to its immediate context, really belongs with the later description of the widow drowning in the woods: it seems to be a case of an epithet transferred from its logical place under the pressure of the widow's feelings. As such, it is of a piece with the mingling of past and present, literal and imagined, which – along with the dirge-like, repetitive movement of the lament – helps to create the impression of a consciousness dazed with sorrow.

from *Spring and All*

The volume which first appeared under this title in 1923 has become a kind of bible for more recent American poets such as Charles Olson and Robert Creeley. Written, like a religious meditation, in prose punctuated by poetry, it offers at once a statement and a demonstration of Williams' cardinal beliefs. The prose offers us the statement, and the poetry the imaginative demonstration, along the lines of the distinction made by Williams himself in the course of the book: '...prose has to do with the fact of an emotion; poetry has to do with dynamisation of emotion into a separate form. This is the force of imagination.'

Essentially, the message of *Spring and All* is one we are familiar with already: that, as Williams once put it, there should be 'No ideas but in things.' The aim of the poet, he argues, should be to discover 'things' (a moment, an object) and then see what he has discovered clearly and separately. But at the same time (since seeing is a continuous process) he should, through the creative force of his seeing, be able to realise the paradox of continuity in change, relatedness in non-relatedness, the universal in the particular. The implicit claim is not that the poet sees things and then articulates their meaning but that they are there, ready to express themselves for one's seeing. All the poet has to do, therefore, is to *see* this meaning, by performing the necessary act of imaginative sympathy, and then find the words which will re-create it.

The numbers given to the following poems refer to their places in the original sequence.

Poem I] The particular occasion of this poem is mundane: Dr Williams is driving to work at the hospital. But through the sheer energy of his vision he perceives the individuality of this isolated moment and its latent significance. Without ever once departing from the specific, Williams' re-creation of a day in early spring – when the new vegetation is just beginning to stir – consequently becomes a celebration of rebirth and the vital principle in general: the seasonal revival of Nature is implied, the 'rebirth' of man through his offspring, the resurrection of the human spirit, and (an appropriate subject for the first poem in a sequence) the quickening of the poetic imagination.

1] *contagious hospital:* a place of death, and new life.
2–5] Spring, the season of recovery and new life, was a favourite poetic subject for Williams.
16] *They:* The word is purposely vague, and could refer either to the 'twiggy stuff' described in lines 10–11 or to the babies being born in the 'contagious hospital'.
22–4] Notice how Williams associates life with the process of clarification.
23] *It:* Again, this is purposefully vague, referring perhaps to the vital principle as well as the individual thing. The rhythms of the verse have been quickening, too, during the course of the poem.
27] There is no full stop after 'awaken'.

Poem II] This, by implication, is partly about the abundance of Spring (as opposed to the 'stark dignity' of its early stages described in poem I) and partly about the rich profusion of material from which the poet separates out his chosen object: but first and last, of course it is a verbal re-creation of one such object, a 'pot of flowers'.

Poem III] The poem begins as a portrait of the farmer, inspecting his fields, with the new year's harvest as yet planted only in his head. Then, in lines 17–18, a fresh dimension is opened up. The farmer now also suggests the artist, whose mind is beginning to stir with the blessèd rage for order. He is to give new life to the earth, thanks to his work, just as the farmer is.

19] *antagonist*: The artist/farmer contends in an athletic struggle for mastery with the chaos without or within (i.e. the kinds of chaos figured in poem II).

Poem XXI] Here, Williams' belief that 'emotions gather around small things', is communicated to us via a strategy of reversed expectations. The deliberately vague, but enormously suggestive, opening leads the reader more accustomed to traditional poetry to expect some grandiose statement of theory (i.e. along the lines of 'Beauty is Truth, Truth Beauty'). All he is offered instead is an individual object (a wheel-barrow), at an individual time (after rain), and in an individual place (beside the chickens). A yearning towards what might or could be is quietly checked by the homely beauty of what *is*.

2] *upon*: Notice the enormous expectations aroused by placing this word in isolation, and before a heavy pause.

Young Sycamore

This, perhaps, is the perfect epitome of Williams' earlier work, the verse written during what has been called his 'objectivist' period. The discovery of the object as a 'thing in itself', the absence of figurative language or any attempt to make it stand for anything else, the organising of the poem around a pattern of verbs and dynamic rhythms which are meant to re-create the life and growth of the object, the tactile imagery and feeling for the intrinsic energy of words: all these are typical of a poet who sees poetry as 'an extension of nature's processes... transfused with the same forces which transfuse the earth' – and whose own verse is best compared, not with the work of any other writer, but with the paintings of Vincent Van Gogh.

1] The first line seizes our attention, with a characteristic informality and sense of urgency.

3] The rest of the poem, from this line on, is a subordinate clause which describes the tree from trunk to topmost twig. The sentence with which the poem begins is never completed; and the reader is consequently left at the end with that sense of rising anticipation which Williams saw as natural to the person meditating on a world governed by change.

round and firm: This is the first in a series of tactile images which help articulate the way the poet lives the life of the tree.

7] The sense of the tree as an activity rather than a passive object is empha-sised by means of the pattern of verbs and verbals which make up the frame-work of the poem: 'rises', 'undulant / thrust', 'dividing and waning', 'sending out', 'hung', 'thins', 'knotted', 'bending'.

8] Placed by itself, 'bodily' assumes a roundness and substance, as we linger over it, which makes it a dramatic equivalent of its meaning.

12] Notice the pause at the end of the line, full of breathless expectation.

24] *hornlike* : This, suggesting the animal-like power of the young sycamore, is the only figurative word in the poem.

Raleigh Was Right

The title refers to a poem by Sir Walter Raleigh, 'The Nymph's Reply to the Shepherd', which offers a jaundiced view of the pastoral dream, suggesting that it is obsolete.

4–7] Note the loving details of this description. The poem as a whole conveys a profound yearning for country pleasures even while the notion of escape into the country is being rejected.

17–18] There may be an implied reference to the poetry of T. S. Eliot here, and particularly 'The Waste Land'. Williams disliked Eliot's poetry intensely, because of what he saw as its rejection of America (where they were both born), the urban present, and new art forms in favour of Europe, an Arcad dreamian of the past, and tradition.

The Night Rider

In his earliest poetry, Williams concentrated on the discovery of individual 'things'. In his later, however, he began to trying to weave things into patterns and then sqeeze ideas out of the patterns he had made; and occasionally he would even move from the specific to the general, by a progression very like that of inductive logic. All this was the product of a growing belief that, while the poet's basic fidelity to the object should remain unchanged, it was possible and perhaps necessary for him to introduce comment. As part of this change of emphasis, Williams talked more than he ever had before about structure: the organising of the poem so that a significant combination of detail would result, or subjective statement be included without the entire work toppling over into didacticism.

Here is a miniature example of Williams' new technique; in which a series of 'things' are brought together in a mosaic, to suggest by their juxtaposition a feeling of calm after fulfilment. By inference the whole notion of life as a rhythmic ebb-and-flow is touched upon.

The form of the poem is characteristic of those Williams wrote in the early forties: regular stanzas (in this case four-line), with lines of varying length but with a fixed number of stresses per line (in this case, two stresses). The aim was to combine flexibility with a firmer sense of rhythmic structure, and led Williams eventually to the invention of the 'variable foot'.

1–4] The conch has presumably been thrown up by the high tide and left at the ebb; the moon is on the wane (its growth and decline, according to legend, govern the sea's ebb and flow); the narrator has just left his lover; the 'damp night' follows a hot midsummer day. All suggest what Spenser called 'peace after stormy seas'.

7] Another ebb motion (autumn) is anticipated.

8] The inner world of the lover and the outer world of 'things' are explicitly linked.

12] This could mean that the peace of this moment has been bought at a high price, a price worth paying, or a price paid with affection. The meanings, of course, reinforce each other.

13–16] These lines refer primarily to the conch, 'smoothed' by the turbulent sea and carrying the memory of that turbulence within it (i.e. in the 'pulse' we hear when we raise a shell to our ear). But line 13 could also refer to the moon, 14 to the sea, and 15–16 to the lover and the summer's day. The mosaic is complete, and with it the re-creation of 'an even mood'.

Preface to *Paterson*: Book One

Book One of Williams' personal epic was published in 1946, and he was working on Book six at the time of his death. Long before he died, Williams had said that there would never be an end to the poem because, like all his work, it had to remain open to the world of growth and change.

Paterson is as much concerned with the reverent investigation of the particular as Williams' other poems are, the particular in this case being an imaginative version of his home town of Rutherford, New Jersey, and, by extension, America. The purpose is to *see* Paterson, to achieve contact with it, and thereby to discover forces that can build a new world. Universal 'ideas' are to be found, once again, by means of a close study of 'things', only now the enterprise is on a much larger scale than ever before. It has to be, since Paterson is itself a conglomerate of particular moments and objects, which have each to be seen properly before being brought together to form a total pattern of meaning.

The form of the poem is the same as that of 'The Night Rider', a 'design' (see Notes to 'The Orchestra'); and it is this along with Williams' thematic intentions which provide the subject of the Preface.

1] Williams begins by making the statement of purpose traditional to the epic (compare the opening of *Paradise Lost*).

remonstrance: protest.

3–16] This answers the question of line 2. How is beauty to be discovered? By the study and gathering up of particulars.

7–16] A self-deprecatory image. The lame dog digs the earth for his bone, just as Williams searches the earth of Paterson for meaning; while other dogs run off in search of juicier meat, just as Eliot and Pound ran off to Europe.

17–20] A terse reply to Eliot's line, 'In my beginning is my end', in 'East Coker'. Eliot's poem is about the transcendence of the cycle of life and death by means of a spiritual resurrection. Williams' poem, he tells us, is about the acceptance of that cycle, the world of process and change.

22] *no return*: i.e. we have only one life in which to discover 'rigor of beauty'.

chaos: see Notes to 'Spring and All', poem II.

23] *nine months' wonder*: man, and everything that lives. The emphasis falls on 'wonder'.

26] *interpenetration*: of man and city, subject and object.

26–9] A quick series of examples of the many 'things' Paterson contains.

29–31] By starting off without preconceptions, the illusion of knowledge, we can then learn by means of a reverent of study particulars. The knowledgeable man, relying on the vast abstractions supplied to him by his intelligence, is the really ignorant one.

32–6] When knowledge remains 'undispersed' into particulars, then the various potential of life ('multiple seed') is lost in a chaos of undifferentiated detail ('flux') and the mind ends in confusion ('floats off in...scum').

37–8] The idea is of knowledge as a globe slowly growing as it is pushed on, gathering more detail.

39–41] Each day brings a new world, and a new and innocent ('ignorant') sun filling the empty space left by the old suns, for the man who never relies on stale knowledge.

41–5] In order to 'live well' and know the truth, a man must accept his own mortality and mutability.

46–7] *addition and subtraction:* adding up particulars to create a design, or idea, and then dispersing those particulars preparatory to creating a new design. The pursuit of knowledge is a continuous, never-ending process (see Notes on 'The Orchestra', line 26).

48–54] Received ideas ('thought') are also the death of poetry ('the craft').

55–56] A celebration of the cyclical process which man imitates in his quest for knowledge, from 'things' to 'ideas' and then back immediately to 'things' again; a quest which now (66) begins with the exploration of Paterson.

59] *mathematics to particulars:* the study of particulars leads us to the science of combinations ('mathematics'), which in turn should lead us back to the study of particulars.

The Descent

This is the poem in which Williams invented the 'variable foot', the final solution as he saw it to a problem which had vexed him all his life: how to create a new rhythmic structure, welded to 'the American idiom', that would enable its users to combine the maximum flexibility with the discipline necessary to place the emphases and pauses where they were required. Total freedom had never been his aim, only the sort of 'open' structure which could best be altered to suit the exigencies of the occasion; and now Williams believed he had found it.

The 'variable foot' is a metric pattern in which 'time is the real matter of measure, and not stress. Elapsed time is the whole story' (Williams). Measure, that is, becomes a relative quantity and a matter of duration, with each foot taking up the same amount of time in the reading regardless of whether it consists of seven or eight words read quickly or one syllable and a long pause. In this poem, each line is divided into three feet, which are indicated by the typographical arrangement.

1–2] The poem is about the 'descent' into memory, the probing of old experiences and problems, which Williams saw as a form of psychic renewal and a necessary preliminary to the writing of poetry.

2] The last foot in this line consists of one word, 'even'. In order to let it take up the same amount of time in the reading as the previous two feet we have to make an immense pause after it; which reproduces for us the voice and breath of the poet, reaching out tentatively for a further definition. This is a good example of how the 'variable foot' could enable Williams to place the emphases and pauses *exactly* where he wanted them.

The Orchestra

This poem, constructed as an imitation of an orchestral piece in five parts, is an attempt to discover an idea of order which is capable of uniting man with man, man with nature, and the different parts of an art-work with one another; and to do all this without betraying the individuality of the elements involved. By inference it becomes a celebration of many of Williams' later poems; arranged as they are like mosaics, in a significant combination of detail (see Notes to 'The Night Rider').

Section I (1–9)] This introduces the organising image of the orchestra, which offers a key to the musical structure of the poem; and which eventually provides a solution to the problem of design. For a good orchestral piece represents a weaving together of different notes and instruments into a coherent pattern, and this is precisely the kind of pattern for which Williams is searching.

1] *cacophony of birds:* This introduces the second crucial element in the poem, the world of natural objects the individuality of which must not be forfeited in the interests of the design.

4] *us all:* The third element is the world of human beings, whose individuality must not be sacrificed either.

9] This states a theme which is to be given a number of variations in the following lines. An order that does not deny the individuality of its component parts is one founded on the different operations of 'love': the sympathy that unites man to man; the empathetic response that involves man in nature; and the imaginative energy that gives organic unity to a work of art.

Section II (10–16)] This is the 'lento' movement, the slowness of which is a result of the prevalence of open vowels, the frequent pauses required by the syntax and punctuation and by the short feet, and the final emphasis of the spaced periods. All this is appropriate to a section which is almost prosaic in its statement of the problem.

Section III (17–23)] In this, the 'allegro' movement, the themes are developed with greater energy. Words swirl around, disappearing and reappearing, and it seems as impossible to pin them down as it is to pin down things for long.

Section IV (23–32)] The themes of the poem are stated again: but now instead of being stated in the abstract (as in 9) they are offered in experiential terms. The development is from an idea believed in theory to an idea proved on the pulses. This is achieved in two ways: first, by using metaphor rather than discursive argument to articulate the ideas; and second, by introducing an urgent personal element into the poem.

23] *tears:* This, and the reference to the heart in line 26, evokes one level of experience with which Williams is concerned, the level of personal relationships.

22–5] *dreams...memory...voices:* These images invoke the world of art, since as Williams sees it they are elements crucial to the writing of poetry (see Notes to 'The Descent').

25] *French horns:* These suggest both the 'assembled order' of music and the world of nature, horns being a traditional emblem of outdoor activity.

26] The personal note is introduced. The poet now feels the principle of love. Feeling it, he can understand its full nature. It is an 'innocent' and empathetic response to experience which must be renewed every day; and consequently the design it fosters must be reshaped every day as well. Each day must be like that 'first day' on which Adam gave names, and so a type of order, to the objects around him.

32] Paradoxically, each day must be like the last day too because the design it witnesses must die with it.

Section V (33–4)] This is the coda, in which the opposing terms of the poem are recapitulated: the birds whose 'twitter' introduced the problem posed by things, and the design created by love into which those birds are absorbed, and within which they may be said only fully to live.

A Negro Woman

Compare to 'Proletarian Portrait'. Notice how Williams uses metaphor here to capture the unique qualities of the woman; to keep our eyes on the object.

from *Asphodel, That Greeny Flower*

The poem from which these lines are taken is addressed to Williams' wife, Florence. In its clarity, expansiveness, and grace it is characteristic of the verse he wrote during his last years. The asphodel mentioned in the title acquires many associations as the poet meditates upon it, with love, with the imagination, and with memory: but it is always, first and last, a tangible, particular flower.

from *Pictures from Brueghel*

These two poems are from the title sequence in Williams' final collection. Towards the end of his life, although he continued to experiment with the 'variable foot', he also went back to the regularly stressed tercets and quatrains he had used in the forties (see Notes to 'The Night Rider') and even to the still 'freer' verse of his early years (see Notes to 'The Revelation'). There was a general sense of recapitulation, of the poet drawing on his hard-won achievements, as well as of fresh beginnings.

Poem I] This illustrates Williams' growing interest in art, and particularly painting, as a formative principle and as the product of the humane impulses in man. Williams had always been interested in painting, of course. Indeed, there is a strong connection between his own early verse and the experimental work he saw at the famous 'Armory Show' in New York, in 1913. But now his sympathies veered towards more traditional painters; and especially Pieter Brueghel whom he regarded as an artist like himself, whose primary concern was with the meaning of simple things and the pleasures of ordinary people.

Poem II] The contrast in the poem, and the painting by Brueghel it describes, is between the catastrophes taking place in the great world and the alternative of commitment to a few, cherished particulars; or between death and the continuing processes of life.

Marianne Moore

The Steeple-Jack

Marianne Moore's poems are founded on a belief in discipline, and the acceptance of boundaries. This acceptance is necessary, she suggests, for two, associated reasons: (i) because, in accepting limitations, the mind discovers a safeguard against danger. 'A good deal of her poetry', Randall Jarrell has pointed out, 'is...about armour,... protection, places to hide'; and it is so, probably, because Moore sees life in terms of risk – the threats our environment faces us with, the menace likely to overcome us if ever we should lose control. (ii) because, in accepting limitations, the mind also discovers fulfilment. Freedom and happiness, Moore suggests, are to be found only in the service of forms: the needs and restrictions of our natures, the scope of our particular world. To an extent, the second idea is a paradoxical one, and its paradoxes are registered for us in the actual patterns of her verse. For these, as another poet Charles Tomlinson has indicated, 'embody and reinforce by technical means our sense' of 'a world where spontaneity and order are not at odds and where the marriage between them results in "spiritual poise"'.

This particular poem at once illustrates the poise which Tomlinson is describing, and supports it. It illustrates it in the sense that it creates a small world; a limited space in which people like the steeple-jack can, according to their creator, enjoy as much freedom as they ever can. And it supports it in the sense that the world described here is, without pretence, a *fictional* one. What 'The Steeple Jack' offers for our inspection is an *idea* of order: a place, and a plainly imaginary place at that, which, in its special combination of the ordained and the haphazard, seems to provide the poet with her own special refuge.

1–6] The peculiar quality of Moore's verse, poised as it is between the controlled and the spontaneous, results from her use of the medieval device of 'rime-breaking'. The formal outlines are severe: the stanzas based on syllable count, the lines so arranged on the page as to repeat specific and often quite complicated patterns. But these 'strict proportions' are rendered much less strict by making the stanza, rather than the line, the basic unit. Rhymes are sparse, enjambement the rule, and the sense of run-on lines is redoubled by ending lines with unimportant words and hyphenations. There is a frequent use of internal rhyme, too, to break up the apparently formal pattern; and the pattern itself, which depends upon such extreme differences in length of line (e.g. nine syllables in line 5 of each stanza, three syllables in line 6), seems to participate in the liveliness of the material quite as much as to organise, or set it off.

1] *Dürer:* Albrecht Dürer (1471–1528), German painter and sculptor. The reference helps to establish the town as an imaginative construct, and to give it a certain order or regularity of outline. The reader beholds it, and more particularly the sea beside it, 'with all the strength and light of all he can remember of Dürer's water-etchings, formal and right as the scales on a fish' (R. P. Blackmur).

2] *eight stranded whales:* Gratuitously specific details such as this endow the town with a fairy-tale atmosphere, the qualities of a definitely imagined world.

5] *waves:* The sea is commonly a symbol of the hazards of life, and the unconscious, in Moore's verse. See, 'A Grave'.

10–13] Note the evocative use of rhythm here. The line seems to rise with the gulls, thanks largely to the anapaestic second foot; and then pause at the end of the stanza, half-questioningly, as the eye follows them out to sea.

13–16] The sea appears to change colour exactly as trees changed colour under the imagining eye of the artist Dürer.

17–22] Here, as elsewhere in the poem, Moore tries to capture the precise contours of things: not because, like Williams, she wished to be appropriated by them or live their life – but because she believed that, by observing an object lovingly, she could discover a significance *in* it which extended *beyond* it. 'Precision,' she said, 'economy of statement, logic employed to means that are disinterested, drawing and identifying, liberate…the imagination.' Characteristically, she regarded the discipline of close perception as a means to imaginative release.

31–5] Another important function of the catalogues, and rapturously observed details, in Moore's verse is to communicate mixed feelings of spontaneity and order. In one sense, the details are random, and so capture the haphazard abundance of the world: but in another they are, as the critic R. H. Pearce has suggested, clear proof of 'the poet's controlling presence'. This seemingly chaotic collection of objects is only there, we infer, because the poet has put them there, sifted them from observation and memory. Paradoxically, they affect us as arbitrary and yet quite as contrived as any part of this patently contrived poem.

36–9] The exotic, which exists outside the limits of this world, is rejected.

40–5] The limitations of the scene are emphasised again. Note that what seems to be excluded, above all, is danger: dangerous animals ('serpent', 'cobra') and emotions ('ambitions').

55–9] The steeple-jack may be dressed in a flamboyant colour, stand high above the town, and even seem to belong to the world of fiction: but he is not, after all, a hero, epic or exotic. He is an ordinary man, performing his duties with the minimum of fuss or wasted effort; devoted to his craft, and doing his best to avoid all the dangers he can during the course of his day. As such, he is the perfect embodiment of the values described by the town, and the poem.

63–7] The function of the town as refuge is emphasised.

64–73] The finely nerved energy of the diction here is characteristic. As a rule, Moore's language is precise but suggestive; controlled to the point of epigram, and yet full of surprises and fresh insights.

73] *at home:* in a restricted space, safe.

77–8] The gilded star, combining the homely and the heroic, is an apt symbol of the mind liberating itself by accepting its limitations.

No Swan So Fine

The conflict between art (the china swans) and life (the real swans) is discussed here, but no definite conclusion is reached. Instead, the poet adopts her familiar strategy of paradox to investigate particulars and probabilities while, eventually, leaving the case open. On one level, the poem says that art is superior to life. On another, the level of irony, it implies that life is superior to art. And on still another, it qualifies this qualification – by virtue of the fact that it is itself an art-work, and an extraordinarily refined one at that. It is proof positive that the artifice it *may* be disparaging *may* not be so bad, after all.

1–2] 'Percy Phillips, *New York Times Magazine*, May 10, 1931' (Moore's Note). Moore frequently uses quotations in this way, placing them in inverted commas and then identifying them in the Notes. 'I've always felt', she explained, 'that if a thing has been said in the very best way, how can you say it better? If I wanted to say something and somebody had said it ideally, then I'd take it but give the person credit for it.'

4] *gondoliering:* The gondolier moves his boat by paddling from the stern. Notice the ironic emphasis placed upon 'fine' at the end of the line.

7] 'A pair of Louis XV candelabra with Dresden figures of swans belonging to Lord Balfour' (Moore's Note). The live swans that once inhabited the 'dead fountains' at Versailles lead, by association, to the artificial swans – which may be alive, or dead, or neither.

9] The age of Louis XV (1715–74) was noted for the opulent and sometimes delicate style known as rococo.

14] 'The king is dead': This phrase collects the ambiguities of the poem together, without resolving them. From one angle, what it says is that King Louis XV and the rococo style his reign witnessed are both dead; that is, literally passed and done with and perhaps figuratively deadening and uninspiring as well. By extension, this may apply to all art, in all styles. From another angle, though, what the phrase does is to remind us of the proverbial saying from which it is taken ('The King is dead. Long live the King!'). and so registers the peculiar type of 'long life' enjoyed by art. Life changes, the implication is, actual swans come and go: but art continues, enjoying its own kind of 'resurrection' from one generation to the next.

The Frigate Pelican

'We must', Marianne Moore once said, 'have the courage of our peculiarities.' We must, in other words, fulfil the needs and accept the limitations of our natures. Here, in one of her many 'animal poems', she offers us an example of a creature who does exactly that. In her Notes, Moore acknowledges the influence of Audubon's portrait of 'Fregata aquila. The Frigate Pelican' upon this work.

2] *Rasselas's friend's project:* In chapter VI of *Rasselas* (1759) by Samuel Johnson, an artist is introduced who has invented wings for human beings to fly with. The description of the wings in line 3 is taken from this source.

4–6] Moore's aim is not to anthropomorphise animals in the way that Aesop does in his *Fables*. What she intends to do, rather, is to register their essential properties or 'hacceitas' (see the Notes on Williams); and then, only then, to try if possible to discover some meaning in these properties which extends beyond the animal to the human sphere. So in these opening lines, before she has done anything else, she insists on the bird's remoteness from man's special concerns. Man, apparently, has even found it difficult to find 'the proper word' for this creature, and may perhaps have misnamed him.

9–14] Besides being beyond the scope of human language, the frigate pelican is also beyond the reach of human standards of morality. For he lives in a way that we might well regard as makeshift and ruthless: by bullying other birds, and forcing them to surrender what they have caught.

19–20] The reference here is to the swan in the fairy-tale, 'Hansel and Gretel', who carried the two children home to their father. It at once emphasises the frigate pelican's independence (*he* would never serve human beings as this swan did); and involves an ironic dig at the age-old tendency to see animals in human terms.

20–2] Moore now emphasises the gap between bird and man ('a less / limber animal') by quoting some of the mottoes, or proverbial statements of value, which the latter has devised for himself. All of these mottoes offer a distinct contrast to the life-style of the frigate pelican; expressing respect as they do for thrift, industry, and a stern sense of social responsibility.

26–32] These lines announce the turn in the poem's argument. The frigate pelican may exist apart from human concerns: but in the very act of doing this he seems to offer us what John Crowe Ransom called 'an exemplum of right-ness and beauty'. His capacity for following the dictates of his own nature can be translated into *strictly human terms*, as it was by the composer Georg Friedrich Handel (1685–1759); who followed the path marked out by *his* own temperament without permitting himself to be distracted by either sentimentalities or trivia. So, paradoxically, the bird is 'like' the good man in being so 'unlike' him (and the apparent incongruity of the frigate pelican–Handel comparison merely serves to enforce the paradox).

36] *'Festina lente'* : 'Make haste slowly.' This is one motto which the frigate pelican does illustrate *in his own way*; instructing us to act deliberately and with caution.

37–9] *'If I do well...'* : 'Hindu saying' (Moore's Note). This is another motto which the frigate pelican may be taken to illustrate. The idea here is that we are blessed, automatically, by accepting the truths of our own natures.

39–40] This sentence describes two actions which are each in their different ways eminently simple and 'natural': the action of the moon rising, and the action of people watching the moon. The author's girlhood home lies just west of the Susquehanna river in Pennsylvania.

40–3] 'In his own way' the frigate pelican also behaves naturally, by flying home to sleep.

40–7] The meaning of these last lines seems to be that in accepting the dictates of our natures we find not only fulfilment (40–3) but safety; safety from the dangers within us (46) and around us (47).

Poetry

This is a critique of the derivative work of 'half poets', and a plea for the original and 'genuine'. These terms are defined in the course of the poem in a way characteristic of Moore: the initial idea is extended by metaphoric devices to a new dimension of wit, and expressed in language that is all sinew, severe and pure.

1–3] In a witty reversal, the critique of all poetry is suddenly limited to derivative poetry only.

8

4-5] The genuine is defined by analogy, using the signs of the emotional animal.

8] 'Useful' has a double function here. It mocks the purely aesthetic attitude to ·literature; and it supplies an example of Moore's characteristic mode of understatement – poetry is useful (or 'use-full') in the sense that all things necessary to the perpetuation of life are.

Notice the witty lengthening of the word 'unintelligible' achieved by placing it on its own.

11-15] As examples of the subjects of genuine poetry, these things are the reverse of 'high-sounding'.

17-18] In her Notes, Moore informs us that this is from *The Diaries of Leo Tolstoy* (New York, 1917): '...poetry is everything with the exception of business documents and school books'.

20-2] A fresh subject matter is not enough. A poet must imagine so exactly and astutely that he can 'see the visible at the focus of intelligence where sight and concept coincide and where it becomes transformed into the pure and total realism of ideas' (Morton Zabel). For another formulation of the same idea, see the Notes on 'The Steeple-Jack', lines 18-22.

21-2] This quotation, Moore's Note tells us, is from W. B. Yeats, *Ideas of Good and Evil* (London, 1903): 'The limitation of his [William Blake's] view was from the very intensity of his vision; he was a too literal realist of the imagination...' The phrase, as Moore uses it, signifies the ability to perceive a fact with such intensity as to translate it into a truth.

24] Invented by Moore, and placed in quotation marks for emphasis, this phrase offers a symbol for the aesthetic order, the arrangement of 'these phenomena' in a modifying structure and texture. Without this, the subject will not be assimilated into the poem and will acquire no new reality, while losing its original own. There will be no poem, in short, only a half-poem.

When I Buy Pictures

'The accuracy of the vernacular! It's enviable. That's the kind of thing I am interested in' (Moore). This poem, which assimilates a 'cultivated contemporary idiom, heightened...because set apart' (Blackmur) into its free verse rhythms, illustrates her interest. It offers us a different, more relaxed formulation of the ideas expressed in 'Poetry': about what is good in verse, or in art generally (the genuine, the precise, the simple), and what is bad (the pretentious, or derivative, the vague, the needlessly ornate).

1] As in several of Moore's other poems, the title is the opening line. This follows on from it.

2] *imaginary possessor:* Every one of Moore's poems could perhaps be described as an act of 'imaginary possession'; in which she perceives an object closely, and with reverence, and then attempts to absorb it – to grasp its significance in her mind.

12] *silver fence:* '"A silver fence was erected by Constantine to enclose the grave of Adam" *Literary Digest*, Jan. 5, 1948' (Moore's Note).

14] *disarm:* In this context, the word brings neatly together the idea of an artist trying to ingratiate himself with his audience, by injecting a false emotionalism into his work; and the idea of a soldier tricking his enemy out of his weapon. Sentimentality, it is implied, the surrender to any mawkish emotion, is one way of letting our defences slip.

17] Moore's Note informs us that this phrase, which so aptly describes her own work, is taken from A. P. Gordon, *The Poets of the Old Testament* (New York, 1936).

A Grave

This poem, like 'When I Buy Pictures', is written in free verse. Its subject is what the novelist Joseph Conrad called 'the destructive element': the sea, as an actual threat to man, and as a symbol of all the possible dangers which confront him during his life.

4] *you cannot stand in the middle:* Man cannot assume a central and controlling position vis-à-vis the ocean. He can only stand apart from it, trying to protect himself against its challenges as best he may.

5] *grave:* literally, and in the sense that it threatens the destruction of human plans.

6] The firs, standing in line, introduce a series of images describing man's feeble attempts to control the ocean, to see it as part of an ordered environment.

9–15] Moore here brings together the idea of the ocean as a grave, as a challenge to human ambition, and as a symbol of the unconscious – those hidden parts of the mind which man explores only cautiously, and at immense risk to himself.

16] *networks of foam:* This punning image, picking up the reference to 'nets' in line 13, continues the reference to man's organising tendencies.

20] *lighthouses...bell buoys:* other means man employs to control the ocean, or at least to avoid some of its hazards.

22] The ocean deprives man of will and consciousness. So, in a sense, do those malignant forces of life and subliminal processes of the mind which the ocean symbolises.

An Egyptian Pulled Glass Bottle in the Shape of a Fish

This is the perfect epitome of what William Carlos Williams meant when he called the typical Moore poem 'an anthology of transit...moving rapidly from one thing to the next' and thereby communicating 'the impression of a passage through...of...swiftness impaling beauty'. In a manner reminiscent of Imagist verse, the object mentioned in the title is associated with a series of sense-impressions, all of which are intended to help us discover it. To paraphrase two lines from 'When I Buy Pictures', the aim of the piece is to achieve an act of imaginative possession; to offer us some piercing glances into the life of the thing described.

1] *thirst:* a witty reference both to the function of the 'pulled glass bottle' and to the element in which the 'fish' imitated in the shape of the bottle lives.

3–4] Fact is translated into truth, and the object (fish, bottle) endowed with a permanent value – by the creator of the 'pulled glass bottle' and the creator of the poem alike.

To a Snail

This poem celebrates the snail, and the snail-like qualities of compression, caution, and guarded understatement which its own lines exemplify.

1] '"The very first grace of style is that which comes from compression." *Demetrius on Style*, translated by W. Hamilton Fyfe (London, 1932)' (Moore's Note).

2–3] Note the characteristic weaving together of concrete and abstract here (and in lines 10–12).

10] *absence of feet*: a witty reference to the snail and to Moore's own verse, in which the syllable is the measure rather than the metrical foot.

10–11] Here, as in *Poetry*, phrases invented by Moore are placed in quotation marks so as 'to impale their contents for close examination' (Blackmur).

12] *occipital*: of, or belonging to, the head. This is a reference both to the curious head of the snail; and to the idiosyncratic 'head' or mind of the poet.

What Are Years?

During the decade of the forties, Moore's verse tended to become less intricate. The juxtaposition of images was no longer so abrupt, the diction more straightforward, and words were rarely broken up to accommodate syllabic count or rhyme scheme. As a result, a subtle change of tone occurred, away from the cryptic, the visual and the witty, and towards the meditative, the accents and abstractions of quiet reasoning. This, the title poem from the 1941 collection, illustrates the development. In it Moore asks simply, what is life? What can give it purpose and direction? The answer she comes up with is the one offered in the earlier poems as well, but she never perhaps stated it quite so directly there. It is courage, she says, which can give meaning to life: the courage to accept our limitatons, and to work within them for fulfilment and joy.

2–3] Since man lives in a dangerous, a-moral environment, against which he has no natural protection, the notions of guilt and innocence are irrelevant. Good works offer no safety.

4] The only possible safety lies in courage: an inner armouring of the self which may compensate for man's innate defencelessness.

6] 'That' refers to 'courage', thus continuing the question about its origins which was asked in lines 3–4. The parenthesis of two-and-a-half lines, however, and the stress given to 'that' by placing it at the end of the line, makes lines 6–10 sound rather like a statement, answering the original question of the poem (i.e. 'What gives meaning to life?' 'Courage. *That* in misfortune ...' etc.).

10–18] The paradox contained in the idea of liberating oneself by accepting the boundaries of the human is expressed here in the image of the sea rising upon itself (15–18); in the ambiguity of 'accedes' (line 12, which means to assent to, but also suggests 'succeeds' and 'exceeds'); and in the balanced participles of 17–18.

20] *behaves*: Strictly speaking, the word means to conduct oneself. It is used here in the colloquial sense, of conducting oneself *well* and showing a proper respect for the decencies.

20–2] The image of the bird steeling itself to rise upward in song possibly reminds us that the strategy of the poem is to demonstrate its theme. It communicates intense feelings, of fulfilment and joy, by accepting the rigours of a meticulous verse-pattern.

26–7] The two lines encapsulate the paradox of the poem; the idea that only in accepting our humanity and mortality do we find a way of giving our lives some permanent meaning.

Melchior Vulpius

The immediate subject of this poem is Melchior Vulpius, a German composer principally of songs and hymns. Its real subject, however, is the creative process: the mysterious power a great artist feels within himself but which he is unable either to name or explain. The poem is typical of most of the later verse, written after the forties, in that it reproduces the abrupt transitions and the kaleidoscopic impressionism of the earlier work – although without being as cryptic, condensed, or as difficult to decipher as that earlier work sometimes is.

1] *contrapuntalist :* one skilled in the art of counterpoint.

8–9] *this mastery . . . :* '"And not only is the great artist mysterious to us but is that to himself. The nature of the power he feels is unknown to him, and yet he has acquired it and succeeds in directing it." Arsène Alexander, *Malvina Hoffman – Critique and Catalogue* (Paris, 1930)' (Moore's Note).

11] *Mouse-skin-bellows'-breath :* '"Bird in a Bush. . . The bird flies from stem to stem while he warbles. His lungs, as in all automatons, consist of tiny bellows constructed from mouse-skin." Danial Alain, *Réalités*, April 1957, p. 58' (Moore's Note). The idea here is that Vulpius, and other artists, 'sing' or compose almost automatically just as this bird does.

17] *antidoting death :* providing an antidote for and relief from the prospect of death.

Robinson Jeffers

Divinely Superfluous Beauty

Robinson Jeffers' aim was, as he once put it, to 'uncentre the human mind from itself'. He wanted his verse to break away from all the versions of experience which emphasised its exclusively human properties, and to rediscover our relationship with elemental Nature. Man, Jeffers insisted, must acknowledge the superior value of the instinctive life, of natural action, simplicity, and self-expression. He must try to imitate the rocks in their coldness and endurance, the hawks in their isolation, and all physical nature in its surrender to the wild, primeval levels of being. This necessarily meant a repudiation of traditional, humanistic philosophies in favour of what the poet liked to call 'Inhumanism'. It meant, he admitted, 'a shifting of emphasis and significance from man to not-man' with a consequent loss of those values which, for centuries, we have been taught to cherish – among them, reason and self-restraint, urbanity and decorum. But, Jeffers was quick to add, it also meant the recovery of an older freedom, aligning us with the peoples of primitive cultures; and an escape, too, from the involuted self-consciousness, the entanglements and dark internecine conflicts, which make our present world such a painful one.

This particular piece, from Jeffers' third volume, is divided into two almost equal parts. In the first part (1-7), the poet presents us with a vision of the spontaneous energy running through all natural things; and in the second (7-12) he expresses the desire to be identified with this energy, to become one with all that is 'divinely superfluous'.

1-6] The characteristic technique by which Jeffers expresses his philosophy of Inhumanism, here as in all of his shorter poems, involves an emphasis upon perspective. Human life is seen from an extreme distance, placed within the larger dimensions of the mountains, the sea and the sky. The poet-philosopher who speaks in these pieces helps to place the subject as well, for his voice, primitive and oracular, seems to align him with the older freedoms he is celebrating. This is largely the result of the style Jeffers developed from his third volume on, in which the tones of colloquial speech are reproduced without weakening formal control of the line. Of great flexibility, hovering somewhere between free verse and iambic pentameter, the rhythms are precise and emphatic without being regular. Together with the unelaborate syntax, and comparatively simple diction, they help to give to the poems a feeling of rugged exactitude; to communicate 'power and reality..., substance and sense' (Jeffers).

3-7] Notice how the beauty of the earth is associated with power or the 'life-force'. It is conceived of as an activity, and an essentially amoral and irrational activity at that: it is 'divinely superfluous' and has no use for purely human notions of economy.

7-12] The perception of natural beauty flows uninterrupted, in line 7, into an expression of the desire to merge with it. This desire means more to the poet, apparently, than the love for any human being could.

To the Stone-Cutters

This plays a characteristic variation on the ancient theme of the conquest of Time by Art. Both the stone-cutters and the poet who describes them are trying to defy time, to achieve a kind of permanence through their creations, and to some extent they are admired for this. Admired though they may be, however, they are clearly being mocked as well, for ever supposing that their work can equal the rocks and hills in its enduring power; or that they themselves can properly escape from the pain of being men and the plight of being mortal. They are cut off from Nature by their own natures, their art is bound by the fact that it is a specifically human product, and no amount of effort on their part can ever alter this.

This second point needs emphasising because it accounts for the tension in most of Jeffers' verse, and not just in this poem. Jeffers may long to identify himself with 'divinely superfluous beauty' but usually he remains aware that complete identification is impossible. The simple fact, which he must acknowledge, is that human beings cannot rid themselves of their humanity. They must remain caught between the demands of their instincts and the requirements of their consciousness and, caught there, their lives become the stuff of poetry (and, sometimes, they themselves become poets).

1] This poem was written while Tor House was being built.

6] *mockingly*: The mockery is directed against time, which he is trying to defy; and himself, for ever supposing that he can defy time completely.

Continent's End

The scene is a familiar one in Jeffers' poetry. The poet-philosopher stands on the Californian coast-line, watching the Pacific Ocean. As he watches, and meditates, it occurs to him (i) that the sea represents a form of life much older than human history – a form from which human beings, in the progressive stages of their development, have moved ever further away; and (ii) that within man, nevertheless, lie ways of being and knowing which antedate even the sea. Both man and the ocean, he recognises, evolved out of 'tides of fire', the primeval chaos which preceded the universe as we now know it; and both contain within them still a few traces of their origins.

1] *equinox*: the time at which the sun crosses the equator and day and night are equal. The reference here is to the vernal equinox.

5] *Aleutian*: the Aleutian Islands, off the coast of Alaska.

7] *long migrations*: the westward movement of civilisation. This, and the poem's title refer us to Jeffers' belief that the West Coast of America, and 'the final Pacific', represent 'the world's end'. With the conquest of the American continent, he argued, *human* history was over; although, of course, cosmic history would continue.

8] *the womb*: the sea, from which came the earliest forms of organic life.

15] This describes beautifully one of the major aims of Jeffers' line, which was to reproduce the pulse of the sea, the movements of the blood.

from *Roan Stallion*

'*Roan Stallion* originated from an abandoned cabin that we discovered in a roadless hollow of the hills. When later we asked about its history no one was able to tell us anything except that the place had been abandoned ever since its owner was killed by a stallion...the Indian woman and her white husband [were] real persons whom I had often seen driving through our village in a ramshackle buggy. The episode of the woman swimming her horse through a storm-swollen ford at night...was part of her actual history' (Jeffers).

This poem, with its origins in local character and events, has the suggestive possibilities of myth. Like many of Jeffers' longer narratives it belongs at once to a particular place and people and to the world of common human experience. Its central action suggests its larger dimensions; when the heroine rides a stallion by moonlight to the hilltop, and there falls upon the ground prostrating herself beneath his hooves. Reading this in context, we cannot help being reminded of one of the most persistent of ancient legends, in which a god comes to a woman in the shape of a beast, and there is sexual contact between them. It recalls, for example, the stories of Leda and the swan; Europa, who was carried away by Zeus in the form of a bull; and Hippodamia, who on the day of her marriage was violated by the great centaur, the stallion Eurytion. This, in turn, encourages us to see the entire narrative as a symbolic one, with several possible meanings:

(i) The name of the heroine, California, and the fact that she is one quarter Indian, one quarter Spanish, and one half Anglo-Saxon, alerts us to one possibility: that the poem is a myth of the American West. According to this reading, California represents a new land and a new breed of people; and her moment of communion with the horse suggests the close contact with Nature which that land and those people can enjoy. Jeffers said as much elsewhere: 'the Monterey mountains', he declared, were the only place where he ever found 'people living...essentially as they did in the Idyls or the Sagas, or in Homer's Ithaca. Here was life purged of its ephemeral accretions. Here was contemporary life that was also permanent life...'

(ii) A second possibility, closely related to the first, is that the poem represents a kind of racial myth which has as its subject myths and the mythologising process in general. Jeffers presents us with a legendary union between a mortal woman and a god in the shape of a beast, and then proceeds to explain to us why, since the beginning of time, man has created such legends. This reading is supported by lines 194–5, which connect the central incident with other mythical annunciations; and every one of these, in turn, with

> ...the phantom rulers of humanity
>
> That without being are yet more real than what they are born of, and without
>
> shape, shape that which makes them.

All of these stories, the poet is telling us, exist because we need them. They serve to remind us of the power and glory latent in ourselves, which we share with the elements; and which can only find a partial expression in the lives that we lead, the societies we build.

(iii) This leads us to the third, and most important, level of meaning in the poem. Above all, 'Roan Stallion' is about the gospel of 'Inhumanism'. The stallion figures the power of Nature just as the creatures in 'Divinely Superfluous Beauty' do; and in surrendering to it, the woman momentarily identifies herself with that power, just as Jeffers had always longed to.

The poem is divided into three sections, or movements. The version given here is slightly abridged.

Section I (1–93)] In this opening movement, we are told about California's journey to Monterey on Christmas Eve, to buy the presents for her daughter which her husband has forgotten. On her way home she has to ford a stream swollen by the floods. Her mare is frightened, and so she climbs upon its back to force it across.

1–2] Notice how the longer line gives a sense of expansiveness to the poem; a movement, somewhere between that of the speaking and that of the chanting voice, which serves to remind us of the origins of verse.

8] *bucksin mare:* a horse the yellow-grey colour of tanned buckskin.

10–17] The husband represents all that is worst in humanity; all that prompts California to turn from man to the beast-god of Nature. Notice how cryptic the conversation of husband and wife is: their language seems to belong to the early ages of the race, just as their lives do.

18] *Monterey:* a town situated about five miles to the north of Carmel, the setting for most of the poem.

26] *Carmel Valley:* a valley, reaching towards the sea, near Carmel.

48–51] California imagines that the water and the stallion are one. This vision of a 'water-stallion', figuring the power of elemental Nature, prepares us for the principal events of the story. It also has several legendary associations. It recalls, for example, the stories of Poseidon, the sea-god who created the first horse; of Poseidon's union with Medusa, which produced the winged horse, Pegasus; and of Pegasus, who was befriended by the water nymphs.

64–72] Primitive myth and Christianity are mingled in California's second vision, just as they are in the folklore of the Spanish-American peoples.

64] *little Jesus:* Jesus Christ was himself born of the union between a mortal woman and an immortal deity.

68] *a noise of wing-feathers:* This is a reference to the legend of Leda and the swan. Jupiter visited Leda in the shape of a swan, begetting upon her Helen of Troy, and the twins Castor and Pollux.

69] *birds' heads, hawks' heads:* These angels are appropriately wild heralds of the union with Nature that California is about to achieve. They are also reminiscent of certain deities worshipped by the Indians of the Southwest and Central America.

71] *snake with golden eyes:* the serpent in Eden (*Genesis* 3), and the snake gods of the Southwestern Indians. This, like the reference to angels with heads like birds, associates the 'religious' dimension of this poem with the primitive worship of Nature; and emphasises Jeffers' profound disagreement with anthropomorphic religions such as Christianity.

80–90] Climbing on the back of the mare, California becomes identified with her mount: a 'horse-woman', and therefore an appropriate mate for a 'horse-god'. Immersing herself in the water, she is meeting and mingling with the 'water-stallion', *and* undergoing a kind of baptism into the religion of Nature.

83] *Cataracts of light and Latin singing:* The vision includes the memory of the sights and sounds of the Church: the light streaming through the windows, the singing of the Latin mass.

Section II (93–205)] The second movement is concerned with the central incident of the poem: the ride by moonlight, and the moment of surrender to the horse.

110] The Annunciation is frequently represented, in paintings, in similar terms, with the Holy Ghost appearing to the Virgin as a flood of light.

126–36] These lines are a clear statement of the philosophy of Inhumanism: the idea that man must try, somehow, to break out of the limits of his humanity and re-discover his identity with the elements. There are many routes, Jeffers suggests, leading us to momentary glimpses of a possible release; among them the routes of poetry and vision, of knowledge and passion. Each one of these reminds us that God is certainly not like humanity and 'hardly a friend' to it either – that, in effect, Nature has nothing in common with man at all.

128] *The atom to be split:* At the time when this poem was written, the possibility of splitting the atom had been recognised. The metaphor combines an acknowledgement of the violence and difficulty involved in breaking away from humanity, with belief in the raw power which might thereby be released.

Tragedy: Jeffers saw the tragic poet as a person who, by recognising the problem and attacking it, might help us to 'break away': 'I think one of the most common intentions in tragic stories', he said, 'is to build up the strain for the sake of the explosion of its release – like winding up a ballista.'

130] *Slit eyes in the mask:* openings, ways of seeing through the mask of our humanity.

133] *He:* i.e. God.

171] *the silent calvary:* The Latin word, *calvaria*, means a skull. 'Calvary' is the hill on which Christ was crucified. Notice how the lines immediately prior to this capture, in their rhythms, the pounding movements of the horse and the growing excitement of the woman.

176] *world's end:* See the Notes on 'Continent's End', line 7. This also picks up the implied reference to the Crucifixion, in line 171, and the reference to the woman leaving her 'world' (i.e. the boundaries of her farm, the limits of normal consciousness) in line 164.

179] The stallion is now identified with the 'possible God' described in lines 194–7; and with the 'possible God' of Calvary (compare 104, 110).

184-93] This, the pivot of the narrative, describes the instant in which the human shell is momentarily broken. It is Jeffers' own equivalent of a mystical experience, transcending reason and illuminating all that surrounds it. In the first five lines, the poet uses the metaphor of the stone to suggest that a rapprochement between man and nature is occurring (California's "small dark head" is compared to a "small round stone"); that a gulf, nevertheless, continues to exist between them (the head, unlike a stone, is said to be full of the 'lightning' of self-consciousness); and that still more effort is therefore required to bridge the gulf and turn rapprochement into union (for 'lightning' could also refer to the power generated in the struggle to escape from self-consciousness). Then, in lines 190–3, union *does* occur. Reverting to the imagery of science, Jeffers tells us that the atom *is* finally split; and for a brief enchanted moment man assumes the status of 'not-man'.

191] *microcosm:* This refers us to the ancient idea that man, the microcosm, is an infinitely small reproduction of the world, or 'macrocosm'. Here, the two become one.

193-202] See the introductory Notes to this poem.

202-5] The mystical experience ends with a vision which brings together the figure of the beast-god; the numerous references to the deities of the water and the air; and the complex images of stones, fire, and lightning.

Section III (206-54)] The poem ends with three deaths. California is pursued by her husband to the corral; and there she watches him, caught by the stallion, being trampled to death. She does not intervene to save him. On the contrary, she contributes to his death by killing the guard-dog which rushes to his defence. But, then, when he *is* dead, she suddenly turns on the stallion and shoots *him*.

222] The woman is pursued like an animal. Notice how many times men are compared to animals in this poem.

250-3] The woman has achieved a momentary identification with Nature: but that has not purged her, completely, of her human nature. She has discovered new allegiances, but she has not rid herself entirely of her old ones – and perhaps never can (see the introductory Notes to 'To the Stone-Cutters'). So having once known her 'god', and realised a communion with him; she then betrays him, almost despite herself, by killing him.

253-4] The sense of an imperfect union, and of consequent betrayal, is emphasised in these closing lines by the implicit references to the historic

betrayal of the Crucifixion. California fires her gun three times, just as St
Peter denied Jesus three times (*John*, 13, xxxviii); and after she has killed
the stallion she smells the spilled wine, emblem of the spilled, sacramental
blood of Christ.

Hurt Hawks

In describing the deaths of two birds, the poet presents us with two concrete
illustrations – of what men should think about dying, and how they should
die. The hawk, as a symbol of pride, courage, and isolation, appears frequently in Jeffers' verse.

1–2] The arrogance of the hawk, his pride even in death, is suggested here
by the imagery of empire and battle. Like 'a broken pillar', the hawk's broken
wing still serves as a reminder of former glory; like 'a banner in defeat', it
trails with a certain mad defiance.

11] *death the redeemer:* Jeffers often uses Christian figures or terminology to
emphasise his own status as heretic. This phrase, for example, depends for
its power upon our recognising how it reverses an orthodox idea: instead of
looking for a means of redemption *from* death, the poet describes *death itself*
as a redemption. Compare line 7.

13–19] Compare the description of 'God' in 'Roan Stallion', lines 194–7.

15] *communal people:* people who huddle together in a mass, unlike the
lonely hawk.

18] The *intellectual* basis or raison d'être of this line is suggested by something that Jeffers wrote about death later. 'I believe', he said, 'that the universe is one being, all its parts are different expressions of the same energy...
The parts change and pass, or die, people and races and rocks and stars;
none of them seems to me important in itself, but only the whole.' Jeffers
regarded death, in other words, or at least tried to regard death, as natural
– almost to be welcomed, as part of a larger process. That does not mean, of
course, that he thought we should actively invite death or accelerate the
process: he is not to be taken too literally here. The *emotional* or *rhetorical*
raison d'être of the line, in fact, is not so much to inform us as to outrage us.
What it says is less important than what it does; which is to make us feel
just how negligible death must be, for the poet-philosopher, if he can even
think of making a declaration such as this.

24] *lead gift:* a bullet.

24–7] At first the movement of these lines is relaxed, their rhythms languid,
the figures rank with suggestions of softness, effeminacy, and collapse. Then,
abruptly, as Jeffers describes the final 'fierce rush' of the bird into the air,
the rhythms become more driving and angular, and the metaphors begin
to express a quite aggressive masculinity. The end, the poet-philosopher
shows us, is at once a dying away, to be accepted; and an affirmation of
sustained growth or renewal to be defiantly, even joyfully, embraced.

The Eye

'Inhumanism', Jeffers claimed, 'is neither misanthropic nor pessimistic...
It...is a means of maintaining sanity in slippery times. It offers a reasonable
detachment as a rule of conduct...and satisfies our need to admire greatness
and rejoice in beauty.' This poem, written during the Second World War,

is an illustration of what he meant: the timelessness of the earth here offers the poet a source of peace, the recognition that within the context of universal history the pain of human history is negligible.

2] *old garden:* a reference to the myth of Eden, and to the idea that the Mediterranean area was the cradle of civilisation.

6] *brave dwarfs:* the Japanese.

My Burial Place

As this and the preceding poem indicate, there is a distinct shift of emphasis in Jeffers' later verse, away from the tragic and towards the mystical. The sense of an inescapable conflict between Nature and human nature becomes of less concern; and Jeffers concentrates instead on the possibility of union. Of course, the idea or even the fact of union is often present in the earliest work, but there it is normally qualified by a recognition of the needs and limits of the human character. In the work of Jeffers' last years, by contrast, this recognition tends to lose its power, and the poet is consequently left freer to contemplate those moments in which, as he once put it, there is 'no passion but peace'. The separateness and intrinsic pefection of the mystical experience becomes the principal subject of his reveries; or, as in this poem, the severe and immaculate instant of death.

8] *necropolis:* a cemetery.

9] *columbarium:* a building with tiers of niches for cinerary urns.

John Crowe Ransom
Winter Remembered

'To an astonishing degree, the problems which engage Ransom's attention turn out to be aspects of one situation; that of man's divided sensibility... The desperation of Ransom's characters springs finally from the fact that they cannot attain unity of being' (Cleanth Brooks). In this poem, the narrator represents the characteristic inability Brooks is referring to. Separated off from his beloved, he comes to typify the sense of fragmentation, estrangement, and sheer vacuum which all those who have failed to achieve wholeness must experience. His particular feeling of 'absence', in other words, charts out a more general situation of emptiness and loss.

2] Note how the alliterated 'l' sounds and long vowels give a mournful, elongated effect to this line.

4] *winter:* This, and the other images of cold in the poem, act as a physical equivalent of 'absence', and contrast effectively with the metaphors of heat which describe all the narrator has lost – passion, and the warmth of a full and developing life.

10] Note how the rhythm falters here, as the lover meditates on what he *might* do.

20] *Ten frozen parsnips:* This mundane image, contrasting sharply with the romantic framework of the rest of the poem, brings together the conflicting figures of heat and cold: the 'parsnips', capable normally of warmth and growth, have been frozen into lifelessness just as, in a way, the poet and his limbs have. The particular tone or attitude inspired toward the subject by this comparison is characteristic of Ransom, and has been variously described as one of 'acid gaiety' (Mark Van Doren) or 'wrinkled laughter'

(Christopher Morley), as 'ambiguous and unhappy' (Yvor Winters) or 'detached, mock-pedantic, wittily complicated' (Randall Jarrell). Perhaps the best description is Ransom's own. For when he referred to that 'irony' which, by combining the dream of the ideal with the dismay of the actual, becomes 'the rarest of the states of mind, because...the most inclusive', he was implicitly describing the tone of his own work. In these last two lines, in fact, the poet himself seems to step forward, to establish the kind of 'mellow wisdom' (Ransom), or ironic inclusiveness of vision, of which the narrator-lover himself is incapable.

Dead Boy

This is characteristic of many of Ransom's poems in that it demonstrates a series of antithetical responses to one event. The different responses, suggested by radical alterations of diction, metaphor, and rhythm, do not belong to different people but to one complex personality, that of the poet, who can love the dead boy and yet recognise his frailty; regret his death but know that his world was doomed in any case; realise the 'poor pretense' involved in the talk of 'forebears' and in the funeral rites, while still acknowledging the value of the beliefs, in tradition and ceremony, thus illustrated. So Ransom effectively dramatises here that 'unity of being', or marriage of thought and feeling, which the narrator-lover of 'Winter Remembered' so conspicuously lacks.

1–3] The orotund, Latinate diction ('subtraction'), and the elevated image in the second line, suggest one reaction to death, which is to distance it with the help of ceremonious language and gesture.

4] Phrases like 'outer dark', 'black cloud full of storms' (6), and 'first-fruits' (18), echo the King James version of the Bible and place the death within a larger, religious context where it is seen as part of a universal process.

9] The dismissive image, the staccato movement of the line, the heavy emphases and harsh alliteration, represent the intrusion of a more realistic assessment.

13] *box of death:* compare the mundane particularity of this with the grandiose phrases borrowed from the Bible.

15] *bruit:* noise. Archaisms like this, derived from the Latin, offer an extreme contrast with such colloquialisms as 'cookies' (10) as well as such terse Anglo-Saxon derived words as 'wrenched' (19).

16] Compare the mellifluous alliteration and movement of this with, for example, the harshness of line 9.

Bells for John Whiteside's Daughter

Death, Ransom said, is 'the greatest subject of poetry, the most serious subject,...there's no recourse from death, except that we learn to face it'. The death to be faced here is, again, the death of a child and the facing of it leads the poet to consider one of his favourite themes; that, in a fragmented society such as our own, only the child's world is whole. Only this world does not suffer from dissociation, and a consequent feeling of spiritual loss; and even so it presents a less than satisfying possibility because it is innocent, limited, and frail. It must be destroyed eventually, either by the process of growing up or, as here, by a much sterner enemy still.

1–4] Note the carefully wrought syntax of the poem. The opening and closing stanzas, establishing the context (of death) within which the child's world is observed, form two separate, self-contained, and quite cryptic syntactical units. The middle three stanzas, which describe this world directly, form on the contrary one long continuous unit; so producing a mood appropriate to the subject, of decorous breathlessness.

1–2] *little...lightness*: These and similar words help establish the frailty of the child's world.

3] *brown study*: a bad mood. The idea here, an appropriately ironic and elliptical one, is that the death of the little girl has breached the decorum, or radically limited order, of the world described in stanzas 2–4 – just as a fit of sulks would. 'Brown' contrasts with the vivid, primary colours in which that world is painted.

5] *bruited*: an archaic term for making a noise. The archaisms also help to place the childhood world for us, to make us see it as quite as ordered and limited as any society governed by a repressive code of manners would be.

12] Even the geese are so refined that they do not honk, but cry out like well-mannered young ladies.

15] *noon apple-dreams*: This is symptomatic of Ransom's tendency to associate the world of the child with Eden: a place of perfect innocence, which is viewed with a certain wistfulness and nostalgia perhaps, but also with a firm sense of its restrictions.

20] *primly propped*: The phrase almost summarises the experience of the poem. 'Primly' recalls all the decorous associations that the child's world inspires: its refinement, grace, and its insularity. 'Propped', rhyming harshly with 'stopped' *and* contrasting with such archaisms as 'bruited' and 'harried' (8), reminds us of what has destroyed this world. Joined together by alliteration but quite separate in their terms of reference, the two words suggest the mixture of sympathy and shrewd knowingness (or what Ransom called the tone of 'tragic irony') with the help of which the death of the little girl is placed.

Parting at Dawn

Like 'Winter Remembered' this sonnet is about that ancient theme, the transience of love: by extension, it is also about the experience of fragmentation and emptiness. The lovers described here, parting in the morning light, are possessed by a feeling of 'absence in the heart', a sense of profound spiritual loss for which the poet can offer them only the coldest of possible compensation.

3] *white*: used here, and often in Ransom's verse, as a metaphor for withdrawal and depletion.

4] The dawn, associated with the moment of loss, teaches men how to suffer and, by inference, how to be stoical.

8] *cenobite*: a member of a monastic community. This continues the idea of depletion, the loss incurred by the lovers as they part, developed in the preceding seven lines.

9–11] Having elevated the lovers above the ordinary world, the poet abruptly brings them back to that world now: the realm of 'wars and wounds' and suffering from which their love no longer protects them.

12] *Lethe:* the river of forgetfulness in classical myth. Returning to the exalted world of the lovers for a moment, the poet recovers a more exalted language; which nevertheless has acquired a slightly ironic tinge now, because of the preceding lines.

13] *effacement:* i.e. of the memory of their love.

Blue Girls

The process of ageing which is the subject of this poem is, like the transience of love and the reality of death, a recurrent theme in Ransom's verse. One reason for this has to do with the 'base of ideas' that Ransom apparently needed, and thought out, 'before his imagination could freely explore his forms and subjects' (John Stewart). The human personality, he believed, is dual; composed of the reason and the sensibility. The reason man employs to understand experience, to discover the universal patterns latent in his world and then use them. The sensibility, on the other hand, enables man to enjoy experience, the fine qualities of particulars, including all those which cannot be absorbed into any pattern formulated by the rational element *and thereby controlled.* In more traditional societies, where man is whole, these two faculties (Ransom thought) hold equal sway. In our society, however, reason has become dominant and man has consequently acquired an exaggerated idea of his own power: he assumes that he, and his idealistic programmes, can rule the world. One thing Ransom is trying to do in his poetry, therefore, is dwell on precisely those aspects of experience which deny this assumption: death, the passing of time, the imminence of old age. By emphasising these, as well as by imitating in the texture of his verse the dualistic character of all life, he is offering what is in part a corrective to his own fragmented times -- an argument in cautious praise of humility.

1–8] Note how the light, tripping movement of these lines, spun forward by the participles and the light 't' and 'w' alliteration, make the verse imitate the actions described.

5–8] The simple but vivid imagery evoking the gaiety and vitality of the girls ('white', 'bluebirds', 'blue' in 1) is contrasted with the figures of the teachers 'old and contrary' (3) looming behind them like the seminary towers.

9] *Practise:* This word, suggesting the effort and even artifice required to retain vitality, marks a turning-point in the poem, which is further emphasised by the 'fail'–'frail' rhyme. The poet, himself another 'old and contrary' teacher, comes forward to remind the girls of transience.

12] Note the appropriate sense of a dying fall produced by this short, monosyllabic line.

14–17] The two movements of the poem coalesce in these lines. The lady described here offers a reminder that age must overtake the girls, and so a warning that they should not value their loveliness too highly. She is, however, praised for being even lovelier, once, than they are now: so it is clear the poet is not dismissing the idea of beauty entirely. Beauty is a quality seen critically, or rather one that is placed in 'the sad and wistful perspective of [its] inevitable disappearance' (Stewart): but it is still clearly admired, even cherished. The aim of the poet is to *qualify* our notions of our own power and importance – but not, at all, to destroy them.

Captain Carpenter

The tale of Captain Carpenter is in a sense a parody of chivalric romance, illustrating the suffering that idealism and an exaggerated notion of one's own importance can bring upon themselves. It is told with typically inclusive irony, which enables us to pity the Captain – and even admire him in a certain bewildered way – even while we are laughing at his presumption and innocence.

4] *rout:* a large evening party. There is a characteristic interplay in the poem between archaisms such as this, which are used in a light, almost mincing fashion, and aggressively colloquial terms like 'bitch' in line 24.

5–8] Note the ironic distance here between the violence of the action described and the decorum of tone and language.

12] *prologue:* The jarring half-rhyme produced by this word is wholly unexpected, after the precision and euphony of the previous rhymes.

15] *shinny part:* a self-consciously 'poetic' way of saying 'shin'. A nice contrast is established here between the preciosity of this phrase and the virulent plainness of the next line.

23] *should:* i.e. according to all the 'laws' of romance.

  hind: a deer.

29] *roan:* see the Notes to 'Roan Stallion' by Robinson Jeffers.

43] *mien:* an archaic term for appearance.

48] *alack:* This stylised expression of regret jars effectively with the Captain's far from stylish appearance.

55] *enow:* an archaic term for enough. The irony is that, for all the multiplicity of the rules mentioned here, the Captain was clearly a 'half-man' (Ransom): so dependent upon a single, isolated part of himself, his reason (see the Notes to 'Blue Girls'), that his dismemberment comes to assume symbolic proportions (i.e. he is 'fragmented' literally by the end of the poem, just as he was 'fragmented' in a moral sense at the beginning).

57–64] Note the interplay between pity and laughter here: the seriousness of the curse is qualified by the details of the Captain's end, so macabre as to approach the absurd. As is usual in Ransom's poems, the reader is being offered a double vision of the event, the doubleness of which must act as our standard of judgement (see the Notes to 'Dead Boy').

64] *kites:* birds of prey.

  clack clack: This phrase, imitating the sound the kites make, is at once chilling and comic – like the tale it completes.

Vision by Sweetwater

'Ransom's poems...are limited to retrospection. Their subjects do not move; their emotions are over. They...are...elegaic and ruminative...' (Donald Stauffer). This piece, which describes a premonition of death experienced during childhood, illustrates exactly what Stauffer meant.

7] *if:* as if.

Antique Harvesters

Usually Ransom depends upon the *style* of his verse to dramatise his positives for us; the style describes the complex personality of the narrator, and that personality in turn defines the kind of unified sensibility of which the *subjects* of the poems seem incapable. In just a few poems, however, he attempts to be more explicit. This is the case in 'Antique Harvesters', in which his own native region is presented as a place where wholeness of being is still available. The poem is not simply intended as a factual account of the South. What Ransom is trying to do, rather, is to develop and extend certain possibilities he finds there so as to create out of them a realm of myth: an ideal world of the imagination by which our own circumstances can be judged and accurately criticised.

1] The poem is set in autumn: a season which, as in Keats' 'Ode to Autumn', reminds man of his mortality but also permits him to see that mortality as part of a general cycle of growth and decay.

2] *what...produce?*: Autumn offers a moment of pause, also, an opportunity for man to consider his 'harvest', material and spiritual.

3–4] One thing reaped from the land is suggested here: patience, the mildness of old men who are as 'dry' and 'spare' as the earth they love.

7] *raven's...wing*: This implies something else offered by the land: an intimation of death and human limits.

13–17] These lines introduce yet another thing yielded by the land, which is the sense of a usable past and a perpetuated life-style; in other words, tradition.

17] The metaphor of the hunt here prepares us for the subsequent description of the hunters.

19–22] With the eruption of the hunters, a new sense of ceremony enters the description.

20–1] Notice how the more romantic associations inspired by this portrait are qualified by such mundane details as 'lank' and 'straddled'. This is characteristic of the entire poem (including its title): an equilibrium is maintained throughout between high rhetoric and the colloquial, a sense of the ritualistic and an acceptance of the commonplace.

25] The sense of ceremony is carried over into the description of the harvesters, who are asked to 'resume' as if they too were participants in a ritual.

26] *the Lady*: the earth, and by extension the South as conceived of in this poem. The word contains overtones of earthly love and religious veneration such as are found in chivalric romance.

28] The line, uniting men and land, effectively continues the sense of mortality and of an underlying seasonal rhythm introduced earlier.

31–2] Note how the rhythm here enacts the meaning.

33–6] The human and seasonal cycles are juxtaposed in these lines, where the old men watch the young harvesters at work in the autumn landscape.

43–8] The closing lines are a triumphant illustration, both of the scope of Ransom's dualism and of that ideal state of unity in which opposites are reconciled. They affirm the dignity of the antique harvesters, the sense of decorum with which their involvement in the land is accepted; and yet they **do** so without rejecting the original recognition of the facts in the case of the agricultural labourer or in the case of any man destined to work and then die. Here, in this special kingdom, the ceremonious and mundane levels of experience are brought together; and life transformed into ritual by the achievement of exactly that wholeness of being which eludes most of Ransom's other characters.

Painted Head

Of the small number of poems Ransom has published since 1927, most are written in unrhymed stanzas and, although nominally regular in metrics, turn out in practice to be quite loose and flexible. There are other developments in this later work as well, including a more severely economical use of language and syntax and a tighter, more elliptical and metaphysical, imagery: but despite all this the subject remains much the same. The 'mind divided within itself' (Ransom) is a major preoccupation just as it was in the earlier work, and so too is the possibility of a state in which such divisions are reconciled. In this poem, for example, these familiar subjects are approached via a meditation on a portrait. The portrait is of a head; and by a series of daring conceits it comes to figure for the narrator a tendency, which he finds everywhere, to depend far too much upon abstractions – to use the theorems devised by the mind to explain away the complexities of experience.

1] *apparition*: an appearance, especially of a startling or ghostly kind.

2] *capital*: a pun on the Latin root word, *caput*, meaning 'head'.

3] *Platonic*: Plato (c. 429–347), the idealist philosopher, is the subject of repeated criticism in Ransom's verse because of what Ransom saw as his habitual retreat into abstractions.

4] Note how the end-words in this stanza ('head', 'no', 'head', 'nothing') emphasise Ransom's belief that the reason divorced from the sensibility offers us only a vacuous interpretation of experience.

7] *decapitation*: the removal of the head from the body. The associations of treason and death which the word normally carries are not irrelevant here.

8] *body bush*: The idea of flowering and fertility associated with the body and concrete experience is to be developed in subsequent lines.

9–12] This head, the narrator suggests, seems too happy to be classed with the heads described in preceding lines. It is the head, perhaps, of a man of thirty who has never sought escape from 'the world's body' (Ransom).

12] *faithful stem*: the body. Compare line 8.

15] *tart*: sharp, acrimonious.

17–20] Since this particular head has never actually been allowed to separate itself from the body, it seems a nicely ironic touch of the artist to remove it from there in his portrait.

18] *this once head*: i.e. the actual head, that existed once, of which the painted head is an imitation.

19] *capital*: superb. This is another pun on *caput*.

21–4] The particular ironies contained in the portrait (and poem) force those whose minds have ignored their bodies, and ordinary concrete experience, to realise their mistake; a mistake which is in any case obvious from the self-destructive consequences of 'decapitation'.

22–4] In an elaborate conceit, the process of separating the reason from the sensibility is compared to the process of dipping an egg in vinegar so as to preserve it as a hard, 'deathlike' object. A pun on the colloquial term 'egg-head', meaning an intellectual, is also implied.

25–9] The portrait illustrates a further point for us; that reason and sensibility, head and body, are inseparable parts of the same process. Without the *two* of them, there can be neither wholeness nor beauty.

29–36] It has been argued that the details included in these lines have a specific, allegorical meaning: with 'big blue birds' referring to the eyes, 'sea shell flats' to the ears, and so on. What is more probable, however, is that Ransom is attempting an imagistic portrait here, of the process whereby the dry, hard world of the mind is charged into life by the operations of the sensibility. The language is *suggestive* rather than denotative, appealing to the senses and the imagination more than to the reason; and as such, it passes its own implicit comment on the limitations that reason is heir to.

E. E. Cummings

in *Just-*

The goal directing Cummings' poetry is the goal of freedom and self-expression; he belongs to a tradition of extreme individualism which dates back at least as far as Ralph Waldo Emerson and Thoreau. 'To be nobody-but-yourself,' as he once put it, 'in a world which is doing its best, night and day, to make you everybody else – means to fight the hardest battle which any human being can fight.' And to win that fight, Cummings believed, is to discover a world transformed, in which love transcends time, natural spontaneity prevails over the demands of habit and convention, and the dreams of the individual become the supreme reality. Such a world transformed is the subject of this particular poem; where it emerges as a place of Spring and infinite hope – a child's world, almost, in which all the necessities of the heart are answered.

'As for expressing nobody-but-yourself in words, that means working just a little harder than anybody who isn't a poet can possibly imagine' (Cummings). Cummings' irregular typographical habits, his word coinages and syntactical distortions, his use of free verse and his highly original development of traditional verse forms: all of these practices are a necessary consequence of his search for individuality. His aim is to create a unique, and sometimes eccentric, voice to express his unique, and sometimes eccentric, personality.

1] *Just :* The word is capitalised to emphasise that this is the *very moment* at which Spring begins.

4] *balloonman :* 'The first and most exciting sign spring had really come was the balloon man. First you heard his whistle in the distance; then he would come walking down the street...' (Elizabeth Cummings, the poet's sister).

5] Note how the spacing of this line helps to capture the echoing, distant quality of the balloonman's whistle.

10] *puddle-wonderful :* a characteristic word-coinage, yoking together abstract and concrete.

13–14] *wee | and bettyandisbel :* The lengthening of the first word, and the merging of the last three words, recreate the excitement and breathlessness of the children. 'Wee' (we) puns on 'whee': exactly the kind of noise children might make as they run, to express their exhilaration.

16–20] 'I am abnormally fond of that precision which creates movement' (Cummings). The precision of the rhythm and spacing here evoke the limping movement of the balloonman, the skipping of the children at play, and the bouncing of the balloons in the air.

21] *balloonMan:* The 'm' is capitalised in order to stress the individuality of the balloonman. He is, the poet emphasises, a separate and significant 'Man' and not just an anonymous part of 'mankind' (or, as Cummings sometimes put it, 'manunkind').

24] The poem ends on a characteristic note of possibility; with the grammatical and syntactical structure left unfinished.

Buffalo Bill's defunct

Written in a more colloquial style than the previous piece, this poem celebrates a hero of the American West, one of Cummings' supreme individualists.

Dick Mid's large bluish face

This irregularly rhyming sonnet is a cameo of what Cummings called the 'unworld'; that is, the ordinary world in which most of us live governed by the stock response, by cruelty and death. The poet takes the imagery and jargon of criminal life as his subject here, and so makes a further, implicit point: that 'manunkind', the people who do what they are told and never think for themselves, are really quite as unfeeling and inhuman as the gangster is.

2] *two-bit:* twenty-five cent.

3] *bulls:* the police.

pull his joint: raid his premises.

4] *dude:* an expensively equipped person, a 'dandy'.

7] *over percent:* i.e. over the amount of money she should pay Dick for her earnings. The sister was a prostitute, apparently, and Dick her pimp.

8] *it / operated in the hundreds ands:* It was located and worked in that area of New York with the street names in the hundreds (e.g. 101st Street, 102nd Street).

9] *chips:* prostitutes.

10] *stewed:* went to a brothel.

12] *Yonkers:* a section of New York City.

14] Jimmie, it seems, was convicted of a crime he did not commit, thanks to Dick Mid's cunning. This line is left unfinished, as if Dick can no longer contain his sadistic glee in words.

'next to of course god america i'

Another excursion into the 'unworld', this poem brings together patriotic cant of all descriptions, in one headlong verbal assault. The aim is parody: to mock, by imitating and exaggerating it, the mindless rhetoric of those who would prefer to obey rather than think, lose their identity in some anonymous mass rather than discover an identity for themselves.

3–4] These lines are borrowed from the American national anthem and 'My country 'tis of thee', a popular patriotic song.

14] *drank:* to cleanse his mouth, probably, as well as slake his thirst.

since feeling is first

This poem, one of Cummings' many lyrics of love and persuasion, is addressed to an anonymous lady; who, the speaker argues, is much closer to the truth, thanks to her spontaneity and gently intuitive nature, than he with all his thoughts and poetry can ever be.

3] *syntax*: the rules and regulations of language, thought, or anything else. This introduces a series of witty, grammatical images, by means of which the poet mocks the very discipline he is using.

5] *wholly*: There is probably a pun on 'holy' intended here. The fool, according to the poem's frame of reference, is more blessed than the wise man because he/she does not see matters from the 'sane' or logical point of view.

7] *approves*: approves of, and proves.

15] *paragraph*: i.e. a separate unit, with a definite beginning and end.

16] Death is transcended by love in the ideal, dream world of the individual (see the Notes to 'in Just-'). It can no longer cut life off in the way that, for example, a parenthesis cuts the words it encloses off from the rest of the sentence.

somewhere I have never travelled, gladly beyond

The person who is 'incorrigibly and actually alive', Cummings asserted, who tries to discover his own special identity, 'prefers above everything and within everything the unique dimension of intensity'. This intensity is found especially, he believed, in the experience of love: 'love is the courage to hope, the determination to be oneself, the ability to dream, the capacity for surrender, and the desire for life... If Mind is the dehumanized Satan of Cummings' universe, Love is its humanized Christ' (Norman Friedman). So Cummings returned to love again and again, usually treating it in the way he does here: as a kind of mystery or semi-religious voyage, by means of which the individual journeys toward truth.

3] *frail gesture*: This introduces a series of references to the hands, or the sense of touch, which remind us of the closeness of the lovers and the fundamentally physical nature of their love.

5] *unclose me*: i.e. as a flower is unclosed by the sun. Imagery of Nature, of the seasons and the elements, runs through the poem, emphasising the spontaneity of the lovers, their preference for intuition or feeling over thought.

7] Note how Cummings alters the conventional word-order, here and throughout the poem; thus obliging us to pause while we read, and experience that attitude of patient meditation which is, apparently, one of the special blessings of love.

8] *(touching skilfully, mysteriously)*: Another reason for the gently ruminative tone of the poem is Cummings' use of adverbs and parentheses, by means of which he lingers over particular words or phrases so as to qualify and define them more exactly.

IN) all those who got

This poem, illustrating Cummings' often idiosyncratic use of punctuation, is an epitaph for 'manunkind': the people who follow the crowd rather than their own inclinations.

1] *IN)*: The bracket here, and in line 4, acts as a means of marking a pause more emphatic than a comma; and reduces the importance of the people referred to still further. They are so 'small', the implication is, so non-existent as individuals, that they can be dismissed between the space of one word and the next. They do not deserve mention for themselves at all: but only for the fact that they are dead, either literally or (more probably) in the spiritual sense.

3] *athlete's mouth*: They have worn their voices out expressing received opinions.

my father moved through dooms of love

Of his father Cummings once said: 'He was...a crack shot and a famous fly fisherman and a first-rate sailor...an expert photographer...and an actor...and a painter...and a better carpenter than any professional... a teacher...and later...a preacher who...horribly shocked his pewholders by crying "the Kingdom of Heaven is no spiritual roofgarden: it's inside you."' This exceptional individual, and supreme individualist, is the subject here.

1] *moved through*: and so defied.

dooms of love: i.e. those pronouncing doom upon, and situations encouraging the destruction of, love.

2] *sames of am*: This is characteritic of Cummings' wholesale transformation of verbs and adjectives into nouns. 'Sames' is roughly an equivalent of 'sameness', and describes the levelling tendencies of the ordinary world. 'Am', a key word in Cummings' vocabulary, is an equivalent of 'being' and refers us to the special and intense type of existence enjoyed by the individualist. Thus, the meaning of the entire phrase is that the father habitually defied convention and the threat posed by the commonplace to (his and other people's) independence.

haves of give: the constraints visited upon man's natural generosity by the meanness of the ordinary 'unworld'.

5–6] *where...here*: The father lived for the moment, to discover fulfilment in the present; and so created his ideal, kingdom here and now upon the earth.

7] *if*: used here as a noun, to describe all the tentative hopes and possibilities which sprang into being and fruition, thanks to the father.

9–12] These lines describe how the father's revivifying ('april') presence could awaken those around him: prompting them to ascend from anonymity ('which') to individuality ('who'), and escape from the sleep of non-being into the ideal, dream world of pure being.

13–14] The father could still any self-doubts or querulous uncertainty ('some why').

16] *mountains*: The mountain occurs frequently in Cummings' verse, as a symbol of natural harmony and the sense of repose this harmony encourages.

19] *moon*: another common symbol of the true life of the individual, and the dreaming imagination.

20] *singing desire into begin*: transforming the possible into the actual, realising the ideal.

22] *heart of star*: a heart or person devoted to the ideal world.

23] This line is a condensed and memorable way of saying that the father lived a positive ('yes') life, devoting himself to getting the most he could out of the immediate moment ('now').

24] *wrists of twilight*: Note how, here and elsewhere, Cummings emphasises the close relationship between this man and nature by describing the natural in human terms, or vice versa.

25–8] The 'unique dimension of intensity' created by the father surpassed ordinary experience as much as the heat of the midsummer sun surpasses our idea or memory of it.

33] *must and shall*: rules and conventions.

37–40] The father offered man a richer gift than the autumn harvest does: the secret of being, the pure freedom of the individual ('is').

40–4] Note how, at this point, the father is being compared to the entire earth. The individual, it is implied, both has and is his own world.

46] *in the head*: in the face.

48] *snow*: another common symbol for the transforming powers of the individual heart. The world made new by the individual is like a world made new by a snowfall.

49] *theys of we*: the barriers set between man and man by the ordinary world.

50] This line describes how the imagination of the father, or his 'song', made his environment appear to be born anew.

55] This and the following eleven lines follow on from lines 53–4. The meaning of this line is: 'even if imagination should become a matter of contrivance and scheming, and passion something which has to be willed...'

57–60] Even if the world degenerated to the point at which cruelty came to be called kindness and giving was replaced by stealing; at which the heart seemed made to fear and the mind to doubt; at which nonconformity was branded as a weakness or disease, and conformity hailed as the aim of all existence...

63] *minus*: a preposition used here as a noun, to signify absence or emptiness.

65] *least*: unimportant.

67–8] Because this man fulfilled the demands of his own soul, Cummings concludes, he offers all the proof we need that the individual and his loving imagination form the ultimate, all-encompassing value.

afloat on some

This is an example of Cummings at his most extreme, pushing his typographical innovations to the limit. The subject of this highly idiosyncratic piece is the moon, which is transformed even as it is described into a symbol of the dream world of the liberated individual.

3] *?*: Cummings replaces the second syllable of 'something' with a question mark, the implication being that 'thing' is too definite and mundane a word to use in describing the shifting, delicate presence of the twilight.

6–8] *an in/-ch/of an if*: the slip of the moon, which is so evanescent, apparently, that it must be referred to as an 'if', a faint guess or possibility; and so indistinct and shadowy that it can only be evoked in a series of hesitant, broken words.

13]): It is characteristic of Cummings' 'poempictures', as he liked to call them, that he should use a punctuation mark here for its visual effect – because it traces, on the page, the gentle curve of the moon.

14–17] The moon, as it occurs in the poem, belongs more to the world of the dreaming heart than it does to the ordinary world of change and decay. It is 'profoundly alive' (Cummings), figuring the intense forms of experience enjoyed by the individualist, and not just a product of some sterile imagining.

enter no (silence is the blood whose flesh

This poem, written towards the end of Cummings' life, treats the entry into death in characteristic fashion: as a unique experience which, in its possible wonder and intensity, can match anything else the individual may ever have to confront.

1–2] *no.../...silence: but unsinging:* The poet is making a distinction here between the various kinds of silence we may experience during life; and the kinds that characterise death. The first are necessary complement of all the sounds or 'songs' which make up our vital existence. 'Sound' and 'silence', in this sense, depend on each other, and imply each other, just as much as the flesh and blood of the body do, or the systole-diastole, ebb-and-flow motions of all organic life. The second, however, form a separate entity, a self-contained thing: far from being part of the living world they constitute a complete, deathly, and 'unsinging' world of their own.

3] *spectral such hugest how hush:* These words are being used almost as if they were talismanic objects: to conjure up and (with the help of their hissing sibilants and softly insinuating aspirates) even to dramatise the strange and silent nature of death.

6] *april:* Characteristically, Cummings takes early Spring as the supreme instance of life, its epitome.

7] Death is now conceived of as a state of anonymity and absence ('perpetually roaming'); one in which the ordinary connections and explanations of existence no longer apply ('whylessness').

8] *autumn:* old age.

winter: death. There may be an ironic echo of Shelley's 'If Winter comes, can Spring be far behind?' ('Ode to the West Wind') intended in this line; the point being that, whereas Shelley evades the finality of death by anticipating renewal, Cummings clearly embraces it.

10] *minus:* see the Notes to 'My father moved through dooms of love', line 63.

11] *millionary:* million-fold.

12] Note how here, and throughout the poem, Cummings uses a vocabulary that emphasises the *nothingness* of death, the way that it manages to deny absolutely everything we know.

13–16] These beautifully cadenced lines seem to dramatise the gradual relaxation of the consciousness, the slipping away of life.

16] *descend:* The poem is left syntactically and grammatically unfinished, so as to imply that the experience of death is rich in possibilities.

Hart Crane

Black Tambourine

Crane called this poem 'a description and bundle of insinuations bearing on the Negro's place somewhere between man and beast': but, characteristically, a series of significant associations makes it something more than that. The black man described in the first stanza is juxtaposed with a black *poet*, Aesop, in the second. As a result, in the last lines Crane appears to be talking about Negro and poet at once. Both are in exile, we infer, either literally or metaphorically; both are caught within a series of degrading alternatives; both, somehow, have to make something out of a radically delimited reality.

1] *cellar*: Because of the context in which it occurs (i.e. a description of the closed world of the American Negro), this word also suggests 'cell'. This is a very simple example of the strategy of verbal enrichment which Crane used in nearly all of his verse. 'As a poet,' he said, 'I may very probably be more interested in the so-called illogical impingements of the connotations of words on the consciousness (and their combinations and interplay in metaphor on this basis) than I am interested in the preservation of their logically rigid signification.' He saw each word, almost, as a cumulus of possibilities and latent associations many, but not all, of which could be fired into life by their verbal surrounds – by the words, and combinations of words, with which they were juxtaposed. The overtones of his language, consequently, tend to matter more than its strictly denotative meaning. What echoes in our minds forms an important part of what is being said.

2] Originally this read, 'Mark an old judgement on the world.' Crane's revision is symptomatic of his development at about this time: from a rather flaccid type of free verse to the tough, and highly original, use of traditional forms which characterised his mature work. The revision introduces a rhyme and gives an appropriately sombre, yet incisive, movement to the line.

3–4] The Negro is surrounded by animals which define his condition.

4] *spans*: The word suggests the bridging of a large space (i.e. in ironic contrast to the dark narrowness of the Negro's 'world').

5] *Aesop*: the author of the famous *Fables*, who lived c. 550 B.C. He was black, a slave, and an exile.

6] The reference to the fable of the tortoise and the hare picks up the description of the insects in lines 3–4 (and, perhaps, the word 'tardy' in 2). Aesop surrounded himself with imaginary animals just as the 'black man' in stanza 1 is surrounded by real ones.

7] This description of the animal remains surrounding Aesop's grave continues, like line 6, the association between man and beast.

8] *mingling incantations*: Deliberately vague, this could refer either to Aesop, still singing to us in his *Fables*; or to the animal remains mentioned in line 7, which magically summon Aesop back to us. In either case, the idea – of life-in-death as opposed to the 'black man's' death-in-life – remains the same. The use of a present participle ('mingling') where an active verb ('mingle') would normally be expected is characteristic, its effect being to emphasise the 'present-ness' or immediacy of the event: Aesop, in his stories, seems to live *now*.

9–12] An intricate verbal collage here brings the poem to an end, without providing us with a paraphrasable conclusion. What we are offered is not an argument, but a complex of 'inter-relationships...raised on the organic principle of a 'logic of metaphor' which antedates our so-called pure logic' (Crane). So the 'mid-kingdom, dark' does not define a particular area so much as take up meanings suggested and expectations aroused in previous lines: the 'cellar' of the black man is implied, the kingdom in exile of Aesop, and perhaps the world between heaven and hell generally. Similarly, the 'tambourine' reminds us both of a degrading alternative (the minstrel stereotype imposed on the Negro, the poet as allowed fool), and a redemptive possibility (music, and all it signifies, as a means of escape from the 'cellar'); and Africa describes a place which is at once literal (the home of the black man), imaginative (the Great Good Place of the poet), and spiritual (heaven, the Absolute). The subtle play of allusion continues on into the last four words. A 'carcass' (describing another alternative available to the black man) is a term normally used to describe the body of a dead animal: but here the very flies which are usually the symptoms of death appear to be the agents of life as well (since 'quick' means alive or vigorous). There is death-in-life here, we must infer, but there is the possibility of life-in-death too: suggestions of decay and recovery neatly balance one another. Further than this we cannot go when we try to paraphrase; and this because what the poem has done, in a way, is supply us with 'a single new *word*, never before spoken, and impossible to actually enunciate, but self-evident in the... consciousness henceforward' (Crane). It has created a language rather than used one.

Chaplinesque

Crane here compares the situation of the poet in modern times with that of the little tramp whom Charles Chaplin (b. 1889) made famous in his films; this poem was in fact inspired by Crane's having seen Chaplin in *The Kid* in 1921. The idea of the artist as a divine fool, who knows more about reality than all the sensible people around him and who evades disaster with the help of this knowledge, is an ancient one: compare the Fool in *King Lear* or the traditional character of Pierrot. This is a modern version of the same idea.

1] Crane said that he felt 'moved to put Chaplin with the poets'; hence the 'we'.

3] The pun on 'deposits' emphasises the apparent poverty of the poet-fool. He has no bank account, only what the 'wind' gives him; which may be a great deal, since the wind was used by the Romantic poets as an image of creative inspiration.

7] 'Poetry, the human feelings, "the kitten", is so crowded out of the humdrum, rushing, mechanical scramble of to-day that the man who would preserve them must duck and camouflage for dear life to keep them or keep himself from annihilation' (Crane).

9–13] The verse also 'sidesteps' here. With almost any Chaplin film in mind, it is possible to assign the 'inevitable thumb' to the city policeman who is the persistent enemy of Chaplin's tramp. The policeman tries to block the tramp, but he manages to step around him with an ingratiating 'smirk'.

The words 'doom' and 'inevitable' add to the larger meaning of the scene, suggesting that the thumb belongs to Death as well as to the policeman. The poet evades mortality through the cunning of his artistic manoeuvres just as the tramp does the authorities by virtue of his physical dexterity.

14] And yet the tactic of verbal trickery and the pose of humility only conceal the search for the truth. They do not violate it.

16] *obsequies:* The primary meaning of 'funeral' refers to the rites performed by the poet as a means of at once acknowledging and defying death; and to the tricks performed by the tramp as a way of evading authority even while paying apparent homage to it. 'Enterprise' is being used in an unusual way, to suggest purposeless endeavour (i.e. the kind of enterprise Crane rejected when he left his father's business).

17] *you:* authority, death, and perhaps the reader (referring to the indirect ways by which the poet communicates the truth to his audience).

18] *if:* as long as.

19–23] The vocation of the poet is revealed when the enforced 'smirk' of daytime experience is changed by the moon (a traditional figure for the imagination) into a kind of holy laughter. The vision of the moon transforming an ash-can into a grail is a paradigm of the imagination seeing in the wilderness of the actual a vessel of supernal beauty.

From *For the Marriage of Faustus and Helen*

The poem from which this passage is taken marks a major transitional stage in Crane's poetic development. Up until the time when it was written, the positive note in his verse had tended to be tentative and partial: even if the possibility of an absolute was affirmed it was usually, as in 'Chaplinesque', hedged about by numerous qualifications and ironies. Now, however, Crane began to discard the scepticism, the detached wit and self-protective wryness that he had learnt in part from T. S. Eliot; and dedicated himself instead to what he called 'a more...ecstatic goal'. His aim was nothing less than the redemption of the actual world, a visionary reconciliation between the real and the ideal.

The immediate occasion of this change was a personal experience. Like the two poets to whom he now turned for inspiration, William Blake and Walt Whitman, Crane had apparently enjoyed a moment of vision, or mystical seizure, which opened out new possibilities in himself, and convinced him that 'we must somehow touch the clearest veins of eternity flowing through the crowds around us'. Here is how he described the moment, later, to a friend:

'Did I tell you of that thrilling experience this last winter in the dentist's chair when under the influence of aether...my mind spiraled to a kind of seventh heaven of consciousness and egoistic dance among the seven spheres – and something...kept saying to me – 'You have the higher consciousness ...'? A happiness, ecstatic such as I have known only twice in 'inspirations' came over me. I felt the two worlds...Today I have made a good start on the first part of "Faustus and Helen." '

As Crane indicates here, 'Faustus and Helen' grew directly out of this mystical experience and, in a sense, tries to recover it, to make it and the knowledge it supplies available to every one of his readers. Faustus, as

Crane explained, is 'the symbol of . . .the poetic and imaginative man of all times', Helen the symbol of an 'abstract "sense of beauty"'; and the 'marriage' between them is not so much an event as a continuing possibility – the moment of communion between the soul and the spirit of essential Beauty, which irradiates all existence ever afterwards.

The poem consists of 139 lines, divided into three sections. The passage given here is the concluding section. In a note on the poem, Crane explained that this was further divided into five parts, entitled 'Tragedy', 'War', 'Resumé', 'Ecstasy', and 'Final Declaration'.

Part I (1–9)] Characteristically, this part is not about tragedy but the *transcendence* of tragedy. The figure addressed is Death: and he is addressed in such a way as to admit his power but suggest the possibility, also, of resurrection.

1] Death is 'capped' like a gangster or soldier, and he presides over the fate of beauty: but only in this world ('in this street').

2] The street narrowing into dawn introduces the first image of possible resurrection. 'Motor' emphasises that the dawn is active, in motion.

3–5] Death is also an emissary from the ranks of the dead (the poem was written shortly after the end of the First World War); and he accompanies the poet, as he does every man, to the grave. The dead, however, seem to arise as they are described, to enjoy a resurrection in which they are stripped of the 'steel' instruments of death.

5] Death is, finally, a gunman, working for other-than-worldly powers.

6] This announcement, that Death himself will die soon, does not mean that death as a fact will disappear, but simply the obsession with it. The discovery of an absolute, beyond the reach of time, will make it seem unimportant.

7–9] The idea is that, when Death dies, it will not be a quiet, almost imperceptible, affair like the wind settling on the bridges. It will be a moment of triumph, causing us to raise our voices in song.

9] *fear and pity:* The emotions with which the tragic poet deals, according to Aristotle's *Poetics.* The song sung at the death of Death is purged of the sense of tragedy.

Part II (10–23)] Crane referred to this part as 'violence clothed in pathos'. It describes an airplane attack, occurring presumably in the First World War, but the description is couched in terms which discover a redemptive possibility even here.

12] *corymbulous:* a cluster, a flat or slightly convex head of a flower. The word conveys the picture of planes flying in a geometric pattern and, as a botanical term, it introduces a series of natural references ('hill breezes', 'meadows', 'blue plateaus' etc.) which effectively surround the description of death with intimations of revival, and continuing life.

16] The houses with holes gouged in their walls are compared to old women without teeth, and therefore unable to flash a smile. The figure suggests the wastage of the land and of life simultaneously.

21] *saddled sky:* The pilot is transformed into an American cowboy for a moment, riding the sky.

22] *hypogeum:* an underground vault. The idea is that nothing could withstand the machine-gun fire from the planes. The highly wrought diction and phrasing of this passage are meant to endow the particular event described with a sense of cosmic significance.

23] The disjunctive rhythm of this line and its predecessors helps to dramatise the throbbing movement of the plane, the spatter of machine-gun fire, and the ferocious activities of war. 'Unless poetry can absorb the machine,' Crane said, '...then poetry has failed of its full contemporary function... This process...demands...an extraordinary capacity for surrender...to the sensations of urban life. [It] presupposes, of course, that the poet possesses sufficient...gusto to convert this experience into positive terms.' The transformation of the rhythms of war into the rhythms of poetry here, and the absorption of both into a larger context celebrating the notion of Beauty, illustrates exactly what he meant.

Part III (24-9)] The spectres of war, tragedy, and death are dismissed; and 'Faustus', or the poet, prepares for a communion with 'Helen', the essential Beauty informing the world.

24-7] The poet explains that he and his generation did not ask for war. Having survived it, they will continue to speak out against it, against memories of it, and against those obsessed with these memories.

26] *stubble streets :* streets bearing the marks of war, like cropped fields bearing the marks of cropping.

27-9] The poet and his kind will also speak out *to* (another meaning of 'before') those who have never caught a glimpse of absolute Beauty. Beauty, the Helen of the poem, is seen for a moment in almost Biblical terms, like the Jehovah of the Old Testament. She fills us with a sense of 'blessing'; and with 'dismay', as well, as we recognise the poverty of our lives without her.

Part IV (30-43)] The vision of absolute Beauty redeems the world, transforming the particulars of experience into a significant and perfect whole.

30] These are examples of the commonplace, the random details of experience.

31] These details the creative imagination or 'Faustus' sees as partaking of the divine, during and after its communion with 'Helen'.

32-4] The imagination, unhampered by worldly notions of getting and spending, will always be able to transform our actual experience; discovering music in the ordinary and redemptive possibilities in our fleeting lives. In the next nine lines, the poet then turns to address the imagination directly.

35] *Anchises :* the father of Aeneas in Virgil's *Aeneid.* After the fall of Troy, the two sailed for Italy, where Aeneas founded Rome.

36] *Erasmus :* Desiderius Erasmus (c. 1466-1536), Dutch humanist scholar and writer. The meaning of this and the next two lines seems to be that Anchises and Erasmus represent all the spirit can achieve, *except for the vision of Beauty.* They brought together the broken fragments they found (the 'blown blood and vine' of Troy and the Catholic Church), and with them helped create a new City of Man. But now the poet is intent upon creating something more like a City of God, a world made new with the help of the imagination.

39] *brother-thief :* Time is stopped by death, and transcended by the imagination. Both, therefore, can be called thieves of time.

recall : remember, invoke.

40–3] The imagination is called upon to laugh at those dull, sullen spirits who will not accept risks; who do not possess the daring and generosity of spirit necessary to receive illumination.

43] The 'golden' appearance of Helen, and her 'gold hair', figure the mystical experience.

Part V (44–7)] The poet ends by celebrating the marriage between 'Faustus' and 'Helen', the imagination and the absolute.

44] *the years:* a figure for mortal life.

45] The 'hands' of 'the years' reaching up to heaven describe the thrust of the mind, and the continuity between actual and ideal. The wronged and wounded world is perfected, made whole by the vision of Beauty.

46] The imagination is the force which spans or bridges the gap between actual and ideal, creating a dimension beyond despair.

47] The arc traced by the imagination reaches beyond the world of getting and spending, the world of ordinary language and even the world conceived of in prayers. Yet it irradiates these worlds, and our lives beneath it, making everything that exists worthy of thanks and praise.

At Melville's Tomb

This, one of the finest of Crane's lyrics, is a hymn of praise to Herman Melville (1819–91), the author of *Moby Dick*, and to the visionary imagination in general. Crane felt a profound affinity with Melville, whom he was inclined to class with 'the dear great Elizabethans'. Both pursued a certain sublimity of expression; both were made bitterly aware of the predicament of the American artist; both spent their creative lives searching for some absolute which would explain to them, and unite, the appearances of their given world; and both used the figure of the sea, frequently, to describe this search.

Crane wrote a long letter to Harriet Monroe, to explain certain parts of the poem which she had found puzzling. All quotations in the notes are taken from this letter.

1–8] Melville, the poet tells us, was aware that men who have drowned at sea may well have arrived at 'fresh concepts, more inclusive evaluations'; which, however, they are unable to report to the living, and of which their remains are 'the only surviving evidence'.

1] Melville is depicted standing on a promontory ('ledge') looking far ('wide') out and into the sea.

2–4] 'These being the bones of dead men who never completed their voyage, it seems legitimate to refer to them as the...mute evidence of certain things, experiences that the dead mariners might have had to deliver. Dice as a symbol of chance...is also implied.' The bones are envoys from another world, *and* proof of the precariousness of existence.

6] *calyx:* the whorl of leaves that forms the outer covering of a flower. 'This calyx refers in a double ironic sense both to a cornucopia [a horn of plenty] and vortex [whirlpool] made by a sinking vessel. As soon as the water has closed over a ship this pool sends up...wreckage...which can be alluded to as a *livid hieroglyph* making a *scattered chapter*, so far as any complete record of the recent ship and her crew is concerned.'

7] *scattered chapter:* dispersed evidence.

livid hieroglyph: A 'hieroglyph' is a secret symbol. 'Livid' refers to both the colour and the fury of the sea.

8] The strange, roaring sound heard when one raises a sea-shell to the ear is used here as a figure for the knowledge to be reaped from these remains; that is, 'about as much definite knowledge...as anyone might gain from the roar of his own veins'.

9–16] And yet the creative imagination may be able to decipher the messages which drowned men leave behind them, and which the sea utters. Melville managed, by means of vision and visionary language, to see and speak about them.

9–10] The whirlpool is calmed, its destructive circles metamorphosed into a circuit expressive of unity and peace. In these and the next two lines, Crane is describing, and in a sense imitating, the visionary act: the transformation of disparate and warring particulars into a perfect whole.

10] *Its:* the sea's.

11–12] 'A man, not knowing perhaps a definite god yet being endowed with reverence for deity – such a man naturally postulated a deity somehow, and the altar of that deity by the very *action* of the eyes *lifted* in searching.'

11] *Frosted:* Melville's eye-brows were frosted by the sea-spray, and his heart chilled by the world.

13] *Compass, quadrant...sextant:* nautical instruments for measuring distance, altitude, and latitude. 'Hasn't it often occurred that instruments originally invented for...computation have inadvertently so extended the concepts of the entity they were invented to measure...that they may metaphorically be said to have extended the original boundaries of the entity measured?' Crane is here developing the suggestion made in lines 11–12: that Melville's imagination, measuring the possibilities of the sea and exploring the possibility of an absolute, may *figuratively* be said to have extended the first and created the second.

15] *Monody:* elegaic poem or song.

16] *fabulous:* extraordinary, and myth-making. The idea is that the sea alone is a suitable guardian of the spirit of Melville, and of the visionary statements which are his achievement.

from *Voyages*

The six poems brought together under this title were written over a span of about three years. They are, as Crane explained at the time when he was writing them, 'love poems' and 'sea poems' as well: the sea appears in them as a threat to the poet-lover and as a rival, as a partner, an enemy, and eventually as a source of comfort and vision. One reason for this, the constant presence of the sea in the sequence, is that the person to whom they were addressed was a European sailor living temporarily in New York; another, that during their affair (which was probably the most passionate experience in the poet's life), the two lovers stayed in an apartment overlooking the harbour; and still another, that the sea was, of course, always a suggestive figure for Crane. Like Herman Melville, he used it to describe both the hostility or indifference of this 'broken world' – *and* the mysterious 'answers' which might ultimately make the world whole again.

Although the six poems can be read separately they do possess a connecting argument, and a profoundly traditional one at that. The poet begins with an earthly affection, experiences ecstasy and loss, and then discovers consolation for his loss in the love of heaven. The beauty of this passing world is perceived, and then superseded by a vision of Beauty in a timeless paradise.

The numbers given to the poems refer to their places in the original sequence.

Poem I] The poet describes some children playing on the shore, and then tells them never to leave it, never to go to sea.

1] *ruffles :* the folds made by the sea in the sand, and the pounding of the surf.

2] *Bright striped urchins :* children dressed in bathing suits, and perhaps a reference to sea urchins as well.

6] *treble :* high-pitched, and three-fold.

10] *kids :* children and goats (i.e. a reference to their vitality and animal-like innocence).

11] *shells and sticks :* There is a covert sexual reference here, which will be taken up in the other poems.

12–13] *a line | You must not cross :* the shore-line. The sea, in this poem, signifies experience: the voyage through life, the voyage of love, the voyage into the self, and the voyage in quest of truth or the absolute.

14] *Spry cordage :* By comparing their rib cages to the rigging on a sail, Crane seems to be suggesting that the children are like boats about to embark.

15] *lichen-faithful :* an affection that clings like a fungus.

    too wide a breast : i.e. the sea's.

Poem II] Disregarding his own advice in the previous poem, the poet sets sail on a voyage of love; a journey in quest of every possible sensation and perception that the erotic life can afford.

1–5] In the first stanza, the sea is described as a majestic lover; laughing at our limited conceptions of love and opening out vaster possibilities to those willing to attend to her. Notice the elaborate 'logic of metaphor' here, which establishes this multiple identity. 'Wink' leads into the erotic image of line 4, and on to 'laughing' in line 5: a series of descriptive details that present the sea as gay, mocking, and abandoned. On another level, though, 'wink' leads into the optical image 'rimless', a secondary meaning of which in turn suggests 'unfettered' and 'vast'; and all of these words describe the sea, rather, as imperious and boundless.

2] *leewardings :* The word, used to describe the to-and-fro movement of the sea, is borrowed from *Moby Dick* by Herman Melville. The entire poem shows Melville's influence.

3] *Samite :* a rich medieval fabric of silk interwoven with gold. This, together with 'processioned' (which describes the waves as if they were figures in a religious procession), adds to our sense of the majesty of the sea.

4] *undinal :* The fact of the moon's influence on the sea is combined here with the myth of Undine, the water-goddess who yearned for a mortal lover. *Unda*, the Latin word from which Undine is derived, means a wave. The entire line offers us a complex figure of love, cosmic and mythical.

5] *wrapt inflections :* The varieties ('inflections') of human love tend to be 'wrapped', or limited, as well as passionate and 'enraptured'.

6–10] Continuing the regal image, the sea is now presented as a great ruler, passing judgement on nearly every human activity.

6] *diapason:* combinations of notes in an harmonious, and usually majestic, whole. This is an appropriately grandiose description of the sound of the sea, and the voice of the sea-queen.

7] *scrolls:* a flowing line or pattern (of the kind waves make), and a roll of parchment (of the kind on which legal judgements are written).

silver snowy: This refers both to the sight of the sea-foam, sparkling in the sun; and to the eloquent but chilling sound of the sea-queen's voice, giving judgement.

8–9] The sea-queen excites terror as she holds court ('sessions'), and her facial expressions alter to express her decisions.

10] Lovers are exempt from the power of the sea-queen, apparently, because, like her, they enjoy the experience of love and because, by means of this experience, they come very close to the divine. Note how the description here combines the erotic (the lovers' hands fondling one another) and the religious (the lovers' hands raised in prayer).

11–15] As the lovers continue their voyage onward into the full mystery of love, their surroundings seem to assume a magic quality, to partake of the atmosphere of legend.

11] *San Salvador:* a legendary city beneath the sea.

12–13] The bells of this city appear to salute the stars, which glow like crocuses in the night. Islands, passed by, look like meadows full of flowers.

14] *Adagios of islands:* Continuing the musical imagery of the poem, this phrase is meant to capture 'the motion of a boat through islands clustered thickly, the rhythm of the motion etc.' (Crane). 'Adagio' is the term for a slow, graceful movement in music and dance.

my Prodigal: the beloved one. As in 'Faustus and Helen', love is the prerogative of 'the lavish heart'.

15] The idea is that the lovers, through their love, will arrive at a full discovery of the mysteries coursing through the body of the sea.

16–20] The poet-lover now calls upon his beloved to seize the day; to gather, while they still can, all the pleasure and knowledge that the bounty of the sea can offer them.

16] The sea is here seen as a figure winding up a clock, making sure that the hours continue to tick away.

17–18] The sea has no money, but it has other riches to give; the riches of the love it embodies.

18] *superscription:* the engraving on a coin, used here as a synecdoche for coins generally.

19–20] While this bounty is available, the lovers must hasten to enjoy it. Love, carried to its fruition, will give them an instant so perfect and beautiful that it will seem to belong to eternity; all the phases of life will be united in an experience of permanent value.

20] *floating flower:* The flower, floating on the sea of love, figures beauty, fruition, ecstasy.

21–5] The poet prays to the seasons, to commit his lover and himself to the world of time, change, and desire. And he prays to the vessel of love and music on which they have journeyed, not to return them to ordinary life until the experience of love has been exhausted.

21] *awe :* The idea is that the seasons should teach them to reverence Time, in which the cycle of love and fruition occurs.

22] *Carib :* Caribbean.

24] *vortex :* whirlpool. The meaning seems to be that, through love, the poet hopes to experience a kind of spiritual death – which in turn will enable him to catch a glimpse of 'paradise', the world of absolute Beauty.

25] *spindrift :* spray blown across the surface of the sea. Used as an adjective here, the word refers to the eyes of the seal, swept by the spray; and to the visionary imagination, spinning free across the ocean to paradise.

Poem III] The promise of the second poem is fulfilled. The lovers experience a moment of ecstasy which is primarily of the earth, earthy: but which seems, also, to partake of eternity, to offer them a possible escape from the world of time and death.

1–8] The poet is now depicted journeying *towards* his beloved, rather than with him. And the seas he passes over seem now to share in and magnify his love, rather than contrast with it. This is a universe of love over which the poet and his mate preside.

1] *consanguinity :* a blood-relationship, used here to describe a moment of intimate physical contact. The idea is that the erotic act of the lovers is being repeated infinitely in the world around them.

3–4] Notice how the labyrinthine syntax here, and the rocking motions of the verse, deliver to these lines a sense of wild, yet measured, activity; and so help to capture at once the movement of the poet across the sea and the movements of sexual union.

8] *reliquary hands :* hands containing sacred relics. This seems to mean that the sea greets poet, or lover, or both (the syntax leaves this deliberately unclear) as equals in love.

9–14] The poet reaches his beloved across the sea, the erotic act achieves its climax; and as this occurs, the entire world seems to be caught in a similar embrace.

9] *black swollen gates :* This phrase refers to the 'Gates of Hercules', or Straits of Gibralter, through which ships pass to the paradisical world of the Mediterranean; to dark and swelling waves (the journey is both across and *down into* the sea); and it is also, of course, a sexual reference.

11] *pillars...pediments :* architectural features which we normally associate with churches and temples. The erotic and the religious sense are combined throughout the poem.

14–18] At the moment of climax, the lovers experience a kind of death. This is at once 'le petit mort' ('the little death') which the Elizabethan poets and others associated with orgasm; the 'dying into' another dimension of existence which Crane and the Romantics felt accompanied the experience of ecstasy; and a dim perception of the higher, transcendental state which is the subject of poem VI.

14] *shed :* This means at once 'happened' (i.e. 'even if death occurred'); 'spilled out' (a sexual reference); and 'cast aside' (a reference to the idea that death, or the apprehension of death, is cast aside during the erotic act).

15] '...there is such a thing as indestructibility...where flesh becomes transformed, through intensity of response to counter-response' (Crane). The 'intensity of response to counter-response' is what the poet is describing here.

17] As so often in Crane's verse, what the reader is asked to register is the *connotative* meanings of these words rather than their logical, denotative meaning. Thus, 'transmemberment' is a neologism which turns the idea of death, or 'dismemberment', into an idea of *trans*-formation. This, in turn, is enriched by the references to song, rich fabric, and the skill of the religious initiate; all of which have been associated already, in this poem or poem II, with love and the changes wrought by love. An elaborate collage of associations works here, in effect, to express an instant of metamorphosis, in which the lovers 'die away' from ordinary life.

18] This line at once encapsulates the experience of the poem, and concludes it upon a note of serenity and fulfilment.

Poem VI] The moment of erotic fulfilment is over, the poet's lover has gone. But with the death of one love comes the birth of another. The poet comes at last to 'Belle Isle'; a paradisical realm figuring the absolute Beauty, perceived in vision and expressed in verse, which transforms and perfects the beauties of this transitory world.

1–8] In the first two stanzas the poet is depicted, not sailing, but *swimming* – in a sea which appears both to imprison him and to proffer him a hope of vision. He embarked on the journey against which he had warned the children in poem I. He suffered, and still suffers, as a result. But the suffering is seen as possibly creative: the voyage of love and knowledge is necessary, it is implied, if ever Beauty and Truth are to be perceived.

1] Notice how the words used here to describe the sea attack and qualify one another. The sea is, apparently, an 'icy' prison; and a place 'bright' with the possibility of vision, where hearts and eyes may be lifted up.

2] The loss of the poet-lover is identified as a loss of *vision*.

3–4] The borders of this world shift and alter, the skies are strange, because the poet is adrift.

5–6] The sounds made by the 'ocean rivers' are likened to the noises heard in a shell when it is raised to the ear. Here, as in 'At Melville's Tomb', this signifies the visionary message when it is still only half-understood.

8] *kelson :* a line of timber fastening a ship's floor timber to the keel. This is meant to describe the broad streaks of light cast by the setting sun; to develop the pervasive imagery of ships and sailing; and to introduce the idea of some force binding sea and sky together which is so integral to the poem.

9–16] The poet prays for an end to voyaging; and for a spiritual rebirth which will enable him to sing again.

9] The 'rivers mingling toward the sky' figure the poet's movement toward a higher consciousness.

10] *the phoenix :* a mythical bird supposed to arise out of its own ashes, and therefore a symbol of rebirth.

11–12] The poet, still 'blind' and drifting, is compared for a moment to an abandoned shipwreck.

13] *what name, unspoke :* The idea is that the vision of absolute Beauty is necessary for the creation of poetry. It offers the 'Word' which will give meaning to the poet's 'words'. See *John* I, i: 'In the beginning was the Word, and the Word was with God, and the Word was God.'

14–16] The waves, lifting the poet up, will offer him a knowledge more basic to existence than the knowledge of tragedy ('the death of kings').

It will offer him Truth and Beauty, the knowledge of the creative imagination.

16] *splintered garland :* The garland, traditional emblem of the poet or 'seer', is splintered by the lightning of inspiration.

17–32] The poet accomplishes his journey, and is rewarded with vision.

17] *siroccos :* warm, sultry winds. The swimmer is moving away from these, northwards. The north is normally associated in Crane's verse with the realm of the spirit and creative imagination.

18] *solstice :* the time at which the sun is furthest from the equator, and appears to pause before returning. The idea of time standing still prepares us for the moment of vision.

19] The cliff which, to the swimmer, appears to stride across a motionless sea is (like the 'sail') an image of movement: the movement towards 'Belle Isle', the movements of consciousness.

22] *lounged goddess :* There is probably a reference to Aphrodite, the Greek goddess of love, implied here. Her name, derived from the Greek word for 'foam', links her to the sea.

23] *Conceding dialogue :* Like Helen, in 'Faustus and Helen', the goddess is the symbol of an 'abstract "sense of beauty"'. As such, she is also the muse of poetry – which Crane saw as a "dialogue" between Time and Eternity.

25] *covenant :* in the Bible, the word is used to describe the compact between God and the Israelites. Here it refers to the union between the poet and the absolute, which gives significance to his experience and so, in a sense, 'guarantees' it.

Belle Isle : 'Beautiful Island', a place of Crane's own invention.

27–8] Under the radiant light of an absolute vision every personal experience assumes a new splendour. The 'oar', figuring the voyage of life and love, is endowed with an ideal existence ('white echo'). For the symbol of the arc or rainbow, see the Notes on 'Faustus and Helen', line 47.

29–30] The 'Word', perceived in vision and expressed in poetry, transforms our given world. Within its 'glow' the 'willows', emblems of change and death, are stilled.

31–2] The 'Word', the transcendent reality of vision or poem, also perfects the loves of this world: by giving them permanent form and by affording them a proper completion in the love of 'paradise'.

from *The Bridge*
Proem : To Brooklyn Bridge

The Bridge represents Crane's attempt at an American epic. Being an *American* epic it is also a *Romantic* epic, in the tradition of Blake's 'Jerusalem' and Walt Whitman's 'Song of Myself': one that is as much concerned with spiritual possibility as with historical achievement. 'I am concerned with the future of America,' Crane wrote, 'not because I think that America has any so-called par value as a state...It is only because I feel persuaded that here are destined to be discovered certain as yet undefined spiritual quantities... not to be developed so completely elsewhere.' It is the old problem of the American Dream that the poet poses. In a series of eight poems we follow the westward thrust of the bridge into the body of the continent, a movement in time as well as in space; and as we move across America Crane continually presents us with the same question. How, he asks, can the ideal possibilities of men be liberated so as to recover the kingdom of heaven here and else-where upon the earth? How can an arc or bridge be constructed between the world in which we live and the world of the imagination, so that the life of the individual may assume a fresh nobility and the forms of the community approximate to the divine? Having asked the question, he also tries to answer it. For Crane is no less a Romantic in this, that he sees himself as an agent of liberation, formulating in his work the new relation between consciousness and reality which will make the changes he requires possible. His epic, like so much of his verse, offers us a series of visionary acts intended to alter our minds – to propose to us 'a new hierarchy of faith' (Crane) – as a preliminary to altering our surroundings.

This poem, which begins the epic, is a prayer in which the poet beseeches Brooklyn Bridge to act as a mediator between the actual and the ideal. He is appealing, of course, to the bridge as a figure rather than a given object. He has transformed the *actual* bridge into an *ideal*, liberating symbol; and in doing so has, in effect, offered us an example of how the two dimensions can be related – and his prayers consequently answered.

1–4] In these lines, the gull is established as a complex symbol of the abso-lute. Its symbolic status is the product of many factors, which include the suggestive whiteness (purity) of its wings, and the rings (wholeness, harmony) of its flight; the references to the dawn light (spiritual vision) in which it appears and the Statue of Liberty (spiritual freedom) over which it flies; its association with the 'inviolate curve' of the bridge and the sails of voyaging ships; and its paradoxical freedom-in-restraint, and motion-in-rest. The last is also captured in the rhythms here, which alternate between moments of breathless stillness and an unimpeded, lyrical flight.

7–8] The vision is lost, as we turn from the ideal to the real world, and the elevators, taking us up to work, paradoxically 'drop' us from our previous imaginative heights.

9] *sleights:* a pun on 'slides' (i.e. pictures), which suggests at once trickery ('sleights of hand') and triviality ('slight'). The cinema is used here as a figure for false vision, the dreams of man betrayed and prostituted.

10] *bent:* as if in prayer.

13] *Thee:* Brooklyn Bridge, to which the poet now turns as a fresh possibility. It seems to unite the real and the ideal worlds, the worlds of elevators and gulls, because like the first it belongs to the urban, technologi-cal age – but, like the second, it describes its own inviolate curve and contains its own paradoxes of motion-in-rest (line 15) and freedom-in-restraint (line 16).

14] The bridge appears to synchronise the movements of the sun; to order its surroundings just as the imagination does.

18] *bedlamite:* madman. This brief description of a suicidal leap off Brooklyn Bridge returns us to the terrible world of reality for a moment.

19] *momently:* momentarily.

20] The mute, indifferent passers-by seem to mock the suicide.

22] In this world, nature becomes aggressively mechanised. The sunlight, spilling down the streets, is more like the light of acetylene torches; its heat grates, like the sound of a buzz-saw.

24] The bridge still looks out, and partly belongs, to the sea, symbol of the absolute.

25–6] The reward or blessing ('guerdon') offered by the bridge is as mysterious and profound ('obscure') as the promises made by God to the Jews.

26] *Accolade*: sign at bestowal of knighthood and, hence, a blessing.

27] *raise*: rise to, or erase.

28] *Vibrant*: life-giving, and musical.

29] The steel ropes of the bridge are transformed, by the 'fury' of the poet's imagination, into the strings of a harp; the bridge itself, into an altar. Brooklyn Bridge is also a figure for artistic and religious vision, two significant mediators between heaven and earth.

31] *threshold*: The bridge offers a gateway into the absolute, thus fulfilling the promises of the prophet, the prayers of the outcast, the cry of the man who loves the world (the poet is all of these).

33–5] The traffic lights on the bridge seem to 'condense' its dark expanse into a significant pattern. The bridge itself is seen as an unbroken ('unfractioned'), harmonious form of utterance, which in turn seems to express the pure sounds of heaven. (At this point the bridge and the poem about the bridge appear to have become one.)

36] The bridge seems to push the darkness (of the night, of the spirit) away.

39] The spiritual possibilities of the city are seen as glowing parcels, unwrapped only in secret, at night.

40] The weather (a figure for the atmosphere of the city) buries these possibilities deep.

41–4] The bridge is asked to unite river and sea, land and sky; and to act as a revelatory image ('myth') to lead the poet towards the absolute.

44] *curveship*: This associates the bridge, once again, with the inviolate curve made by the gull's flight, and with the 'apparitional' ships.

Royal Palm

Crane visited his mother on the Isle of Pines, Cuba, when he was sixteen and found the palm trees growing there 'perfect delights' because of their 'ornamentation, stateliness, and open-airiness'. This poem is at once a description of them, and a figurative account of the imagination ascending to a vision of the absolute. The calm pauses of the palm's ascent are imitated in the slowly unwinding syntax, the stately rhythm, and the uncluttered passage of the sentences.

2] *tower*: frequently a figure for the inviolable imagination in Crane's verse.

regal: a reference to the imposing appearance of the 'royal palm', and to Crane's belief that the imagination presides over our world.

4–10] Like the imagination, the palm exists in splendid isolation, its growth seemingly a product of its own self-possession. An 'anchorite' is a hermit.

8] *frondings*: foliage.

9–11] The palm does not appear to belong to the world of time and change, flowering and decay, which surrounds it.

14] *a fountain*: This refers to the cascading leaves of the palm, and the creative, life-giving qualities of the imagination.

Theodore Roethke

Open House

'The primary thematic concern in Theodore Roethke's poetry is with the evolution and identity of the self' (Ralph J. Mills Jr). This, the opening poem in Roethke's first volume, is a frank announcement of his intention to use himself as the material of his art. Its style is characteristic of his earliest published work. The language is stripped and bare; the rhythms are driving and insistent, marked by a definite pause at the end of nearly every line; and the stanzas form a series of tight, epigrammatic units, each carefully rhymed.

9–10] The cryptic and witty paradox contained in these lines is typical of Roethke's early verse, which in general shows the influence of English 'metaphysical' poetry.

Cuttings

The poems in Roethke's second volume bear witness to a sudden, radical change of perspective and style. There is a new rooting of poetry in sensuous experience, in the 'greenhouse' or natural landscape of the poet's childhood; and along with this a search for some dynamic concept of correspondence between the vegetable and human worlds. Much of his verse from now on, Roethke later explained, 'begins in the mire, as is man is [sic] no more than a shape writhing from a rock': a being, the birth and growth of whose consciousness can be fruitfully compared to the birth and growth of plants, trees, and all organic matter. This particular poem is about birth, the first stirrings of life.

1–4] 'If we concern ourselves with more primitive effects in poetry,' Roethke said, 'we come inevitably to the consideration...of verse that is closer to prose... The writer...must keep his eye on the object, and his rhythm must move as his mind moves.' Examples of vegetable energy themselves, the greenhouse poems spill over into Roethke's first free verse; reflecting his new-found belief that instead of imposing order on experience (*all* experience, conscious, subconscious, and pre-conscious) he should discover the order latent in it.

8] *tendrilous :* tendril-like.

Cuttings (later)

A further intuition of the intimate relationship existing between man and organic nature, this poem continues the story begun in 'Cuttings' about the birth of consciousness – the poet's own consciousness, as an individual and yet representative instance.

1–4] 'What absorbs his [Roethke's] attention is...the stretching and reaching of the plant, its green force, its invincible Becoming' (Stanley Kunitz). Note how the poet uses the sounds and movements of the verse here to reproduce this process of 'becoming'. The long lines and elaborate alliteration, the preponderance of heavy stresses, open vowels, and participles, all combine to create an effect of enormous effort and evolutionary struggle.

1] *resurrection :* This introduces an implicit comparison, between the perpetual transformation of one form of organic life into another which is Roethke's version of rebirth, and the Christian type of resurrection.

2] *feet*: So as to bring the two terms of man and nature closer together in the imagination, nature is given human attributes.

5] *underground*: below the earth and beneath the skin.

10] The subject of this comparison is left deliberately indeterminate. It might be either the vegetation described in the preceding line or the man described in the succeeding one, or perhaps both. The fish is mentioned frequently in Roethke's verse. As one of the more primeval forms of sentient existence, it is normally used as a corresponding figure for the early, pre-conscious stages of human life, and for the deeper, subconscious levels that remain a crucial part of the psyche even after infancy has passed.

11] 'sheath-wet': still covered in the mucus of the womb, chrysalis, or sheath.

Night Crow

This briefly anticipates Roethke's deeper studies of the 'history of the psyche' (to use his own phrase) in his later verse. The bird described here not only corresponds to certain things within the human mind, it is able to *evoke* them as well. In other words, it functions as an archetypal image, by means of which the poet reaches back into his own early history, and the early history and pre-history of his race: into all that Carl Jung included under the term 'the collective unconscious'.

Unfold! Unfold!

With the series of longer poems that went to make up his third volume, Roethke's journey into the interior of himself took a fresh and more violent turn. His aim now, apparently, was to explore beyond childhood and the natural world to 'the swirling, threatening, inchoate sources of his very being' (Roy Harvey Pearce). He wished, as the title of this poem suggests, to 'unfold' and so reveal the deepest recesses of personal and racial memory.

Talking about the sequence from which 'Unfold! Unfold!' comes, the poet said: 'Each poem...is complete in itself; yet each...is a stage in a...struggle out of the slime; part of a slow spiritual progress... The method is cyclic. I believe that to go forward as a spiritual man it is necessary to go back... There is a perpetual slipping-back, then a going-forward; but there is *some* "progress".' And acting upon the belief stated here he modelled every piece on one simple, archetypal pattern; in which the heroic protagonist journeys into the darkness of another world, conquers the dangers he discovers there, and then returns to lead a fuller, more inclusive life in the day-light realm of ordinary experience. The pattern is an ancient one which we can find, for example, in legends of a night journey under the sea (e.g. the Biblical story of Jonah and the whale); in descriptions given by mystics of the 'dark night of the soul'; and in that movement of withdrawal into the self and memory, followed by recovery and a renewed capacity to deal with events, which Carl Jung saw as necessary to the 'process of individuation'. The only thing that makes it unfamiliar here, perhaps, is Roethke's methods of presentation. He compresses language and syntax into abrupt, dream-like units, which depend upon their total context for explanation; he telescopes imagery and symbols; and he employs rhythms which seem strangely primitive, even oracular in many of their effects. Exactly what

Roethke intends by adopting these methods may appear mysterious enough at first, but in fact it is quite simple: instead of just *reporting* the journey into the interior as most earlier writers have done he is trying, essentially, to *recapture* it. He is aiming at a direct, personal, and intuitive rendering of the experience described, in which – so he hopes – all of his readers can share.

Section I (1–9)] The protagonist is compared here to a mountain-climber. As he approaches the summit, the final stage of his journey into the personal and collective unconscious, so his difficulties seem to increase.

1] *by snails:* with the slow movement of a snail.

spirit: a term frequently used by Roethke to describe the core of the self.

2] *body without skin:* an apt figure for the personality stripped of all accidents.

fish: see the Notes on 'Cuttings (later)', line 10. The idea here is that the self, reduced to its essence, is not prone to the difficulties and diseases of ordinary life.

3–4] The narrator protests here that he cannot continue his journey. He finds it almost intolerable, and longs to find another means of self-discovery.

6] This line refers both to the escape from time that the journey into the unconscious involves; and to the threat of annihilation which accompanies this journey (i.e. the spiritual and psychological annihilation which would occur if the protagonist were unable to re-emerge with his discoveries).

7] *field:* the place of 'light' and illumination. Its benefits, apparently, are not easy to separate from the threats mentioned in the previous line.

8] *soul's crossing time:* a traditional metaphor in mystical literature for the road to salvation.

9] *The dead:* the occupants of the collective unconscious, the human and sub-human ancestors inhabiting memory who speak to the narrator in the next section.

Section II (10–13)] A series of stark questions and declarations, set down side by side without rational connectives, suggest the kind of knowledge the protagonist acquires during his journey into the interior. It is a knowledge, it seems, which depends on the dismissal of reason and the analytic powers; felt instinctively rather than thought out.

10] This, and the subsequent lines which 'the dead speak', have no particular symbolic or allegorical meanings. The poet does not intend any specific information here. He is simply attempting to convey (by means of a speech as primitive as folk-saying; as sub-human, almost, as an animal cry) an immediate sense of a complete spiritual and psychological transformation.

Section III (14–34)] The protagonist remembers other occasions when he has journeyed into himself (the pattern of regression and progression is a continual one). Slipping back into the instinctual life, he says, he has sometimes felt inclined to stay there, rather than go forward into new and more inclusive states of being; to remain in the darkness rather than return with his discoveries to the light.

14] *whelm:* overwhelming number.

proverbs: the cryptic statements and questions of section II.

Mr. Pinch: a character in the *Comedy of Errors* who tries to cure 'Insane' by chanting: 'I charge thee, Satan, hous'd within this man / To yield possession to my holy prayers.' Here the name seems to be used to describe a purely

subjective thrust toward self-purgation and self-discovery; one which succeeds (i.e. in ridding the self of 'Satan' or spiritual torpor) where the attempts
of Shakespeare's character so conspicuously fail.

15] This line, a characteristic mixture of humour and surrealism (both
of which Roethke uses as a means of denying the demands of reason)
continues the description of the purgative process which accompanies the
journey into the interior.

16] The last time the narrator explored his own being, he felt tempted to
remain in the dark and almost silent world he found there.

18–19] *hunted the bird.../Fishing:* both metaphors for the pursuit of the
'spirit'.

20] The protagonist compares himself, in the dazed state with which this
section is largely concerned, to a man driving a car in a condition of half-
sleep – one who seems hypnotised by the advertisement hoardings he travels
swiftly past.

21] *oily fungus...algae:* the 'slime' of personal and racial memory. The next
four lines catalogue the minute forms of life, animal and vegetable, that
inhabit this slime.

26–34] The portrait of a world which lies below the level of consciousness,
and of the protagonist's delight in that world, is completed in two stanzas
which combine, appropriately enough, the strange characters of fairy-tale
(26) with the imagery of dreams (28, 29, 34); the thriving microscopic life
of the mire (27, 31) with incidents that might have come out of primitive
legend (27, 32, 33).

Section IV (35–40)] In the moments immediately prior to revelation, the
protagonist feels his inner struggle intensifying; between the longing to
continue in the darkness of unconscious life and the need to return to the
world of consciousness, responsibility, and evolution.

35] *the life of the mouth:* the life based on instincts as primitive as that of
appetite.

lust for ripeness: This double-edged phrase refers both to the longing to
remain in the fecund 'slime', and to the commitment to 'progress'
demonstrated by the self.

36–7] A series of figures is used here to communicate that sense of growth
and release into the daylight world in which, as yet, the narrator himself
does not share.

38] *small vision:* the vision which cannot include the conscious *and* unconscious levels of experience within its range.

39] *vine:* an appropriately botanical metaphor for inspiration, the knowledge released by the procedure of 'slipping-back'.

40] *dead tongue:* One voice out of memory is now singled out as the force
providing the impetus necessary for the narrator to complete the process
of revelation.

Section V (41–63)] The poem ends with a return and a revelation: a return
to waking life and the revelation, of supreme importance to nearly all of
Roethke's work, that the conscious and unconscious dimensions of experience are quite inseparable. They are so united, it seems, as to make
development in the one dependent upon sustained and satisfactory knowledge of the other; and so precisely analogous that the world we see can be

described as a system of correspondences, enabling us to pierce through to a world which, otherwise, we can only sense.

41] *symbols...simple creatures:* The idea expressed here, and developed in the rest of this section, is a familiar one in mystical literature: that the external and visible world is, in its every detail, a sign or symbol of an internal and spiritual one.

42] *willow-shy:* The drooping outline of the willow is used here as a figure for shyness.

44-5] *light song...light:* traditional symbols of mystical illumination.

47] *father? Father:* The vision of the father completes the revelation. As a being who is elsewhere described as the protector of the greenhouse, and even a personal equivalent of the Biblical God, the father announces by his arrival the recovery of order and the rediscovery of selfhood. Reunited with his father, the protagonist is reunited within himself; finding his father, he finds his true identity.

49] *house...field:* representing, respectively, the limited kind of wisdom available to the reason, and the true knowledge which only the journey into the interior can bring.

50-2] These lines continue the idea expressed in line 41. Stones correspond to stars; the visible reveals to the initiated the light of the invisible, although to those of 'small vision' it may seem only to obscure it.

53-4] *fat...salt:* figures for, respectively, the visible and invisible worlds, 'fat' being an oblique reference to flesh and 'salt' a synecdoche for the sea and its inhabitants. The idea is that the conscious world alone cannot lead us to real happiness. Only the union of the conscious with the unconscious can do that.

55-6] The poet will seek appropriate modes of conduct and salvation within himself, not in the doctrines of organised religion.

57] *The lost:* those who have never made the journey into the self.

58] *The stalks:* a synecdoche for the primitive, natural world, with which 'the lost' are out of step.

59-60] These lines express Roethke's belief in the cyclical nature of life. The pattern of regression and progression repeats itself within the individual existence, and in creation generally.

62] *The dead:* see the Note on line 9. The archetypal occupants of the unconscious, hidden in a bush just as God the Father once was (*Exodus* 3, ii, iii), can help man towards discovery of his 'true self' (Roethke). They have done so here.

Memory

Having established a true sense of himself in such poems as 'Unfold! Unfold!', Roethke then turned outward to affirm his relationship with others. This is the last in a group of poems addressed to his wife; in which the narrator arrives at a fresh understanding of his own independence via a clear recognition of the independence and singularity of his beloved.

3] The ordinary world is replaced by the special, and in a sense inward, world of the lovers.

4] *she knows all I am:* she recognises his 'true self', just as he recognises hers. Their love is, in effect, dependent on shared awareness of, and reverence for, their separate identities.

6] *Half-bird, half-animal:* The beloved, like the lover, belongs to two worlds at once; uniting within herself the air and the earth, the conscious and unconscious levels of existence.

9-12] This stanza links the relationship of lover and beloved to the remembered relationship of child and mother (doe and fawn); and then intimates, through the reference to the poet following after this memory, and through the image of the grass turning to stone (the changing transformed into the changeless), that, as Roethke once put it, 'everything is twice'. Personal associations, in other words, trace a cyclical pattern just as the inner life does: they follow after one another continually, inviting the self into dimensions of being which are partly different, and partly the same.

from *Meditations of an Old Woman*
First Meditation

In his later verse Roethke gradually began to consider ultimate questions: about God, about Eternity – above all, about death and its significance for the living. These, of course, are questions about the self too, the place it occupies within the universal scheme, and so in a sense represent a final stage in the poet's life-long analysis of his own being. They led him, anyway, into writing a number of long meditative pieces, intended to offer new formulations of cherished beliefs; pieces like the one included here, which is the first in a series of five. The speaker, as the title indicates, is a woman: a character based partly on Roethke's mother, and partly on Roethke himself.

Section I (1-19)] The poem begins characteristically, with a landscape that represents the speaker's state of mind. The old woman, sensing the approach of death, expresses a need to understand life; and to understand it as only those who are about to leave it can.

1-7] Note how the lethargic movement of the free verse, the frequent and emphatic pauses, the clogged consonants and long vowels, all help to create a sense of inertia and decay.

8] *not always upward:* its direction is uncertain.

10] *talus:* slope.

13] *rind:* flesh, the body.
   the life within: the life of the spirit.

18] The old woman is referring here to her 'true self', the life of the spirit, which remains unimpaired after the body has been almost worn away. 'Seed' carries suggestions both of erosion (i.e. existence reduced to a minimal level) and of latent vitality.

Section II (20-59)] The second section develops the idea of a journey. The old woman remembers a bus trip she once took to the west. This quickly becomes a figure for the journey through life, the wavelike motion backward and then forward by means of which the self proceeds; and this in turn introduces a journey through time, an excursion into memory. The old woman recalls the greenhouse land of her childhood, when her inner and outer worlds were in perfect harmony and she experienced a kind of spontaneous joy. Then returning to the present, she uses a series of images of journeys not taken, or marred by accident, to describe the quite different situation in which she finds herself now. She is suffering, apparently, from an attack of bewilderment and frustration: faced with the problems of mortality and decay, she has ceased to progress.

21] *western country:* used here in a double sense, to suggest both exploration, the new frontier (e.g. of the American West), and death, the end of a cycle (e.g. the cycle of sunrise and sunset).

27] *The movement...wavers:* see the introductory Notes to 'Unfold! Unfold!'

39–42] The two sparrows described here represent the inner and outer worlds; and the song they sing, a possible union.

59] *Lunging down:* This falling movement is probably meant to remind us of the Fall in Christian mythology; and consequently to refer us both to the voyage from childhood to adulthood which the old woman has already taken, and to the voyage from life into death which she is about to take.

Section III (60–73)] The third section is a turning-point. In describing, tentatively, the journey of the spirit, made against almost intolerable odds, the woman is discovering something to which she can still be committed. No matter how old she may grow or worn she may be, while she lives her 'true self' can continue to seek renewal.

60–5] Note how the long lines, tentative rhythms, and accumulations of words help to enact the movement described.

69] *a salmon:* like the crab (62) a figure drawn from the sea, which is a recurrent symbol of the unconscious in Roethke's verse.

Section IV (74–99)] The meditation ends poised precariously between knowledge of desolation and belief in the spirit's continuing power. There are, the old woman admits, times when affirmation no longer seems possible; indeed, they tend to proliferate the older she becomes. But there remain more positive moments as well, when the self achieves growth by realising a fresh and harmonious relationship with all that is. Such moments more than just make up for the others: they are blessed with a special perfection of their own, a sense of fulfilment or even ecstasy which no deity can ever supply.

74–82] A landscape of nightmare is used here to describe the old woman's occasional feelings of loss and desolation.

82] *no riven tree...eagle:* There is no evidence in this particular world of the power or mercy of God; no indication at all that there is a life of the spirit.

84] *cerulean:* presumably intended to signify here an 'inhabitant of the sky', a bird.

85] *cicada:* an insect.

86] *phoebe:* a small bird.

The Moment

This poem, one of Roethke's variations on the 'carpe diem' theme, is the story of two people who successfully pit their love, and the ecstasy attendant upon it, against the challenges of time and death. 'The act of love', as Karl Malkoff puts it, 'is seen here as a positive, creative assertion of being in the face of nonbeing.'

1–4] The short lines, compressed syntax, and the chiming effect of the repeated, irregular rhymes, all help to create the impression of a swift but controlled movement – the voyage towards an occasion of absolute joy.

1] *ice of pain:* an image of death and nothingness, like the ravine mentioned in line 2 and the abyss in line 4.

3] *the sea:* an image of eternity.

6] The physical, the life of the body, struggled against the flux of time.

7–9] This paradoxical image, enclosing sound and silence, the infinitely large and the infinitely small, dominates the poem. It describes the act of communion, the instant in which the transitory and the permanent meet, thanks to love.

10–14] With union comes a new sense of ecstasy and possibility; the merging of inner and outer worlds in that eternal moment which gives the poem its title.

Once More, The Round

This, the concluding piece in 'Sequence, Sometimes Metaphysical' (a group of related poems included in Roethke's posthumous collection of verse), celebrates the cycle of existence in which, so the poet declares, every living thing participates. Man, bird, and beast, animate and inanimate nature, all share in the same wavelike motions of life, 'going-forward', 'slipping-back', and then 'going-forward' again. All belong to what could perhaps be described, and indeed *is* described here, as a kind of cosmic dance.

1–4] The poem itself seems like a dance, thanks to the chiming rhymes, the repetitions and lilting rhythms of the verse.

1] *Pebble...Pond:* figures, respectively, for the self and the universe – which are united here by belonging to the same cycle.

2] The unknown can be known by means of the journey into the interior, or unconscious. See 'Unfold! Unfold!'.

3] *true self:* see the Notes on 'Meditations of an Old Woman: First Meditation', line 18.

a Hill: used here, as in 'Unfold! Unfold!', to describe the final stages of the journey into the interior.

4] The core of the self becomes more 'visible' the further the journey goes, the more one participates in the cosmic dance.

8] *the Eye:* the faculty of poetic or spiritual vision.

9] *William Blake:* the English poet and mystic (1757–1827) who, like Roethke, celebrated the spirit's journey into the unknown, and the possible union of visible and invisible worlds.

Robert Lowell

Children of Light

In his early work, Lowell is a consciously Catholic poet who chooses to see the world as a 'conflict of opposites': on the one side stands 'the complacent self, the satisfied persistence in evil that is damnation', on the other, 'the realm of freedom, of the Grace that has replaced the Law' (Randall Jarrell). The self-absorption of the isolated individual is set over against the selfless-ness of true faith; the inward and fragmentary nature of Puritanism, or cultures influenced by Puritanism, is contrasted with the serenity and coherence of the traditional Catholic order. As Allen Tate has suggested, this opposition tends to repeat itself in the style of these early poems, in that there is a constant tension noticeable in them between structure and texture. The language, packed and feverish, the contorted syntax and disruptive imagery, the multiple levels of allusion and bitter ironies of feeling, are all barely kept in control by the formal patterns of the verse. Like an unwilling disciple, the poet finds it hard to tolerate the rigours of an inherited form. His speech has to be *willed* into submission, and even then that submission seems only temporary and incomplete.

This poem, from Lowell's first volume, illustrates some of the characteristic tensions. It is divided into two sections, which present us with two historical examples of the crime of Cain or violence committed against the brotherhood of man. In the first section (1–5), the material hardships of the Puritans are paralleled by the more serious failure of their doctrines to provide spiritual nourishment, a failure illustrated by their cruelty towards the Indians. In the second (6–10), the crime committed by the Puritans is magnified into the horrors of the Second World War. The implication of the entire piece is that inwardness finds its issue eventually in the disruption of both the private life and the public.

1] *stocks:* an ironic reference to the traditional Puritan mode of punishment.

2] This line has both a literal and a metaphorical meaning.

3] *Nether Land:* The pun associates the Puritans with an abyss of spiritual ignorance.

4] *unhouseled:* unconsecrated.

Geneva's: The reference is to John Calvin (1509–64), who provided the first logical definition and justification of Protestantism.

The literal meaning of the line is that the Puritans lacked the spiritual support provided by Catholicism, which is founded on the community rather than the individual.

5] *Serpent's seeds:* the seeds which fell on stony ground and withered away in *Matthew* 13, v–vi.

6] *searchlights:* This develops the idea of light as a barren force, introduced in the previous line. See *Luke* 16, viii: '...the children of this world are wiser in their generation than the children of light'.

7] The compressed syntax here suggests that the searchlights threaten the houses built on the rocks of the Massachusetts Bay area, rather than the state of warfare which makes the searchlights necessary.

8] An image for the loss of faith, the 'hall of mirrors' mentioned in this line may also be a reference to the palace at Versailles where the First World War (supposedly the war to end all wars) was brought officially to an end.

9–10] The only light comes from destruction as the descendants of Cain destroy the seeds given them by the Master (see *Matthew* 25, xiv–xxx), the surplus which a single-minded pursuit of gain has produced.

The Holy Innocents

With the help of a complex series of analogies, the poet here transforms an account of a team of oxen labouring up a hill into a visionary description of the year 1945 labouring up the hill of history; and the oxen themselves into 'holy innocents', types of the faithful followers of Christ, who have been born out of their due time and seem alienated from their world.

3] *burlap:* coarse canvas.

4] *ale-wife run:* 'Ale-wife' is a type of fish allied to herring, 'run' a fast-flowing stream. Note the dramatic stress placed upon 'drool' and 'start' in this line, after the distinctive pause at the caesura. The clogged consonants, open vowels, and slow, emphatic rhythms of these opening lines all help to enact the described movement.

6] *St. Peter's:* This reference to one of Christ's disciples, and the supposed founder of the church in Rome, introduces the first analogy.

7] 'These are they which were not defiled with women; for they are virgin. These are they who follow the Lamb whithersoever he goeth' (*Revelation* 14, iii–iv). An equation is being established here between the simple beasts of burden and the simple followers of Christ; both of which groups, apparently, are at odds with the world (8) – and with the modern world in particular (4–5).

9–10] These lines employ a succinct image, drawn from the Bible, to describe the pursuits of the world. Like King Herod (traditionally portrayed as a ranting tyrant in the Morality plays) the world is forever bent on frantic, meaningless activity. As such, it can have no real effect upon Christ and His followers; nor any idea of their more elevated sufferings.

11] *speechless clods and infants:* a familiar description of Christ's followers, which has particular relevance here. It refers us both to the oxen ('clods') and to the 'infants', or 'holy innocents' massacred in His place.

13] *grace:* Note the ironic emphasis given to this word by placing it at the end of the line.

14] *with losses:* another irony, this time of understatement. 1945 was the last bitter year of the Second World War.

15] *purgation:* referring, probably, to the idea that man is redeemed in history by Christ.

15–18] On one level, these lines simply describe the place to which the oxen are returning. On another, they provide us with a series of figures (the manger, the holly, Christmas) which help strengthen the link between oxen, Christ, and the followers of Christ.

18–20] The link is strengthened still further. The oxen, the poet tells us, will probably die 'in the harness', pulling the wagon up a hill; just as the faithful die dragging the weight of the world behind them, and just as Christ died suffering for the world on the Cross.

20] The poem ends, appropriately enough, on a note of serene faith: with the vision of the infant Jesus and all He promises in His stillness.

Colloquy in Black Rock

The colloquy of the title is between the poet and his heart, a term that is used ambiguously in every stanza to refer to both the physical organ and the soul' (Hugh Staples). As a physical organ, the heart is described accelerating rapidly, so producing a catabolic effect upon the body, which is repeated in its surroundings: the entire material world of the poem seems to be dissolving, too, into primal formlessness. But even as this occurs the heart as *soul* seems to benefit from the quickening; in that the destruction of the body and the world are seen as a necessary preliminary to the appearance of the Holy Ghost. The death of matter, the suggestion is, prefaces the life of the spirit.

Black Rock is a part of Bridgeport, an industrial city in Connecticut on Long Island Sound.

1-6] Notice the tension here between texture and structure. The kinaesthetic imagery, the harsh gutturals, the violent rhythms and language: all make the perceived destruction seem immense, even apocalyptic. But the tight, symmetrical form of the poem, a pattern of alternating sestets and quatrains, rhymed and in iambic pentameter, helps the poet to organise this frenzied material; to control it, if only just, and guide it towards some affirmative conclusion.

3] More blood is pumped through the heart as its beat accelerates.

8] *Black Mud*: Even the material form of the 'Black Rock' seems to be reduced to formlessness.

9-10] These lines contain complex suggestions of death *and* life-in-death, appropriate to the double-edged theme of the poem. Bridgeport had a large Hungarian population, who worshipped at a local church of St Stephen. Primarily workers at the armaments factories and so servants of destruction, they are here imagined to be giving blood as a contribution to the war effort; to be trying to redeem their negative efforts through a positive act of sacrifice. St Stephen was the first Christian martyr, stoned to death in Jerusalem about 36 A.D. He affirmed the life of the spirit, in dying, just as the narrator seems to do here.

11-16] The entire phenomenal world is now described in a state of dissolution.

17] *Jericho*: where the walls came tumbling down at the blast of Joshua's trumpets (*Joshua* 6, 7). This is another image of destruction seen as a *positive* act.

22] *Kingfisher*: a symbol of Christ, who now takes possession of the soul. Note how the metaphorical structure of the poem, in contrast to the level of literal description, has witnessed a steady ascent: through the elements of earth and water (stanzas I–III) to air and fire (stanza v).

24] *'Stupor Mundi'*; 'The astonishment of the world'. Originally applied to Frederick II (1197–1250), the Holy Roman Emperor, the phrase is used here as a description of Christ and of the experience of the poem.

Beyond the Alps

Lowell's fifth volume, *Life Studies*, witnesses a radical change of style and approach. The Catholicism of the earlier verse disappears, and with it the elaborate arrangements of stanza and rhythm. In their place is a poetry which, as Gabriel Pearson has suggested, abandons itself 'in the interest of sane, viable living, to the practice of reduced scales, and, not without reluctance, of diminished pretensions'. The lines are limpid and flexible, the syntax and idiom virtually those of colloquial speech, and such rhymes as do occur are almost invariably fleeting and irregular. All this is the eminently appropriate expression of a poet who no longer begins with a predetermined structure for his material: but instead tries to discover structure of a kind, and immutability, in the actual processes of remembering and expressing. The only order tolerated, in other words, is the order of literature. The poem describing the event becomes the one acceptable means of refining and shaping it.

This, the opening poem in *Life Studies*, dramatises Lowell's moment of transition. Its subject is movement; the journey from one mode of being to another, and the discoveries made along the way. And its form situates it somewhere in between the willed patterns of the earlier verse, and the looser textures of the later. It is divided into three stanzas, with fourteen lines of rhymed, blank verse in each: but the rhyme scheme varies in each stanza, the language is idiomatic, even slangy, and the pattern of the blank verse seems to disappear sometimes under the pressure of the poet's flowing speech.

1–2] This reference to the failure of a Swiss expedition to scale Everest introduces the major theme of the poem: the gap between human aspiration and achievement.

5–6] The stewards on the train, banging the gongs for meal-time, also seem to be announcing a revelation – the discovery to be made by the poem.

7] 'Life changed to landscape': The journey now becomes an interior one, of the imagination.

7–8] *I left the City of God:* The journey from Rome is both literal and symbolic. Lowell is taking leave of his former Catholicism: which he now sees as little more than an expression of need. As an aspiration, it represents the absolute order which men have pursued throughout history. As an achievement, it suggests all the weaknesses latent in the human being which make the absolute unavailable – and the pursuit of it even dangerous.

9–11] The description of Benito Mussolini (1883–1945), the Italian dictator, develops the major theme. A contemporary Caesar, he pursued the idea of public order: all he achieved, however, was chaos. His own lusts ('skirt-mad') and his own nature (bound inextricably to the prosaic needs of the earth) saw to that.

11–14] Unable to find a satisfactory image of order in history or religion, the poet is equally unable to adopt the breezy optimism of his ancestors. They had unlimited funds (of money, and of confidence) which are unavailable to him.

15–16] The idea behind these lines is that many, perhaps most, of those who subscribe to the Catholic faith have no clear idea of what they are subscribing to. Their rage for an absolute order finds its satisfaction, not in dogma, but in the figure of the Pope: who is for them a symbol of *power* rather than the vicar of Christ. Their cry to him, 'Papa', is symptomatic of their child-like dependence.

18–19] *electric razor...canary bird:* as ludicrous equivalents of the lightning and the dove, these two objects offer a deflating commentary on the power and mercy of God and the vicar of God. Even the Pope, the poet implies, cannot live up to the idea of order personified in him.

20] 'Candle' suggests a votive offering. This punning line argues that the order of reality offered by science stands no chance against the order of reality represented in religion.

23–5] But the order of religion remains unreal – an impossibility. The human animal, limited by his nature, worships the power and appearance of the absolute and little else.

26 *'coup de grâce':* finishing stroke. In this and the subsequent two lines, the poet uses a condensed piece of description to advance his argument. The

spirit of 'God' herding the people to St Peter's square to hear the Papal announcement offers a bitter parody of the pastoral function: these are sheep in the worst sense. The 'costumed Switzers', or tall Swiss Guards, who protect the Vatican and slope their pikes at the crowd, continue the impression of rising and falling which runs through the poem; and they reinforce our sense, too, of the *temporal* rather than the spiritual power of their leader. Finally, the sequence 'Pius' (the name of the Pope, and the Latin word for 'holy') – 'monstrous' – 'human' charts out, in the simplest manner possible, the gap between ideal and actual.

29] The train comes down from the Alps; the poet descends, temporarily from the heights of his speculations; and the poem intimates, slyly, that any order worthy of respect has to take the moving, mundane realities of the earth into account.

32] *Apollo :* a Greek god sometimes associated with the sun. As the sun rises, the poet looks back, literally, over the plain to the Alps; and, figuratively, to the world of classical antiquity.

35] The Cyclops was the one-eyed creature blinded by Ulysses in the *Odyssey*. Like the comparison of the Alps to the Parthenon in the previous line, this reference helps to bring the literal and figurative journeys closer together. There are further, half-hidden references to legendary voyages in lines 38 and 39.

40] *Minerva :* the Roman equivalent of Athene, the goddess of power and wisdom. For Greek and Roman alike she embodied all kinds of attributes (38); and yet, like other deities, her very strength was also her weakness. The lofty ideas she described were too far above human capabilities (36).

41–2] The poem has explored human limitations, the forces of darkness within ourselves which place absolute ideas of order beyond our reach. In this final couplet, the poet summarises these forces and in the act of summarising them, indicates one type of order still available to us – the order of literature. The individual imagination, modestly grappling with experience and creating out of it, as here, a complex of focussed suggestion: this, it seems, is the only trustworthy repository of value now.

41] *Paris :* the son of Priam, King of Troy, and the lover of Helen. As the person who brought destruction upon Troy, and as a figure whose blackness contrasts him effectively with the snow of the Alps, he suggests all the forces of a buried world: impulse, weakness, and violence.

42] *Etruscan :* used presumably as an example of a remote civilisation and, by extension, as a figure for the pagan, sinister, and mysterious energies running through our veins and the veins of the earth.

For Sale

Many of the poems in *Life Studies* are concerned with Lowell's immediate ancestors. Their aims appear to be (i) to exorcise painful memories (ii) to recover the past, place it, and so give it some coherence and meaning (iii) implicitly, to establish the family tradition as one that is definitely faded and gone, as unavailable to the poet as his former Catholicism. This piece, about the sale of a house and the loss of a father, fulfils, however modestly, all three of these aims.

'To Speak of the Woe that is in Marriage'

Several of the poems in *Life Studies* deal with marriage: Lowell's own experience of marriage, and marriage as an institution – one symptom of the human need to impersonalise, and so fix and order, the personal. Like the pieces about Lowell's family, they describe a state of unceasing conflict, between the rigours of the social unit and the rebelliousness of the individuals involved. Like those pieces, too, the only point of compromise is to be found in the process of recollection rather than in the experience recollected, in the disciplined freedom of the poetic voice.

This poem, spoken as the quotation marks indicate by the woman, describes the almost insane behaviour of the husband. Implicitly, it poses a question: at what point, it asks, does the antagonism between man and wife become intolerable, requiring them to break the ties to which they have committed themselves?

The title of the poem is taken from the Prologue to the Wife of Bath's Tale in Chaucer's *Canterbury Tales*.

The epigraph, a quotation from the German philosopher Arthur Schopenhauer (1788–1860), is presumably meant to suggest that this relationship, violent and macabre as it is, may well reproduce itself in 'the future generation': both literally, through the act of coition described in the last lines, and in the larger, representative sense.

13] *climacteric*: The word combines the literal meaning of crisis with a punning reference to sexual climax.

Skunk Hour

This, the last poem in *Life Studies*, returns us to the bedrock, the ground of being for all the poems in the volume. In it, the poet tries to confront his own madness and despair; and to find through the act of confrontation a type of imaginative release. His purpose, as he intimated in 'Beyond the Alps', is to create order out of the actual process of exploring himself and shaping the agony he discovers there into verse. Appropriate to the stark mood of the poem the diction is flat and severe, the rhythms jagged, and the syntax arranged into a series of sharp declarative sentences.

Elizabeth Bishop (1911–) is the poet on whose 'The Armadillo' this poem is modelled, according to Lowell.

1–24] 'The first four stanzas are meant to give a dawdling...picture of a declining Maine sea town. I move from the ocean inland. Sterility howls through the scenery, but I try to give a tone of tolerance, humour, and randomness to the sad prospect' (Lowell). Random though they may appear to be, the details described here have been rigorously selected so as to communicate feelings of loss, frustration, and self-enclosure: all of which are relevant to the subsequent discussion of the poet's own predicament. This is characteristic of the entire poem, which fuses naturalism and symbolism in the most effective way.

1] A nautilus is a small sea-creature with a chambered shell. This (together with the subsequent comparison of her to a hermit, the reference to her Spartan and isolated existence, and to the fact that she is in her dotage) helps establish the heiress as an immensely isolated figure; who seems (stanza II) even to cherish her isolation.

5] *selectman :* one of the councillors in a New England township.

7-9] The heiress likes to escape into the past, apparently, as well as into the seclusion of her house. Her status, as a member of an old family and so inheritor of the declining New England tradition, is ironically analogous to that of the poet.

13] *The season's ill :* It is winter, the dark season of the year and a moment appropriate to the poem's mood.

14] The millionaire has already escaped to another place. The theme of escape runs through these first four stanzas, describing at once the poet's own sense of loss – and his longing to evade his predicament.

15] *L. L. Bean :* a Maine mail-order sporting-goods firm.

16] *yawl :* a small boat.

18] *red fox stain :* '...meant to describe the rusty colour of autumn on Blue Hill, a Maine mountain near where I was living' (Lowell).

19] *fairy :* a slang term for homosexual.

21-2] *fishnet's...cobbler's :* There is perhaps an ironic reference to the life of Christ contained in these lines.

24] *marry :* This, of course, is purely a dream.

25-36] '...all comes alive in stanzas V and VI. This is the dark night... My night is not gracious, but secular, puritan, and agnostical' (Lowell). The poet confronts his situation directly. The atmosphere of these lines is one of despair and death.

25] *dark night :* both in the literal and the symbolic sense.

20] *Tudor Ford :* The poet's vehicle makes him as much of a quaint anachronism as the three figures previously described.

skull : perhaps a reference to Golgotha, 'a place of a skull', the name given to Calvary in (e.g.) *Matthew* 27, xxxiii: and certainly the first in a series of metaphors of death.

27] *I watched... :* The poet's behaviour betrays his own morbid, almost insane, state of mind at this moment.

28-9] Love and death are associated.

35] *I myself am hell :* Compare Satan's remark in *Paradise Lost*, book IV, line 75.

37-48] 'Out of this [i.e. stanzas V and VI] comes the march of affirmation, an ambiguous one, of my skunks in the last two stanzas. The skunks are both quixotic and barbarously absurd, hence the tone of amusement and defiance' (Lowell).

48] The skunks are a figure for the actual, at once disgusting and amusing, to which the poet has returned. They are a figure for the courage required to confront the actual: they 'will not scare' and neither will the poet while breathing in their 'rich air' (notice how the rhyme emphasises the analogy). And they are, finally, a way of indicating how the poet can master his experience and so avoid despair: by transmuting it into poetry, the kind of condensed and controllable image which is illustrated here.

For the Union Dead

In this, the title piece from Lowell's sixth volume, the civic disorder of the present is contrasted with two alternative ideas of order. The first is the order of the past: old New England, conceived of in consciously mythological terms and figured in the statue of Colonel Shaw, the commander of a Negro regiment during the Civil War. The second is the possible order of present and future registered in the architecture of the poem: 'Colonel Shaw's statue...is replaced... by a superior monument, the poem itself, as a symbol of the quality of the poet's judgement' (Patrick Cosgrave).

The epigraph ('They gave all to serve the state') is the inscription on the statue, slightly altered.

1] *old South Boston Aquarium:* The poem begins with rumours of mortality: the aquarium, and the winter season, remind the poet of times past.

5] *snail:* The snail, like the nautilus mentioned at the beginning of 'Skunk Hour', figures the enclosed self. Once, the poet tells us, he longed to break out of this enclosure into the savage world of the aquarium; an act associated with the gesture of breaking of bubble.

9–11] Returning from times past with the poet, we learn that he fluctuates now between this longing and the more habitual withdrawal into himself.

11–16] These lines establish an analogy between the poet's surroundings and the world of 'cowed, compliant fish'. The steamshovels, like sea-creatures which once inhabited the aquarium, are like the monsters of some prehistoric era; the world, or rather 'underworld', they create reminds us of the 'dark downward...kingdom' described in line 10; and the poet adopts the same attitude towards the construction workers (and, by implication, his contemporaries) as he did towards 'fish and reptile' – that is, one of shocked yet fascinated withdrawal.

18] *sandpiles:* This continues a series of images describing the chaos, or formlessness of the present. Even the memorials to the order of the past are succumbing to this force (see 21, 24).

23] *St. Gaudens:* Augustus St Gaudens (1848-1907) built the monument to Colonel Shaw and his men which stands opposite the State House on Boston Common.

28] *William James:* the philosopher (1842-1910), who unveiled the monument. The rest of the line is borrowed from his speech at the dedication ceremony.

29] *fishbone:* A witty reference to the rectitude of the Colonel, physical (see 40) and moral, and to his anachronistic status, this also develops the pervasive imagery of sea-creatures.

32] *compass-needle:* a word which describes the appearance of the Colonel, and his function as a guide or arbiter of value.

33–4] The comparisons with the wren and greyhound, and the description of the next fourteen lines, help define the values that poem and statue alike embody. What we are offered here is a type of disciplined freedom, a necessary restraint which fulfils rather than represses. Within this context the self is neither locked, snail-like, in the fixity of its own shell, nor released into irresponsibility and formlessness. Instead it is poised exactly between these two alternatives, where it can function with grace and effectiveness.

37] *out of bounds:* the values he represents are no longer acknowledged.

41] *a thousand...New England greens:* The function of the statue is now generalised.

46] *grow...younger:* because the values they embody never die.

53] *The ditch is nearer:* The pit of hell, and the savage underworld, is closer to us now.

54] *last war:* the Second World War.

57] *Mosler Safe:* a safe that escaped destruction in the bombing of Hiroshima, a photograph of which was used by the company to advertise the durability of its products. This and the preceding two lines present us with an ironic measure of the violence, the faithlessness, and the greed of the present.

58] *Space:* the world of space exploration, the vacuum left by the collapse of civic order.

59–60] The poet crouches over his television, just as he crouched towards the aquarium and the construction site, to witness another failure of principle: the present has not kept faith with Negroes (i.e. in the issue of school integration) as Colonel Shaw tried to.

64] *blesséd break:* which 'would activate his values again; that it will not come is shown by the designation of his hope as a bubble' (Cosgrave). The only bubble that will break, that *has* broken indeed, is the one mentioned in 7, loosing anarchy upon the world.

65] 'The Aquarium is gone': literally, and in the sense that the savage forces it contained now roam everywhere.

65–8] This last sentence, describing the present chaos, brings together the several references to sea-monsters, preying upon one another; the imagery of the machine and destructiveness; and the sustained contrast between the ideal of service realised by Colonel Shaw, and the 'cowed, compliant' servility of his successors.

from *Notebook*

Reading Myself

Lowell has said of *Notebook* that it is 'written as one poem, intuitive in arrangement, but not a pile or sequence of related material. It if less an almanac than the story of my life.' This book of irregular, unrhymed sonnets is perhaps the clearest proof yet of the poet's belief, with him since *Life Studies*, that 'literature – with poetry as its most refined incarnation remains a viable and trustworthy means of shaping and mastering experience' (Pearson). Various events in Lowell's life, from June 1967 until June 1970, are translated into verse; ranging from the momentous to the trivial, they are all rescued from oblivion by being metamorphosed into the permanent stuff of art. As the sonnet included here indicates, this is a process which need not necessarily end with this volume. For as long as the poet is alive he will need to place and understand his experience, to give it a certain measure. He will need, in fact, to write poems like this one.

6] *Parnassus:* a mountain sacred to the Greek god Apollo, and the Muses.

7] The image of the honeycomb brings together a number of related ideas about the 'sweetness', or pleasure, of verse, and its permanence.

8] The circle is, traditionally, a figure for eternity.

9] *mausoleum :* Like a mausoleum, the poem acts as a lasting memorial to the poet.

11] This seems to mean that the honey or sweetness of the poem preserves memories, just as amber (a yellow substance, like honey) preserves the remains of insects.

Index of First Lines